MW00606614

REPORTING THE
CUBAN REVOLUTION

Media and Public Affairs

ROBERT MANN, SERIES EDITOR

Gold medal awarded to each of the thirteen American correspondents

REPORTING THE CUBAN REVOLUTION

★ How Castro Manipulated American Journalists ★

LEONARD RAY TEEL

FOREWORD BY PATRICK WASHBURN

Louisiana State University Press
Baton Rouge

Published by Louisiana State University Press
Copyright © 2015 by Louisiana State University Press
All rights reserved
Manufactured in the United States of America
First printing

DESIGNER: Michelle A. Neustrom
TYPEFACE: Cassia
PRINTER AND BINDER: Maple Press

Frontispiece photograph by author, courtesy Herbert L. Matthews
Collection, Rare Books and Manuscript Library, Columbia University.

LIBRARY OF CONGRESS CATALOGING-IN-PUBLICATION DATA

Teel, Leonard Ray.
    Reporting the Cuban Revolution : how Castro manipulated American
journalists / Leonard Ray Teel ; foreword by Patrick Washburn.
        pages cm. — (Media and public affairs)
    Includes bibliographical references and index.
    ISBN 978-0-8071-6092-3 (cloth : alk. paper) — ISBN 978-0-8071-6094-7
(pdf) — ISBN 978-0-8071-6095-4 (epub) — ISBN 978-0-8071-6096-1 (mobi)
    1. Cuba—History—Revolution, 1959—Press coverage—United States. 2.
Castro, Fidel, 1926– —Relations with journalists. 3. Cuba—History—Revolution, 1959—Journalists. 4. Cuba—Foreign public opinion, American.
5. Foreign news—United States—History—20th century. 6. Reporters and
reporting—United States—History—20th century. I. Title.
    F1788.T355 2015
    972.9106'4—dc23

                                                            2015012006

★ CONTENTS ★

★ FOREWORD ★

In thirty-one years of college teaching, I was surprised continually by the students' general lack of historical knowledge. For example, on a journalism history test, they were asked to name one of the two times when John F. Kennedy was president that he became extremely angry with the press. I remember one student writing that the president did not like the press coverage when he dropped "the big bomb" on Japan (an event which happened more than fifteen years before Kennedy became president), and another said he did not like the Pentagon Papers coverage (which, of course, occurred eight years after the president died). And then there was a student who was totally clueless about the answer, but that did not deter him from plunging ahead fearlessly, claiming Kennedy did not like the coverage of his assassination.

I thought back to these answers when I reviewed Leonard Teel's manuscript for Louisiana State University Press. It occurred to me that today's students (as well as many older people) probably believe that there was never a time when Cuban dictator Fidel Castro was not portrayed as an evil, communistic enemy of the United States. But as this book reminds them, he was very much an unknown quantity as he led a small group of revolutionaries in a guerrilla war from December 1956 to January 1959, when they finally overthrew the Cuban government of President Fulgencio Batista. Leaders in the U.S. government became publicly alarmed about Castro, who was sworn in as prime minister in February 1959, only after he began establishing a socialist state, eventually accepting economic and military ties to Russia over the next two years. And in the more than fifty years since then, Castro has been extensively characterized by the U.S. government as a threat to America, with the criticism frequently reflected in the U.S. press.

But while Teel's book will remind readers that there was a time when Americans were basically just curious about Castro rather than fearful of him, that is not the real value of it. Instead, this is a heretofore untold story of a small group of foreign correspondents who were after an important international scoop—an interview with Castro during the revolution—and were willing to risk their lives and undergo hardships to get it as they slogged through jungles and climbed steep mountains, never knowing if they might be ambushed or captured by government troops. The fact that this tale has not been told by other historians is surprising. But even Teel admits that he had doubts about writing this book when he got little encouragement from other mass communication historians to do the study. However, when he asked me what I thought about doing it, I urged him to plunge ahead because I found it a wonderful adventure tale that clearly broke new ground. I am glad that I gave him that advice, but I take no credit for the resulting book. It is solely his—and well deserved, I might add.

Among the things that make this book stand out is Teel's narrative style of writing. Quite simply, he knows how to tell a good story that not only entertains but educates. That should not be a surprise. He worked fourteen years on the editorial side of the *Atlanta Journal* and *Constitution*, where he honed his writing skills and clearly learned a commandment drummed into all newspaper reporters: keep the reader turning the page. Good writing is not a priority with many faculty members, who feel the only thing that matters is saying something important while disregarding if they do it in an interesting fashion. I once made the statement in a graduate research class at Ohio University that I felt 70 percent of the faculty members in university mass communication departments did not communicate well in what they wrote because they paid too much attention trying to impress their academic peers rather than also educating and enlightening a general, college-educated audience. In short, they were stodgy, uninteresting writers, who reveled in the use of the latest fads in academic verbiage, such as the use of a word like "synergy." Teel does not make that mistake in this book, just as he did not make it in his acclaimed 2001 biography of Pulitzer Prize–winning editorialist Ralph McGill of the *Constitution*. He is a gifted storyteller who does not bore readers, and academia needs far more like him.

Another of his virtues is that, like all good historians, he tells readers not only *what* happened but *why* things happened. Given the time and the money to do it, a bright high school student can frequently find out what occurred in history, but explaining why is the real intellectual challenge. Sometimes it is easy when researching and writing history, but frequently it is not, and coming up with the answers, or the probable answers, can be exasperating and time consuming. Teel is one of those historians who does not bang readers loudly over the head with the why answers—now I'm going to stop and tell you why and I want you to listen—but when you get through reading this book you will know why things occurred. It's a subtle way of writing, and he is good at it.

Another thing that Teel is to be commended for is his use of extensive sources, both primary and secondary. He did not throw this book together quickly to get a publication that will get him a bigger annual raise or some other reward; it took time to do the research and the writing and to do it right. And the reader is the one who ultimately benefits in this process.

The bottom line is that this book is an excellent example of how to do historiography. It reminds me of what Richard Kirkendall, a former officer of the Organization of American Historians, said in 1980 on the first day of a graduate history class at Indiana University: "There are many things in history that have not been studied, but who cares? Study something that people care about, study something that is significant." I have never forgotten those words, and Teel follows that advice in this book.

Patrick S. Washburn
Athens, Ohio
November 2014

★ PREFACE ★

This book focuses on the Cuban Revolution during 1957 and 1958 when the reporting by American foreign correspondents misinformed the public and misled Congress and policy makers, with lasting consequences. It was certainly not the first instance of misreporting from foreign conflicts. From 1917 to 1920, the *New York Times*'s coverage of the Russian Revolution was "nothing short of a disaster," one study revealed, because news reports were "dominated by the *hopes* of the men who composed the news organization ... a case of seeing *not what was*, but *what men wished to see*."[1]

I had been interested in Cuba for years, first as a tourist in Havana in the summer of 1957, during a lull in the Cuban Revolution, then in Miami as I listened to Cuban refugees during my years at the University of Miami, and ultimately in Atlanta as a journalism historian. The Cuban Revolution—which historian Samuel Farber called "one of the most important events in twentieth-century Latin America"—provides a unique picture of U.S. correspondents operating in a foreign culture where they were vulnerable to being manipulated. This story follows the experiences and work of a special group of thirteen who, more often than not, reported what they *wished to see*. All thirteen went to Cuba between 1957 and 1959, most of them taking risks to reach the mountains and find Fidel Castro and his rebels. Their reports—in newspapers, magazines, and on network television and radio—repeated and amplified Castro's promises to restore Cuba's democracy and free elections. In "gratitude," Prime Minister Castro awarded them gold medals engraved with their names and his flourishing signature.

This is the first study of the group of thirteen, focusing on what they wrote that Fidel Castro found so very helpful in his quest for U.S. support. The Cuban episode highlights the cumulative impact of "scoop" journalism as well as the important role of homeland editors and producers—media "gatekeepers"—whose responsibility it was to edit and publish or broadcast the stories.

It is understandable how the thirteen—and their gatekeepers—could have misread the revolution by viewing Latin Americans through North American eyes. This has been a common problem for Latin Americans, as stressed by

Gabriel García Márquez in accepting the 1982 Nobel Prize for Literature: "The interpretation of reality through patterns not our own serves only to make us ever more unknown."[2] In Cuba, what most of the U.S. correspondents hoped to see was the defeat of the dictatorship of Fulgencio Batista and the rebirth of democracy, disregarding evidence to the contrary.

While this book is a history—not a theoretical treatise—the reporting from the Cuban Revolution offers ample evidence that could be considered in the light of media theories developed since the 1950s. For instance, a treatise in 1965 explained how Castro's guerrilla warfare defeated the Cuban military. "The scale of the action was miniature," wrote Robert Taber, "but propaganda victories came early and were international in their scope. One followed the other."[3] Since 1968, media scholars have focused on the power of mass media to shape public opinion through the agenda-setting power of the press.[4] Since 1991, media framing theory has become useful in analyzing how the display of stories tells audiences what to think about and also how repetition and reinforced associations "render one basic interpretation more readily discernable, comprehensible, and memorable."[5] Rhetorical concepts—such as empty signifiers—could also be useful in classifying Castro's political rhetoric, notably his pledges to restore "democracy" and "free elections."[6] In today's global mediascape, foreign correspondents and their gatekeepers at home have become ever more vigilant in trying to interpret reality "through patterns not our own."

★ ACKNOWLEDGMENTS ★

I am sincerely grateful to my colleagues in the American Journalism Historians Association. Frankly, this book would not have been written without both their encouragement of the idea and their discouragement of my earlier focus. That first attempt was rejected twice by a review committee, prodding me to reconsider and to discover this story.

Curiously, the new focus for *this* book was contained in a very brief United Press International story that I had undervalued. Only three paragraphs long, the story was published on April 19, 1959, on page 4 of the *New York Times*. The first paragraph reported that Fidel Castro on the first day of his visit to the United States after winning his revolution awarded gold medals to thirteen American correspondents who had publicized his cause. The second paragraph named the eight men and one woman who attended the gold medal ceremony at the Cuban Embassy in Washington and gave their affiliations. The third paragraph identified the four who did not attend.

I wrote a paper on the new topic, and it was quickly accepted for presentation at a conference in New York. In the progression from the paper to the book I have been consistently encouraged by friends and colleagues. I am especially grateful to the author and professor John Maxwell Hamilton of Louisiana State University, who within minutes of hearing of my proposed book led me straight to Robert Mann, series editor for LSU Press, where I received the kind of encouragement that kept the work progressing.

Numerous AJHA members have been helpful, the earliest being Patrick S. Washburn of Ohio University, who kindly wrote the book's foreword. I had support also from my colleagues across disciplines at Georgia State University. I cannot forget the surprised and helpful response by our university provost, Dr. Risa Palm, when my wife explained the core of the story—gold medals for helping Castro win. "That," said Dr. Palm, "seems a dubious honor." Indeed, even in 1959, the honor had become dubious as Fidel Castro's regime raised serious doubts about his promises to those correspondents that he would restore Cuba's democracy and hold free elections.

It was a time-consuming project over six years to collect the print and broadcast works by the twelve men and one woman, as well as biographical and historical information. The research was assisted greatly by my dear friend and colleague Joseph B. Treaster, the John S. and James L. Knight Chair in Cross-Cultural Communication at the University of Miami School of Communication. He sent me his entire Cuban history library, including books by some of the thirteen. His wife, Barbara Dill, gave my early chapters a careful and encouraging reading, as did Jay Mallin, a journalist resident in Havana during the 1950s. For helping me track down much of the primary source research, I thank my several graduate student research assistants. I am also grateful to the many librarians and archivists at Georgia State University, especially Jason Puckett; at the University of Georgia's Peabody Awards for the Charles Shaw Papers; and at Columbia University's Rare Books and Manuscript Library for access to the Herbert L. Matthews Collection, including the gold medal inscribed with Matthews's name and Castro's flourishing signature. I thank also Julio Eduardo Muñoz, executive director of the Inter-American Press Association in Miami, for personally handing me the IAPA archives, and I am grateful to our university's Center for Human Rights and Democracy for the grant for travel to the IAPA offices.

The final text benefited greatly from professional copyediting by my dear friend Phyllis Mueller and by Jo Ann Kiser for LSU Press. More generally, I value the support—and patience—of my colleagues in Georgia State University's Department of Communication and College of Arts and Sciences.

All the while I have been so fortunate in having enthusiastic encouragement from my wife, Katherine, herself a writer and the daughter of a historian of the nineteenth-century South. She and our circle of friends have helped keep the flame lit.

REPORTING THE
CUBAN REVOLUTION

CHAPTER 1

THE THIRTEEN

I n April of 1959, four months after Fidel Castro entered Havana—triumphantly riding atop a tank—he visited Washington as Cuba's new premier. The protocol for his visit was somewhat unusual, however, because he was not invited by the president of the United States, Dwight D. Eisenhower, who actually left town during the visit for a golfing vacation in Augusta, Georgia. Instead, the directors of the American Society of Newspaper Editors had asked Castro to speak at their annual convention in Washington both because he was obviously newsworthy and because they had worrisome questions about his past, his politics, and his intentions—of which they knew nothing for certain. During the two years of the revolutionary war, the editors had relied almost completely on their correspondents' interviews with Castro in the mountains for information about the rebel leader. But now that Castro was officially in power, their questions about him had become urgent.

Fidel Castro was a hero at home and abroad. He had received avid popular attention in France, Spain, and Latin America, but his greatest debt for favorable publicity was to U.S. foreign correspondents, especially to thirteen of them. One after another, these correspondents for newspapers, magazines, radio, and television had risked injury, arrest, and torture in their quest to find and interview Castro in the Sierra Maestra mountains.

The regime of President-General Fulgencio Batista rigidly enforced his periodic decrees of total media censorship. Nothing could be safely said about Castro. The Cuban press was controlled through systemic bribery and, if necessary, coercion. Media representatives from the United States who were based in Havana could be expelled for violating the censorship. Visiting foreign correspondents were closely watched, and army patrols blocked access to the rebels' camps in the southeastern Sierra Maestra mountains. Meanwhile, censors daily scissored unwelcome stories from the *New York Times*, *Time* magazine, and other imported publications.

The thirteen succeeded by disguising themselves, sometimes as tourists, or as a teacher on vacation, or as a Presbyterian minister visiting the congregation. Like hunters returning with big game, they brought home exclusive "scoops." Together with vivid descriptions of their own daring adventures, they wrote what Fidel Castro told them of his plan to defeat the dictator and restore Cuba's democracy and free elections. On newspaper front pages, in national magazines, on radio and network television, the stories portrayed for millions the Cuban rebels' determined struggle against dictatorship, eventually influencing even members of Congress, who in 1958 cut off arms shipments to Batista's dictatorial regime.

On the first day of his April visit to Washington, Castro acknowledged his debt to the U.S. media during a celebration in the Cuban Embassy on 16th Street NW. The occasion was the honoring of his thirteen favorite correspondents. During the two years of his struggle to power, most of the thirteen had worked independently, but they were familiar with one another's work. Some had cooperated on the tasks of finding the rebel camps and gaining access to Fidel or his brother Raúl. In the process, some were arrested and jailed briefly. One was threatened with torture. Two others were injured when rebels' jeeps overturned in the rugged terrain. Another was hospitalized with exhaustion.

Nine of the thirteen showed up at the Cuban Embassy, but all thirteen were named the next day in a perfunctory, three-paragraph story. It was written by United Press International and published in the *New York Times*, very modestly positioned low on page 4. Although two of the honored—Herbert L. Matthews and Homer Bigart—were *New York Times* reporters, the *Times* news editors may have considered the dubious nature of the award. Since taking power in January, the Castro regime had so far provoked protests by conducting summary trials and executions of Batista regime supporters, so-called *Batistianos*.[1]

Foremost among the thirteen was Herbert Matthews, a *Times* editorial writer. He had scored the biggest initial scoop. He was the first to publish, on February 24, 1957, that Castro was *not* dead, as United Press International had reported. Matthews found Castro and wrote that he was "alive and fighting hard and successfully."[2]

That story made headlines internationally and inspired other journalists to follow. One after another during two years, the thirteen spread Castro's message across the full spectrum of mid-twentieth-century mass media. For the Columbia Broadcasting System, Robert Taber used the new documentary film format to show Castro and his "jungle fighters" to millions of

Sunday evening viewers on CBS television. When Taber handed over the microphone, Castro in recognizable English appealed directly to Americans. Magazine writers in words and pictures portrayed Castro and his rebels on guard or on the march. By far the most persistent magazine writer was Andrew St. George, freelancing first with *Cavalier* and eventually hired by *Look, Coronet,* and *Life.* St. George also served as guide and photographer for Sam Halper with *Time* and *Life* magazines and advised the one woman among the thirteen, Dickey Chapelle, a freelancer for the *Reader's Digest.* Jules Dubois, the *Chicago Tribune*'s Latin American correspondent, reported so much of the revolution that by April of 1959 he had published a book. His rival at the *Chicago Sun Times,* Ray Brennan, hospitalized for exhaustion after spending so much time in the mountains, was also working on a book. Some had smaller roles. Morton Silverstein, an associate of Mike Wallace at CBS, had been in Cuba vacationing with his wife when he headed to the mountains and freelanced bulletins for radio and newspapers. A latecomer to Cuba, Robert Branson, representing the *Toledo Blade,* narrowly focused on a Toledo man who abandoned his wife and children to lead a rebel unit.

The four who did not attend the ceremony were also named in the three-paragraph story. A veteran war correspondent, Homer Bigart, got the assignment when the *Times*'s news editors decided to switch to a news reporter rather than continue relying on Matthews. Although Matthews had covered wars, he was by that time an editorial writer accustomed to writing his opinions, and the editors wanted to back away from his evident bias toward Castro. The youngest of the thirteen, Karl E. Meyer, boosted his career with a series of six articles that the *Washington Post* promoted in advance with a photograph of Meyer on horseback. For radio, Charles Shaw, a World War II protégé of CBS icon Edward R. Murrow, had become a prominent broadcaster and news director in Philadelphia. He thought so highly of his radio reports from rebel territory that he submitted them for the 1959 Peabody Award competition. Finally, Wendell Hoffman was Robert Taber's cameraman who lugged the bulky CBS equipment up to Cuba's highest peak; his own story was translated into Spanish for the famous Cuban newspaper *Bohemia.*

Highlighting the embassy ceremony, Premier Castro, dressed in a military uniform, presented each journalist with a gold medal. Since victory in January, the regime had awarded many commercially produced medals and pins, some with Fidel's image, in support of peace, agrarian reform, and solidarity with the regime.[3] But these medals for his favored journalists were far more distinctive. Specially cast in eighteen-karat gold, each was engraved with the journalist's name. And though they did not have Castro's image, they did have the distinctive flourish of his signature. Inscribed were the words "to our American Friend with Gratitude."[4]

Also engraved there was a further message from Castro—four words by which he characterized the journalists' work. The four words—"Sierra Maestra Press Mission"—stated clearly that he believed they had faithfully carried out a "mission." For *la causa* (the cause) and *la lucha* (the struggle), they had served as propagandists.

Although the correspondents did not deny that their work aided the revolution, they did not consider themselves partisans in a "press mission." In fact, their motives were diverse and mostly personal. Herbert Matthews, Ray Brennan, and Charles Shaw rejuvenated their careers. Jules Dubois was a crusader for press freedom and against dictatorships throughout Latin America. The project advanced the careers of Robert Taber at CBS and Karl Meyer at the *Washington Post and Times Herald.* Andrew St. George and Dickey Chapelle freelanced for magazine paychecks. *Time*'s Sam Halper took the assignment to catch up with the competition and perhaps be promoted. Morton Silverstein mainly relished the excitement. And Homer Bigart, Wendell Hoffman, and Robert Branson were just doing their jobs.

Certainly they had not worked for Fidel Castro but for the organizations that paid them and for their publics at home. Their reports had passed peer review by scrupulous gatekeepers—editors, publishers, and network executives. Even the conservative publisher Henry Luce's editors at *Time* and *Life* featured stories and photographs that popularized the rebels' struggle. So, while the correspondents' stories, scripts, and photographs usually portrayed the rebellion as Castro and his rebels presented it, their editors had considered their work as justifiable, even laudable journalism: they were reporting the "other side" of the story, the side rigidly suppressed by the dictatorship's censorship of the Cuban press.

Serving a revolutionary "press mission" would have violated an honored ethical standard established in the twentieth century, that of impartiality. By the 1950s, leaders of American journalism had become committed to objectivity. The American Society of Newspaper Editors in 1923 had adopted the first national code of ethics; objectivity and impartiality had become part of the creed to distinguish American journalism as not only a business but a profession. That ethic, as media critic John Merrill observed, had become "a kind of organizational imperative or belief" so that news stories would be truthful, unbiased, full, and fair.[5] Applied to Cuba, that imperative might have required balancing the reporting on all sides—the dictatorship and the revolutionaries, as well as the Cuban exiles (especially those in Miami actively competing against Castro to overthrow Batista). By that standard, the work of only three of the thirteen showed such an effort for inclusivity.

It served Castro's purpose that this cohort of thirteen, in the war zone, abandoned the code of impartiality as irrelevant. They were reporting on a revolution against a tyrant who had seized power in a military coup and whose regime practiced bribery, torture, state-sponsored murder, and press censorship. The correspondents' hard-gotten stories were, in their opinions and the opinions of their editors, truthful. Another consideration was that there was no code of ethics for international correspondents similar to the one for U.S.-based reporters.[6] In practice, as the media critic J. Herbert Altschull eventually concluded, that ideal of objectivity evidently applied to American journalists "only within the geographic limits of the United States."[7]

None of the thirteen earned Castro's appreciation more than Herbert L. Matthews. Matthews had raised him from the dead to international prominence. The photograph of Castro, alive and well, had appeared on the front page of the Sunday *New York Times*, the paper often considered as the "gold standard for 'fair' and 'balanced.'"[8] Matthews's scoop confounded the Cuban authorities. They had already closed the book on Castro, claiming the army had killed the thirty-year-old rebel and most of his eighty-one followers shortly after their yacht from Mexico ran aground on Cuba's southeastern coast. On December 3, 1956, that information, given to the United Press correspondent in Havana, had appeared on the *New York Times* front page: "Cuba Wipes out Invaders; Leader Is among 40 Dead."

In the following days that story lost credibility. The regime could not display Castro's body. Nor could it explain why the army remained on high alert near the landing site. The dictatorship had little credibility, certainly not with Castro's 26th of July Movement, some of them loyalists since Castro's first aborted uprising in 1953. One week after Castro was allegedly killed, he seemed possibly alive. A *Time* magazine story reported that the "government believed Castro was somewhere on the island," identifying Castro as "a well-born, well-to-do daredevil of 29" and adding that "Batista declared modified martial law in one suspect province," indicative of a continuing threat.[9] In addition to erring on Fidel's age—he was thirty, born on August 18, 1926—the U.S. media did not delve much deeper into the biography of this "wellborn, well-to-do daredevil."

By mid-December of 1956, government authorities conceded that not all the rebels had been killed or captured, and Batista issued an order for the army to suppress the rebellion at the earliest possible time and with the fewest possible casualties. The communiqué from the Presidential Palace, the grand classical home of Cuban presidents since 1920, stated that the military would drop leaflets from planes so the rebels "may surrender with full guarantees for their lives," a promise that some survivors hiding in the sugarcane fields would unfortunately believe. Significantly, the regime did not mention that the air force was bombing the mountains populated by thousands of poor farmers and squatters.[10]

By mid-December, too, reliable news that "Fidel was safe and sound" reached Havana and was printed in twenty thousand copies of the Movement's underground publication, *Revolución*. Its editor, Carlos Franqui, had learned the truth after making the bus trip to Santiago. There he talked with army officers who said that Castro was "still being hunted down." While Franqui was there, Castro smuggled a message to leaders of the Movement that he and eleven others—including his brother Raúl Castro and Argentinian rebel Ernesto Che Guevara—"were safe in the hands of Crescencio Pérez and the peasant militias." They were being guided "into the Sierra."[11]

Publishing that news, Franqui wrote, "played an important part at a moment of confusion, weakness, and hardships." While the Cuban press and radio were censored, Franqui noted that *Revolución* "made the whole country sit up and take notice of the Movement. And it sparked an all-out persecution campaign by the police," who detained suspects and confiscated copies of *Revolución*.[12]

Then one night in mid-January, in the light of a full moon, the rebels went on the offensive, attacking an army camp. "We sneaked up to within 120 feet," Guevara noted. "Fidel opened fire with two bursts from his machine gun and all the available rifles followed suit. The soldiers were practically defenseless and were being mowed down. . . . This was our first victory." At this stage, they were desperate for weapons and Castro was rationing bullets. The victory cost them five hundred rounds, but they took a thousand rounds from the fort, plus eight rifles and one Thompson machine gun.[13]

The foreign press, in its sketchy report on that battle, assumed the rebels were led by Castro, whom they now described as "the swashbuckling young lawyer." *Time* magazine, with information from its Havana-based correspondent, reported that Batista "tried aerial bombing, strafing, napalm attacks and paratroop drops" and then "was forced to give up the waiting game and mount a major offensive," airlifting 1,100 men. "In sharp skirmishes, the rebels captured rifles and machine guns." Batista's well-equipped army "so far has been ineffectual" against Castro's "hit-and-run platoons." Local sympathizers were sending the rebels food and supplies, accepting as payment "personally autographed IOUs, payable 'when the revolution wins.'"[14] Although censors kept this news out of the Cuban press and methodically censored *Time* and other imported publications, news and rumors filtered into Cuba with visitors.

Amid the suppression, Herbert Matthews's scoop lifted the "veil of silence," becoming the first article to give evidence that Castro was very much alive. Working with the 26th of July Movement's contacts in New York, Matthews arranged to interview Fidel in the Sierra. On February 17, under the cover of a forest, they talked for a few hours until dawn. Matthews jotted in his reporter's notebook key words and phrases about what Fidel said, how he said it, and what he looked like. Matthews was obviously impressed with Castro's height, beard, rifle, telescopic lens, confidence, and flair. Returning immediately to New York, this veteran reporter of the Spanish Civil War and World War II converted his six pages of notes into "the biggest scoop of our times."[15]

One week after the interview, on February 24, the *Times* published the story in the most prominent spot on the front page of the Sunday paper, together with a photograph of Castro holding his favorite rifle with its telescopic lens. The headline—"Cuban Rebel Is Visited in Hideout"—drew worldwide attention to Castro and to the reporter who had found him. It was stunning news that Castro was still "alive and fighting hard and successfully in the rugged, almost impenetrable" Sierra Maestra. "President Fulgencio Batista has the cream of his Army around the area, but the Army men are fighting a thus-far losing battle to destroy the most dangerous enemy General Batista has yet faced."

Matthews also emphasized his own triumph. He had broken "the tightest censorship in the history of the Cuban Republic" to deliver "the first sure news" that Castro was in Cuba and that in "the outside world," Matthews alone was the bearer of the truth. "No one connected with the outside world, let alone with the press, has seen Señor Castro except this writer. No one in Havana, not even at the United States Embassy with all its resources for getting information, will know until this report is published that Fidel Castro is really in the Sierra Maestra."[16]

Why did the *Times* consider this the most important front-page story? Apart from breaking the silence, correcting its previous misleading reports, and revealing the dictatorship's big lie, the editors of the nation's "newspaper of record" became the first to assess the strength of the rebellion. Not even the U.S. Embassy in Havana had such information, largely because, as Matthews put it, Ambassador Arthur Gardner "was closely identified and very friendly with the dictator."[17]

In these first descriptions, Matthews framed Castro favorably. He portrayed the rebel leader as charismatic and courageous, a freedom fighter who risked his life against great odds to defeat a dictator and restore Cuba's democracy: "He has strong ideas of liberty, democracy, social justice, the need to restore the Constitution, to hold elections."[18]

The Batista regime responded immediately by attacking Matthews and the *Times*, claiming the story was a complete fiction, that no such interview occurred. That proved to be an embarrassment when the *Times* countered the next day, in the second of the three-part series, by publishing a photograph, taken by one of the rebels, showing Matthews and Castro side by side, smoking Cuban cigars.[19] In Cuba, censors had cut out the first two stories. But a better fate met Matthews's third article. Coincidentally, Batista's censorship decree expired that very day, and Cuban editors eagerly published excerpts.

Matthews expressed some humility about creating such a sensation, saying he was just a journalist doing his job. "There was a story to be got, a censorship to be broken. I got it and I did it."[20] Nonetheless, his scoop had ramifications for American journalism. During the height of the Cold War when international news focused on the Middle East and Asia, Matthews put Castro and his rebels on the nation's news agenda. His revelations of fact and opinion, so framed and highlighted, challenged other correspondents to follow. Immediately, the *Chicago Tribune* reprinted most of Matthews's three articles, a decision supported by one of the thirteen, the *Tribune*'s Latin American correspondent, Jules Dubois.

In New York, the freelancer Andrew St. George was immediately struck with envy and the inspiration to sell a story on Castro to an adventure magazine. His wife Jean remembered "the morning he came out of the bathroom with a towel wrapped around his waist. He was waving a copy of the *New York Times* with Herbert Matthews's article about Fidel in the Sierra. He was so excited and kept saying, 'I wish I had done this.' And then within a few days he got the call from *Cavalier*. It was a dream come true for him."[21]

During the next two years, the other twelve followed Matthews's trail. Each sought new ways to portray the revolution. As Matthews had, they invariably called attention to their personal encounters, thus documenting how they succeeded where several others failed.[22] They stressed their connections with the Movement's operatives in New York and Miami, their escorts and secretive journeys from Havana to the Sierra Maestra mountains, and their ingenuity in outwitting the Cuban police and the army patrols. They mentioned the risks of detection, arrest, and possible torture, and they elaborated on their disguises as tourists and businessmen traveling with friends and relatives. They endured all this because, as Andrew St. George said so well, they *wished* for such a story. They needed Castro.

Then, too, they succeeded because Castro needed *them*. Because the regime's recurrent censorship was relentlessly enforced across Cuba by bribes and terror, the U.S. media were essential to publicize the Movement to the world outside of Cuba from which Castro could draw money, weapons, recruits, and political support. "He needed publicity in the strict sense of calling attention to himself," Matthews wrote. "Without a press, Fidel Castro was a hunted outlaw, leading a small band of youths in a remote jungle area of eastern Cuba, isolated and ineffectual." Matthews regarded Castro's dilemma as the same that had faced the Cuban rebels in the 1890s in their war against Spanish rule. General Máximo Gómez had made "remarkable use" of American newspapers. Gómez used almost the same words half a century earlier: "Without a press we shall get nowhere." With a press, Matthews noted, Gómez "got American intervention."[23]

Having succeeded, all the correspondents returned to the mainland, where their stories were expedited with little or no peer review or editing before being printed or broadcast. Senior staff reservations were few. However, the *New York Times*'s news editors began to worry that Herbert Matthews was too supportive of Castro; they decided to turn the Cuban assignment over to a news reporter, Homer Bigart.

The U.S. media stream during 1957 followed the revolution's progress with photographs, film, maps, and even Castro's voice in broken English. The media story line was that Fidel Castro's force of bearded rebels (*barbudos*) was growing and beginning to come down from their camps in the high Sierra Maestra to attack army outposts. During twenty months of such attention, the rebels (whose beards indicated how long they had fought) became almost legendary, and their leader, El Comandante, as they called Castro, was portrayed as heroic, standing his ground against Batista's land and air assaults.

The coverage of the revolution soon had to deal with Castro's political views. In March, President-General Batista branded Castro as a Communist. In interviews, Castro repeatedly brushed off accusations that he or brother

Raúl or Che Guevara was a Communist, and he emphasized his pledge to restore the constitution of 1940 and democratic elections. Asked about his own political ambitions, Castro often replied that, under the constitution, he was "too young" to be president. Seldom, however, did the thirteen provide much perspective on Castro's earlier political life and rhetoric, as when he had criticized colonialism and U.S. imperialism. When questioned, Fidel maintained he no longer held those views.

Not until after the revolution did some of the thirteen express concerns that they were used as conduits for rebel propaganda. But certainly they did not relate Castro's methods to twentieth-century propaganda strategies developed and used by other revolutionaries, Lenin in Russia and Mao in China. Belatedly, Jules Dubois expressed doubt about Fidel's intentions. In April of 1959, in the same month when Castro gave him the gold medal, Dubois's hurriedly written book about the revolution lauded the victor: "It was not until Fidel Castro came along that the people of that island found the leader they were willing to follow, to fight for their lost liberty." But the book's title raised the central question: "Fidel Castro: Rebel—Liberator or Dictator?"[24]

Nor did the thirteen place Castro in the context of Cuba's history of autocratic regimes. Since gaining independence after hundreds of years of autocratic Spanish rule, Cuba had still tended toward authoritarian regimes supported by the military. During Castro's early childhood, the dictator was General Gerardo Machado. In 1933, a bloody revolution forced Machado into exile and Batista rose to power, becoming the first president under the constitution of 1940, then in 1952 the dictator. That ended the twelve-year experiment with a democracy characterized by widespread corruption that provided paths to wealth for the few. By 1952, as noted by one reformist professor who joined Castro's revolution, "disenchantment with the fraud and corruption of the previous [elected] administrations" stirred up a middle-class reform movement that Batista's coup took advantage of but subsequently suppressed.[25] At the time of the 1952 coup, fundamental weaknesses undermined the democratic experiment, notably underemployment, massive poverty, an insufficiently informed electorate, and a politically motivated corps of military officers.[26]

In 1957, Castro with his armed rebels emerged increasingly as the one challenger with a real chance to defeat the dictator and restore the democracy. Castro's viability grew as other revolutionary alternatives failed. Early in 1957, Havana university students failed in an attempt to assassinate Batista in the Presidential Palace. Later in 1957, an invasion force of Miami exiles funded by former Cuban president Carlos Prío Socarrás was compromised by a Batista spy and quickly defeated. Over time, Castro became the only challenger with the essentials for contesting the military dictatorship: his home-grown image of a leader who defied death and an armed guerrilla force holding the naturally strategic high ground in the Sierra Maestra—his "Free Cuba"—to which over time he could attract money, arms, volunteers, and the foreign press.

Beyond the screen of the dictatorship's strict censorship, the unfolding saga of Castro's revolution would be best told in the U.S. media. And while Castro worked with all of the thirteen correspondents he honored, he always regarded Herbert L. Matthews with special warmth. For it was Matthews's scoop announcing that Castro was not dead, but "alive and fighting hard and successfully," that launched the "Sierra Maestra Press Mission."

CHAPTER 2

SCOOP!

On February 9, 1957, Herbert Matthews arrived at Havana's airport. He and his wife, Nancie, posed as North American vacationers lured by holiday promotions to enjoy the sunshine and casinos in this Caribbean paradise. Nothing, he assumed, "could have looked more innocent than a middle-aged couple of American tourists." He was right, but if questioned he was prepared to lie. A covert assignment required a variance from journalistic ethics.[1]

Since December, police in Havana had become more suspicious because of a cycle of violence attributed to terrorists, as the government branded the recent insurgents. Very public bombings had unsettled nerves. Matthews would soon learn that the situation was far more troubling in eastern Cuba. There, authorities had responded by killing at least thirty young men. Their bodies were hung in public places as gruesome effigies.

Matthews wrote that Havana and the other Cuban cities "crackle with the most astonishing rumors." Cubans generally doubted the government's claim that Castro was dead. Cuban Army officers and the Batista regime at first had cited the United Press story by bureau chief Francis McCarthy that Castro was among those killed during the rebels' landing along the southeast coast. That was on December 2, and within days, the army and air force had pursued the rebels and announced that they killed or captured most of them.[2]

In New York, Matthews had wondered why the government did not display Castro's body. Lacking such proof, the Batista regime offered another explanation: Castro was not with the militants on the yacht, but remained safely behind at their training camp in Mexico. If Castro *had* come with his men, Matthews questioned Castro's wisdom in announcing the timing of his invasion. "How could a revolution, proclaimed in advance, succeed against a regime like General Batista's, which controls the army and its loyalty?"[3]

Then in January, the regime had suddenly decreed a forty-five-day censorship of Cuba's press, radio, and television. Newspaper publishers protested without effect, as did the Inter-American Press Association. Now the regime also required foreign correspondents to clear outgoing dispatches.[4]

And censors continued the practice of removing incoming stories such as a *New York Times* report, attributed to anti-Batista sources, that Castro was alive and fighting government soldiers.[5]

The suppression called more attention to Cuba. In New York, Matthews now questioned why Batista felt so threatened that he needed to gag even his loyal press, whose staff was subsidized by government bribes. "Censorship never helps in such situations. On the contrary, it adds tensions, increases rumors and gives the impression to the world that the government is in desperate straits. This would not seem to be the case." Why was censorship necessary when Batista had a mighty U.S.-equipped and -trained army? And economically, the country appeared to be prospering. In the absence of credible sources, Castro's fate was the one looming question: "If Fidel is alive," Matthews had wondered in January, "why does he not do or say something to show that he is? Since Dec. 2 he has kept absolutely quiet—or he was dead."[6]

As a member of the *Times* editorial board, Matthews had staked out Latin America as his special area of interest. Given his extensive experience reporting on dictatorships in Europe, he felt he understood the dynamics of dictatorships—rule and rebellion—whether he was writing about Argentina's Juan Perón or Cuba's Fulgencio Batista. As a *Times* editorial writer, he wrote about Cuba without the restrictions of the newsroom's codes of objectivity or impartiality. He was expected to express his opinion; in fact, he was paid to be opinionated.

In 1952, shortly after Batista seized power from the democratically elected president, Carlos Prío Socarrás, Matthews went to Cuba, questioning why Cubans had accepted another dictator. The answer, he reasoned, was that incapable or corrupt leaders over time had conditioned Cubans to "adopt an attitude of apathy toward their government." Cuba had become "a republic without citizens," he concluded in a long article that was also translated and reprinted in the Cuban magazine *Bohemia*.[7]

By 1956 Matthews had been following developments in Cuba for more than four years. While Batista's regime prevailed, most news reports focused on economic news, much of it positive. Statistically, Cubans' average income was reputed as among the highest in Latin America, despite chronic unemployment between sugar harvests. While the country still depended on its sugar exports, there were efforts to diversify through industrialization.[8] Batista had launched a massive public works employment project, borrowing $350 million to build a tunnel connecting Havana and East Havana.

Tourism was growing thanks to the rising popularity of leisure air travel. Cubana Airlines made news when it added a sixth daily flight between Miami and Havana on Viscount turbojets. Pan American Airways advertised cheap weekend round-trips from Miami, and Eastern Airlines and Delta Air Lines stopped in Havana.[9] While swift flights appealed to weekenders, the West India Fruit and Steamship Company announced new 104-mile ferry service between Key West and Havana so vacationers could tour the island in their cars. Also more leisurely were the overnight cruises from the Port of Miami aboard the SS *Florida* or the *Evangeline* that by the next morning gave voyagers a picturesque first view of Havana's foreign cityscape, the Malecón shoreline, the old Spanish fort guarding the harbor, and, in the water, Cuban boys diving for passengers' coins.[10]

Havana was the leading tourist destination in the Caribbean, well ahead of rival Puerto Rico. Travel writers reported that Cuba was responding to Puerto Rico's surge in hotel construction with its own surge along Havana's waterfront. Encouraged by financial incentives from the Batista regime, investors were building two new luxury hotels with casinos, the Habana Hilton and the Habana Riviera. The Riviera was being funded by the reputed U.S. mobster Meyer Lansky. "Havana will be a magical city," Lansky said privately. "Hotels like jewels built right on top of the coral reef that supports the Malecón. Fabulous casinos, nightclubs, and bordellos as far as the eye can see. More people than you can imagine."[11] The Riviera was no isolated investment, but part of the mob's long-range plan to develop a new base in a friendly, offshore haven.

Travel writers emphasized Havana's cultural attractions. By then Ernest Hemingway was such an icon that tourists made the rounds of his favorite bars and visited his villa, Finca Vigía, where he had lived on and off since 1939. There he wrote much of *For Whom the Bell Tolls* and the book that in 1954 won the Nobel Prize for Literature, *The Old Man and the Sea*. And there in 1957 he wrote about his early years as a writer in Paris in *A Moveable Feast*.[12] In one bar Hemingway frequented, La Bodeguita del Medio, the management posted the author's signed testament written on butcher paper: "My mojito in La Bodeguita. My daiquiri in La Floridita." Elsewhere in the city, the Tropicana night club and casino—famous for spectacular floorshows and the Afro-Cuban jazz pianist Ramón "Bebo" Valdés Amaro—was open again for business despite the bombing on New Year's morning.[13]

Beneath the optimism, Herbert Matthews noted two persistent "bad spots" in the economy and the regime: "Unemployment is heavy, corruption is rife."[14] Those bad spots had plagued Cuba's experiment with democracy, established by the constitution of 1940. By 1951, the danger of economic and political instability was foreshadowed by investigators from the International Bank for Reconstruction and Development. They warned that "subversive and specious hands" threatened Cuba because consecutive elected presidents neglected three looming problems well known to Cuba's elites: "ill-conceived" spending, "lack of integrity" (a euphemism for corruption), and various unpredictable autocratic "laws by decree."[15] In short, the three elected presidents—Batista in 1940, Ramón Grau San Martin in 1944, and Prío Socarrás in 1948—had been spendthrift and untrustworthy.

In 1952, the predicted "subversive and specious hands" struck suddenly. Fulgencia Batista, again a candidate for president, was polling a poor third when he conspired with dissatisfied army generals. On March 10, they staged a coup and then canceled the election. The coup was bloodless, as President Prío Socarrás sought refuge in the Mexican Embassy and chose exile in Miami.

The coup also sank the political aspirations of Fidel Castro. He was a member of the Ortodoxo Party running for Congress to represent a poor district of Havana where he had a law practice. Castro responded by organizing an anti-Batista resistance movement with his own followers, a nucleus of no more than ten friends. Sixteen months later, his "Fidelista army," largely recruited from working-class followers of the Ortodoxo Party, attacked a stronghold of the Cuban Army—the Moncada army barracks at Santiago de Cuba, in Oriente Province in southeastern Cuba—hoping that an impressive victory there might inspire the people of Oriente to rise in support.

On Sunday, July 26, 1953, armed with an assortment of guns, Castro and 130 rebels assaulted the fortress. Their advantage of surprise was soon lost. After that, undermanned and overwhelmed, the attackers were suppressed in less than thirty minutes. Many were subjected to ghastly torture and then killed. "The final *Fidelista* death toll was sixty-nine, and only five wounded because, as Castro later pointed out, the regime wanted no surviving prisoners."[16]

Within days, both Castro brothers were caught. Raúl was arrested at a roadblock on July 29. Fidel and his companions were captured on August 1. Soldiers found them sleeping in a farm hut and wanted to kill them. According to Fidel, one soldier called him an "assassin" and he yelled back, "It is you who are assassins . . . it is you who kill unarmed prisoners . . . you are the soldiers of a tyrant!" Their leader intervened. Lt. Pedro Manuel Sarría Tartabull had met Fidel at the University of Havana.

Castro later told a biographer, "A corporal shouted to Sarría, 'Lieutenant, we'll kill them!' [Sarría] roared, 'Don't kill them! I order you not to kill them! I am in command here. . . . You can't kill ideas. . . . You can't kill ideas.'"[17]

Held in the Santiago city jail, Fidel Castro soon established himself as a celebrity. Newsmen were permitted to interview him, reporting "widely and amply" that he—not exiled president Prío Socarrás in Miami—was fully responsible for the attack. Castro was also permitted to tell his story in a radio broadcast, during which he proclaimed, "We came to regenerate Cuba." As Castro later reflected, "And at that minute, the second phase of the revolution began."[18]

Fidel was tried for an "act aimed at bringing about an armed uprising against the Constitutional powers of the State." The trial gave him a forum in which to assert that his rebellion was legal and that President-General Batista was a usurper of power, guilty of violating the constitution. In his two-hour defense, Castro contended that "the dictatorship that oppresses the nation is not a Constitutional power, but an unconstitutional one . . . established against the Constitution." He stated, "We have fomented a rebellion against one single power, an illegal power, which has usurped and merged into a single whole both the Legislative and Executive Powers of the nation, and has thus destroyed the entire system that was specifically safeguarded by the Code."[19] He later would publish his defense in a revolutionary pamphlet.[20]

Fidel Castro was sentenced to fifteen years in prison, but he served less than two years. Meanwhile, public pressure led President-General Batista to sign an amnesty for "the boys of Moncada" and other "political prisoners." On May 15, 1955, Castro, his brother Raúl, and their fellow revolutionaries walked out of the Isle of Pines prison. By June 12, Fidel had taken active leadership of the 26th of July Movement that he had organized in prison, naming it for the date of the Moncada assault. Fearing for his safety, on July 7, 1955, he left Cuba to raise and train an army in Mexico and plan an invasion.[21]

B y February of 1957, Herbert Matthews's curiosity about Castro's fate merged with Castro's urgent need to tell his story. For weeks, Matthews suspected that the Cuban government's latest censorship decree was covering up a massive secret. With the Cuban press gagged, any foreign correspondent who discovered what the truth was would come out with a scoop. So Matthews alerted the *Times* bureau chief in Havana, Ruby Hart Phillips, that he would soon be coming on vacation.[22]

In the Sierra Maestra, Castro was trying to arrange a meeting with any journalist who could report that he was alive and fighting. He had already sent a messenger, René Rodríguez, to arrange an interview. In a remarkable chain of connections that led to Matthews, Rodríguez met with the Havana leader of Castro's 26th of July Movement, Faustino Pérez, who delegated a Havana University student, Javier Pazos, "to make the necessary contacts" through his father, the economist Felipe Pazos. The elder Pazos had been a founder of the Cuban National Bank and was serving as the bank's president when he was displaced on the day of the coup in 1952 by one of Batista's long-time political supporters.[23] Now Pazos was among a small cadre of influential middle-class citizens supporting Castro. Among Pazos's many contacts was Ruby Hart Phillips at the *Times*. Phillips already knew that Matthews wanted to visit, so she sent a note to him via her boss, the *Times* foreign news editor, Emmanuel R. "Manny" Freedman. At the end of the chain, Matthews received a mysterious message to "get to Havana as soon as possible."[24]

Without knowing the reason for this urgency, Matthews hastened to Havana with wife Nancie. At the *Times* office, Matthews asked Felipe Pazos if Castro was alive. "I had been strongly inclined to believe in his death," Pazos said later, but "the first convincing indication I had had of his being alive . . . was the message that he wanted to see a foreign correspondent."[25]

Matthews was expecting to step right into the mission. But because Pazos regarded him—a balding, middle-aged man—as unfit for an arduous journey into the mountains, he thought Matthews was the go-between who "would send for someone from New York."

Surprised that Pazos would consider him unfit, Matthews insisted that he would go himself. "Without sufficient care not to show my surprise," Pazos told Matthews later, "I asked whether you were apt at mountain climbing, and you just repeated dryly, but softly, that you would go."[26]

As an economist, Matthews wrote, Pazos "could not have known what makes a journalist tick. As if any newspaperman would pass up an opportunity like that! A newspaperman who will run a big risk for a mediocre story is a fool; one who will not run a big risk for a big story should go into the public relations business." This was an opportunity to "break the tightest censorship in the history of the Cuban Republic." Finding Castro before any other journalist would be "the biggest scoop of our times. There is no thrill in journalism like getting a scoop."[27]

Matthews had not had such an opportunity since his years as a war correspondent in the 1930s and 1940s. Early on he had been eager to go to war.

At the age of eighteen, he had volunteered to fight in France in 1918, but he arrived as the world war was winding down and saw no action. After getting a degree in Romance languages at Columbia University, Matthews got his first job at the *Times* in 1922—as a secretary-stenographer for the assistant business manager. He wrote he was thankful that journalism "has always attracted young graduates—like myself in 1922—trained for nothing in particular, with no technical or professional knowledge, but with a belief that they can write." Working steadfastly, he rose to a reporter's position and then in 1931 returned to Europe, assigned to the *Times*'s Paris Bureau.[28]

During the next decade, he got himself assigned to report on a succession of wars, close to the fighting, often in the position of covering only one side. In 1935, he volunteered to go to Italy and accompanied Mussolini's army invading Abyssinia (Ethiopia). For the other side's story, the *Times* alternated dispatches from the reporter for the *Times* of London, George Steer, who was pro-Abyssinian. As one historian noted, that war attracted a mix of esteemed and young correspondents, some "wide-eyed youngsters" including a recent bridegroom and a sports reporter, and some notables such as the British novelist Evelyn Waugh, who later championed Italian colonization and satirized "left wing" reporters in his novel *Scoop*. Matthews, in his mid-thirties, was described as "a tall, gangling, ex-secretary-stenographer."[29]

The war correspondents were notably biased. While some sought to rouse world sympathy for the "hopelessly outmatched Ethiopians," Matthews considered his coverage as being "as straightforward and frank as censorship would allow," yet conceded that he nonetheless favored the successful Fascist army. On the one hand, he reflected, he had been "content to be a mere spectator, to applaud [Italian] success because it was success, and to refrain from any moral judgment." At another time, he explained his pro-Italian slant another way: "If you start from the premise that a lot of rascals are having a fight, it is not unnatural to want to see the victory of the rascal you like and I liked the Italians during that scrimmage more than I did the British [ally] or the Abyssinians."[30]

After the Italians triumphed in 1936, the *Times* managing editor, Edwin James, granted Matthews a leave from the Paris Bureau to cover the Spanish Civil War. As it turned out, Matthews would be reporting on the Loyalist Republican forces defending Madrid while another *Times* reporter, William P. Carney, was assigned to cover the attacking army of Generalissimo Francisco Franco's Nationalists. Matthews worked out of Madrid's Hotel Florida—home to a number of noted writers and journalists, among them the novelist John

Dos Passos, the Hungarian émigré photojournalist Robert Capa, and Ernest Hemingway, the latter reporting for *Collier's* magazine. Matthews and Hemingway shared the belief that a writer could not cover the war from a hotel. Rather than depend upon military news releases, they set out to find the fighting at the front.

In one battle in March of 1937, Matthews scored a scoop when he discovered that "the attacking divisions had been Italian," not Spanish, indicating that the Italians were backing Franco with troops. "The story was a very big one. This was the first positive evidence that Mussolini had not merely sent planes, cannons, tanks, technicians, and advisers—he had sent an expeditionary force." Ironically, because Matthews was "alone in emphasizing [the] Italian angle," explained the assistant managing editor in New York, the story was considered "obvious propaganda" for the Loyalist side. Matthews learned that the editor had "ordered the copyreaders to substitute the word 'Insurgent' wherever I had sent 'Italian.'"[31]

In fact, editors in New York consistently edited his dispatches, seeking to eliminate what they considered Loyalist bias. "The story that I had told—of bravery, of tenacity, of discipline and constant decency—had been scoffed at by many," Matthews wrote years later. "But the lessons I had learned! They seemed worth a great deal. Even then, heartsick and discouraged as I was, something sang inside of me. I, like the Spaniards, had fought my war and lost, but I could not be persuaded that I had set too bad an example."[32]

Afterward, Matthews became part of the *Times* team that covered the Second World War. In 1946, after a decade of reporting from war zones, he reflected on his urge "to seek adventure, risk life and take joy in comradeship and danger—these are deep feelings, so deep that even I who love life and family and luxury and books have yielded to them. . . . I still say, 'Let him who loves life, risk it,' for it is only in danger, and in surviving it, that one can learn how good it is to be alive."[33]

As such experiences were his fondest memories, it was almost like retirement from active duty when in 1949, at the age of forty-nine, the war horse came home to the *Times* building in Manhattan to the routine of writing editorials and reacting to others' stories. His desk on the sedate tenth floor was separated from the action in the newsroom seven floors below. Soon he developed a specialization that would get him outside New York: He began writing about political turmoil in Latin America.

n February of 1957, Matthews's spirits had risen at the thought of being inside Cuba's civil war. This time the "rascal" he disliked was easily the military dictator, the general and president Fulgencio Batista. The "rascals" he
longed to meet—and possibly like—were the rebels and their elusive chieftain
who most people thought was dead. "Only those fighting with him and those
who had faith and hope knew he was alive," Matthews wrote, "and those who
knew were very few and in utmost peril of their lives if their knowledge was
traced. . . . To arrange for me to penetrate the Sierra Maestra and meet Fidel
Castro, dozens of men and women in Oriente Province ran a truly terrible
risk because their lives would be forfeit." For rebels, "torture always came
first"—before execution—because Batista's police "would want to extract
whatever information they could get." In this, Americans had no idea of "the
fierceness and viciousness with which the General [Batista] was fighting back
against the terrorism and the rising wave of revolutionary opposition."[34]

It is unlikely that Castro could have found a more suitable correspondent.
Besides writing for a prestigious newspaper—in Matthews's opinion "the
most powerful journalistic instrument that has ever been forged in the free
world"—here was a senior correspondent who had long ago found his voice
and style, as well as his intellectual reach, for interpreting news in broader
political and cultural contexts. His reporting since the Spanish Civil War
demonstrated his distaste for fascism and dictators, as well as his sympathy
for the oppressed. Experience, knowledge, and fluency in Spanish had led
him to this rare moment.

Matthews understood why Castro needed him. "He needed publicity in
the strict sense of calling public attention to himself," Matthews wrote.[35] Fidel
had said he would return to the homeland and he "desperately needed to
let his followers in the cities know that he had kept his promise," observed
Matthews's biographer. Castro had "survived the dictator's best efforts to liq-
uidate him. . . . An interview would be the first volley."[36] With press, he could
strike the dictatorship even from isolation in the Sierra Maestra.

Castro was following the examples of Cuba's heroes of the war against
Spain in the 1890s. José Martí and General Máximo Gómez had sought the
support of American newspapers, among them the *New York Herald*. "Without a press we shall get nowhere," Gómez had said. "With a press," Matthews
noted, Gómez "got American intervention."[37]

Sixty years later, Castro was seeking the same remedy. "Without a press,"
Matthews wrote, "Fidel Castro was a hunted outlaw, leading a small band of
youths in a remote jungle area of eastern Cuba, isolated and ineffectual."[38]

Matthews's story in the *Times* would circumvent Cuba's censorship and break the silence. As Matthews later reflected, he gave Castro and his guerrilla band "a nationwide and even a worldwide fame."[39]

Matthews's trek into the mountains began six days after he and Nancie arrived in Havana. At 5:30 p.m. on Friday, February 15, three Cubans posing as companions met them at their hotel, the Sevilla Biltmore. Matthews told the hotel staff that they were going on a fishing trip. "All I knew was that the rendezvous with Fidel Castro had been fixed for midnight the next night in the Sierra Maestra."[40] The three escorts were the university student leader Javier Pazos; Faustino Pérez, who had told Pazos that Castro wanted the interview; and Liliam Mesa, a young woman from Cuba's upper class so devoted to the revolution that some considered her "fanatical."[41] Matthews was told that the trip would be about five hundred miles, sixteen hours by car, and the last part a climb on foot in a forest. Castro had made allowances for Matthews's age. He "would take the chance of coming a little way toward the edge of the range so that I would not have to do much climbing. There were no roads there and, where we would meet, no horses could go." During the car trip there were some nervous moments. Nancie recalled, "We stopped so many times for thimblefuls of Cuban coffee that a long trail of people had every chance to examine us in detail. By 5 a.m. we were cold. I was hideously depressed." In the sugar country, she worried because Liliam was driving in circles and three times asked directions from the "same pleasant policeman. That charming girl, I thought, is a dangerous wife for a revolutionary." Once a soldier stopped them, and Nancie nearly panicked. But, "he merely peered at us in friendly fashion . . . and we were waved on."[42]

On Saturday the sixteenth, they reached Manzanillo, where Nancie stayed with a family. Matthews was now within sight of the mountains, but was told of a new obstacle. The guide assigned to drive them into the mountains reported that four soldiers were patroling the road. Pazos refused to delay the mission because Castro was already coming down from the high Sierra. "I knew," he said, "the only excuse Fidel would accept for our not going on that day was our getting killed trying."[43]

At 7 p.m., Pazos, Matthews, and three others climbed into a jeep and drove off. Matthews was now posing as "an American sugar planter who could not speak a word of Spanish and who was going out to look over a plantation in a certain village. Our story convinced the Army guard when he stopped us, although he looked dubious for a while. Then came hours of driving through sugar cane and rice fields, across rivers that only jeeps could manage." A heavy rain the day before had turned the path into a morass. At midnight, "after slithering through miles of mud," they went on foot and at last "slid down a hillside to where a stream, dark brown under the nearly full moon, rushed its muddy way. I waded through with the water almost up to my knees. Fifty yards up the other slope was the meeting place."[44]

Nobody was there. In the dark, two of the group set out into the wilderness and found their way back by signaling with a double whistle. "One of us replied in kind, and this had to be kept up for a while, like two groups meeting in a dense fog, until we got together." Their guides had linked up with Castro's scout, who led them "swiftly and unerringly across fields, up steep hills, floundering in the mud. The ground leveled out blessedly at last and then dipped suddenly." There the scout double-whistled softly. "The return whistle came. There was a short parley." Matthews had to go farther. "We were motioned on, sliding down into a heavy groove. The dripping leaves and boughs, the dense vegetation, the mud underfoot, the moonlight—all gave the impression of a tropical forest." There they were told to wait in the grove until dawn on Sunday. They sat on a blanket, eating soda crackers and talking, then napping.[45]

Such detail authenticated the journey. Describing the danger and geography underscored the adventure and focused very much on Matthews himself: Thanks to *his* legs and eyes and ears, a story was being revealed that nobody else had been able to get. He was again proving himself a courageous foreign correspondent, as he had twenty years earlier in Spain when he dared death at the front. This time he was piercing a dictator's veil of silence—"the tightest censorship in the history of the Cuban republic." A journalist, not the dictator, would determine what should be written about the rebel leader and his movement.[46]

Just after dawn, Castro's brother, Raúl, arrived. A few minutes later, "Fidel himself strode in." This Castro was far from dead. "Taking him, as one would at first, by physique and personality, this was quite a man—a powerful six-footer, olive-skinned, full-faced, with a straggly beard." He was "dressed in an olive gray fatigue uniform and carried a rifle with a telescopic sight, of which he was very proud." Castro lowered his voice. Army patrols were possibly nearby. Matthews noted, "No one could speak above a whisper."[47]

In the midst of danger, the scene seemed surreal: the journalist from Forty-third Street sitting with this hunted man in the midst of a Cuban forest. One more time in his long career Matthews was in a war zone among warriors who had so far survived against the dictator's army. Matthews opened his reporter's notebook. "Señor Castro speaks some English but he preferred to speak in Spanish, which he did with extraordinary eloquence." In the low light Matthews recorded his words and anything to authenticate his character and the surrounding danger. "This section surrounded by cols [columns] of soldiers—many fights, [ditto] losses. Bomb every day. 79 days we [have] been fighting."[48]

Castro was proud of his rifle scope. He said Batista's soldiers feared scopes. "We can pick them off at a thousand yards with these guns." Matthews got the impression that "his men have something more than fifty of these." Breakfast was brought. There was tomato juice, ham and crackers made into sandwiches, coffee, and "a box of good Havana cigars." A photo of the occasion showed Matthews smoking while writing in his notebook as Castro worked at lighting his cigar.[49]

They talked for three hours, Castro always with his rifle at the ready and Matthews struggling to frame this character who was so awesome that he threatened a mighty regime. "The personality of the man is overpowering. It was easy to see that his men adore him and also to see why he has caught the imagination of the youth of Cuba all over the island. Here was an educated, dedicated fanatic, a man of ideals, of courage and of remarkable qualities of leadership."[50] Matthews needed more to tell this story. How did Castro expect his band of rebels in the mountains to overthrow the entrenched dictator with a large and equipped army? How many men did he have? What was the goal of his rebellion? The correspondent determined to tell the story as Castro told it to him.

He portrayed Castro as confident of victory. Castro told how he had a tactical advantage by fighting in the mountains. "We have been fighting for seventy-nine days now and are stronger than ever. The soldiers are fighting badly; their morale is low and ours could not be higher." The state of the Cuban Army's morale had been discovered by questioning captured soldiers, who, Castro said, were afterward freed. "We are killing many, but when we take prisoners they are never shot. We question them, talk kindly to them, take their arms and equipment, and then set them free. I know that they are always arrested afterward and we heard some were shot as examples to the others, but they don't want to fight, and they don't know how to fight this kind of mountain warfare. We do."[51]

How had the rebels survived? The peasants who lived in the Sierra, *guajiros,* were helpful because the rebels treated them fairly. This was in stark contrast to their treatment by the area's bandits and by the military. Since

December, the army had herded the *guajiros* out of the mountains, and the air force bombed the forest. The rebels made friends by paying cash for food and supplies. Castro summoned one of his men, who showed Matthews the money to be paid to the peasants—"a stack of peso bills at least a foot high"—equivalent to about $4,000.[52]

In Castro's political imagination, he had already liberated part of the Sierra, and the *guajiros* were the first inhabitants of his "Free Cuba." As Castro explained, this "Free Cuba" of rocks and trees represented a reality that his followers were willing to die for. From here he could strike the plains and sabotage the sugar plantations and return to a safe haven. When he was stronger in men and arms, he could open a second front.[53]

When Matthews turned the conversation to politics, Castro emphasized his commitment to restoring the democracy and elections. "Above all," he told Matthews, "we are fighting for a democratic Cuba, and an end to the dictatorship." Matthews attested to Castro's credibility. "His is a political mind rather than a military one. He has strong ideas of liberty, democracy, social justice, the need to restore the Constitution, to hold elections."[54]

In emphasizing democracy, Castro claimed the moral high ground that President-General Batista could not claim, having usurped power and abrogated the constitution. Batista's power was impressive, but instead rested upon his command of the Cuban Treasury and the army, as well as upon the support of the U.S. ambassador and State Department and the support of U.S. military aid. In Cold War *realpolitik,* Washington regularly armed and trained the Cuban Army as a deterrent against communism in the hemisphere.

Castro stressed one complaint about U.S. policy. Those military weapons sent to Cuba to defend the hemisphere were instead being used "against all the Cuban people. They have bazookas, mortars, machine guns, planes and bombs." The Cuban Air Force flew reconnaissance and bombing missions over the mountains every day, Castro told him, "but we are safe in here in the Sierra; they must come and get us and they cannot."[55]

Around nine in the morning Matthews got a glimpse of Batista's air campaign when "a plane did fly over.... The troops took up positions; a man in a white shirt was hastily covered up. But the plane went on to bomb higher in the mountains."[56]

What was Castro's opinion of the United States? What about Castro's past "bitterness" toward U.S. policy? Matthews knew that Castro as a student leader had identified with the fervent anti-imperialist, anticolonial sentiment in Africa and Asia in the 1950s. When the Juan Perón regime in Argentina proposed an "anti-imperialist" association of students, Castro reportedly had "embraced it with total enthusiasm."[57]

Castro assured Matthews that the past was past. "You can be sure we have no animosity toward the United States and the American people."[58]

What else did he stand for? With lawyerly finesse, Castro told Matthews what he was not. "We are not anti-military; that is why we let the soldier prisoners go. There is no hatred of the army as such, for we know the men are good and so are many of the officers."

Politics aside, Matthews made a passing reference to Castro's economic ideas. "He has strong ideas on economy, too, but an economist would consider them weak."[59]

As the interview ended in the early morning light, Castro arranged for Matthews's safe passage past army patrols. "They never know where we are," Castro told him, "but we always know where they are. You have taken quite a risk in coming here, but we have the whole area covered, and we will get you out safely." Their scout led Matthews down through woods and across fields to a farmer's house at the edge of the mountains, where he hid until their jeep came. "There was one road block to get through with an Army guard so suspicious our hearts sank, but he let us through."[60]

Matthews arranged one more clandestine rendezvous. After returning to Havana he slipped away to meet with four members of the Student University Federation. "They told me they had a plan which would put a definitive end to the dictatorship." Their president, José Antonio Echevarría, told Matthews, "Cuban students were never afraid to die."[61]

On Tuesday, February 19, after eleven days in Cuba, Herbert and Nancie assumed the guise of tourists who had dutifully left American dollars at the casino table. As they boarded their plane to New York, to Matthews's relief, "no one bothered us."[62] During the flight he wrote and he continued writing for the next few days. At last he completed not one story, but a three-part series that presented a living Castro, a beleaguered Batista, and a troubled Cuba, together with his own opinions of the whole business. The *Times*'s newsroom editors decided to publish the blockbuster first installment on February 24, a Sunday when the *Times*'s circulation was 1.1 million, twice the daily readership. Matthews's editors—journalism's "gatekeepers"—decided that his scoop on Castro's survival was major news, more important than any other story that Sunday. They placed it in the most important news spot on the front page, topped with a three-column headline: "Castro Is Still Alive and Still Fighting in Mountains." With it was an eye-catching photograph of Castro in a militant pose, holding his rifle. An editor's note explained that Matthews "has just returned from a visit to Cuba." The story continued on page 34, across five columns next to a map with a cross marking where Matthews met with Castro.[63]

The *Times*'s treatment emphasized the importance of Matthews's achievement. He had foiled the military, found and interviewed Castro, and defeated the censorship. Matthews's credibility was furthered by documenting his own hero's journey, how this relentless seeker of truth took risks to get this story out of Cuba. The risks enhanced his experience, in keeping with his old "urge to go out and fight . . . to seek adventure."[64] In Cuba as Matthews revealed it, readers could share in the intrigues of the revolutionary underground: his traveling in disguise along the road to the east, avoiding arrest, slogging through mud and forest, and then the prize—Fidel. Scoop!

As finding Castro validated Matthews's quest, Matthews in turn validated Castro's heroism. "As the story unfolded of how he had at first gathered the few remnants of the Eighty-two around him; kept the Government troops at bay while youths came in from other parts of Oriente as Batista's counter-terrorism aroused them; got arms and supplies and then began the series of raids and counter-attacks of guerrilla warfare, one got a feeling that he is now invincible. Perhaps he isn't, but that is the faith he inspires in his followers."[65]

Although not one of the "followers," Matthews accepted Castro's word that the rebels had "many fights and inflicted many losses." But as a reporter, he wanted to state the size of the rebel force. Castro declined to give an exact number, answering in generalities, giving the impression that he had at least forty men. "I will not tell you how many men we have, for obvious reasons. He works in columns of 200; we in groups of ten to forty, and we are winning. Batista has 3,000 men in the field against us. . . . It is a battle against time and time is on our side." Castro later told how he misled Matthews by having his eighteen men march through the campsite several times.[66]

T he first installment of Matthews's series caused political consternation inside the Cuban regime, extending from its embassy on Washington's Massachusetts Avenue to the Presidential Palace in Havana. The U.S. ambassador in Cuba, Arthur Gardner, was uncomfortably blindsided. Matthews maintained that he had not consulted with the American embassy in advance because he distrusted Gardner, who had developed a friendly relationship with President-General Batista. "No one in Havana," Matthews declared in the story, "not even at the United States Embassy with all its resources for getting information, will know until this report is published that Fidel Castro is really in the Sierra Maestra." In any case, Matthews knew that Gardner was relying on the word of Batista's press spokesman, Edmund Chester, who maintained that Castro had been killed and buried by December 9, as reported by the UP's Francis McCarthy.[67]

In Havana, where the regime's current press censorship decree was in effect for two more days until February 26, government censors cut the offending articles from the Sunday *Times* and made sure that the story did not get into Cuban newspapers or on radio. At the palace, Batista turned to Chester to frame a new statement attacking Matthews as a liar. Chester had numerous connections with U.S. and Latin American journalists. His association with Batista dated from when Chester directed the Associated Press Latin American Department and served as vice president of the AP's Latin American news service, *Las Prensa Associada*. Then in 1948 at Columba Broadcasting System in New York he became director of CBS's young television news operation. There, he stunned the ambitious television news team with his propensity to suppress negative news stories that affected network profits. During one memorable morning meeting, Chester told the news team that CBS television news henceforth should avoid criticizing U.S. government policy. His reason: Oldsmobile was a significant new CBS sponsor, and its parent company, General Motors, made vehicles for the government.[68] As the Cuban regime's publicity agent since 1953, Chester helped bolster the dictator's relationship with American journalists. In 1954, he arranged for the famous American muckraking columnist Drew Pearson to interview Batista. After a two-hour private session, Pearson came away with the positive impression that the dictator was "an extraordinarily gracious person, not at all the military tyrant he is depicted."[69]

Now, reacting to Matthews's story, Chester devised a strategy of denial. He advised that the government should insist that Matthews had faked the interview and written a piece of fiction. Chosen to read the statement to the press, Minister of National Defense Santiago Verdeja said: "The Government does not know whether Fidel Castro is alive or dead ... [but] at no time did the said correspondent have an interview" with Castro. He referred to Castro as "the pro-Communist insurgent" who "at no time has been able to build a popular organization to win popular support for his unsuccessful terroristic attempts."[70]

Meanwhile, Matthews's second installment departed from standard journalism. While the scoop on Sunday reported on Matthews's journey and Castro's survival and professed ideals, the article printed on Monday verged away from news reporting into opinion writing as Matthews wrote what he *believed* to be true. The tone and content of the article indicated his sympathy with the rebels and cited evidence from Cuban sources whom he did not name. In news reporting, such practices usually made editorial gatekeepers uncomfortable, but in this case Matthews prevailed. First, he had earned editorial freedom because of his astonishing feat. Second, the Cubans he was quoting, if named, might be jailed or tortured. Finally, while editors in the mid-1950s generally preferred transparency to anonymity, increasingly national reporters were offering anonymity in exchange for "deep background," and foreign correspondents "used the method primarily for foreign diplomatic reporting."[71]

Herbert Matthews himself was confident in drawing conclusions about the Cuban conflict. As an editorial opinion writer, he was not restricted by newsroom expectations for impartiality and identification of his sources of information. Thus he stated that the rebels and other "forces lined up against General Batista are strong and getting stronger every day." And he also noted Cuban citizens' uncertainty about the outcome. "Even the best-informed Cubans do not know what is happening outside their immediate circles." And while the regime branded Castro as a "pro-Communist," Matthews personally vouched that "there is no communism to speak of in Fidel Castro's 26th of July Movement, the student movement or the disaffected elements in the Army."[72]

Thus, Matthews characterized Castro as "the rebel leader of Cuba's youth," even though the Havana university students were planning their own insurgency. In declaring that "the cream" of President Batista's army was "fighting a thus-far losing battle," Matthews accepted Castro's word and overlooked the reality that the rebels were confined to a small part of the Sierra.[73]

Matthews conceded that Batista "has the upper hand," because the economy seemed good, strengthened by U.S investments and propped up by massive government borrowing for public works to stimulate employment. "There are profitable sugar, coffee and tobacco crops. Tourism has been satisfactory."[74]

Politically, as an ardent anti-Communist in the Cold War, President-General Fulgencio Batista had influential friends in Washington, especially in the State Department and the Pentagon. "General Batista has been made to feel he has the United States behind him," Matthews noted. In fact, American diplomacy in the 1950s usually sided with the existing power structure, even dictatorships, if they were anti-Communist.[75] During the Cold War, U.S. *realpolitik* favored a stable, reliable partner in Latin America. As with Batista's predecessor, whom he deposed—Carlos Prío Socarrás—Batista's staunch anti-Communist stance was rewarded with U.S. weapons and military training intended for defense of the hemisphere. However, Matthews asserted, Castro's challenge meant that Batista would also need "luck" to survive, "for Cubans are a violent, unpredictable people.... Their anger and disappointment have been rising steadily."[76]

Matthews's second story also reported events that had been censored since Castro landed in December. The Cuban Air Force had been bombing the forest-covered Sierra Maestra, where victims were almost always the *guajiros*. The army had become frustrated that their few thousand soldiers had no luck in catching Castro or drawing the rebels out of the Sierra and into a decisive battle. In the cities, however, suspected insurgents could not hide so easily. There the regime had made a horrific impact. In Santiago, police rounded up young men, tortured them, and, as a method of terror, left their bodies in plain sight. That strategy was backfiring, Matthews contended. Batista's "horrifying" brutality against his own people was driving them to sympathize with Castro, who "dominates the Sierra Maestra" and was the only apparent challenge to the dictatorship. "The dictator has lost the young generation of Cuba."[77]

Matthews stressed that the "brutality of Cuban to Cuban, is always horrifying to foreigners." In Holguin in the east, "the tough Army commander sent by General Batista gave what citizens now ironically call 'Batista's Christmas present.' The bodies of youths began showing up in the mornings in the streets, until there were twenty-six by the turn of the year. At the same time in Santiago, down on the southeastern coast, four bodies turned up, one of a 15-year-old boy who, according to medical testimony, had been tortured for twenty-four hours before being killed. Eight hundred women of Santiago, including the mother of the boy, marched through the streets with placards on Jan. 4 in one of the city's most bitterly impressive demonstrations."[78]

Stark revelations underscored Matthews's own courage. "The only way to get complete information about Cuba today is to go there, as this writer did, to talk with every type of Cuban, to travel around the island. One must then leave the country to write the story. On such a trip one gets to understand why President Batista is so generally unpopular and why such a formidable opposition is building up against him."[79]

Matthews pieced together a pattern of corruption that he traced to the dictator and the core of army officers who backed Batista's *cuartelazo* (barracks coup) on the morning of March 10, 1952. By day's end, Batista had replaced all of the country's top officials.[80] Leaders of the army since then appeared to be partners in supporting a corrupt and murderous regime. "It is universally agreed that there is more corruption than ever under the Batista regime," Matthews wrote. The dictator and his generals shared "enormous peculations" with "smuggling on a great scale." Recently, U.S. mobsters moving into Havana had made deals with the regime, involving huge payoffs for securing Cuba as a protected haven for investments in new and lavish hotel-casinos, notably the "most grandiose" hotel, leisure, and entertainment complex ever constructed, the Monte Carlo de La Habana. With Batista's support, mobsters were making Havana the haven Las Vegas could never be: Meyer Lansky's dream—since first being summoned to Cuba by Batista in 1937—of a wide-open city for gambling and prostitution, as well as for "the filthiest of all rackets—the smuggling and peddling of heroin and other narcotic drugs." All would be beyond the reach of U.S. government investigations and prosecutions.[81]

Coincidentally, Cuba had become a safe haven for the mob partly because the U.S. State Department and military steadfastly supported the Batista regime. In the perspective of Cold War politics, President-General Batista provided a predictably stable government while the Eisenhower Administration's foreign policy in the 1950s focused on the Communist "menace" elsewhere, in Eastern Europe, the Middle East, and Asia.

Latin America generally seemed off-limits to the spread of communism. One exception, in Guatemala, had been dealt with. In June 1954, as was eventually revealed, the U.S. Central Intelligence Agency, under the direction of Allen Dulles, joined with the United Fruit Company and Guatemalan exiles to organize and finance a military invasion that overthrew the reformist government of President Jacobo Árbenz Guzmán. He had adopted leftist, allegedly Communist-style policies, nationalizing American-owned agricultural land of the United Fruit Company, meanwhile giving "free vent to anti-American sentiment," a passion related to the general anti-imperialist ferment in Latin America in the 1950s.[82]

The overthrow of Guzmán resounded as a warning to Castro while he was still in prison for the Moncada attack. Reminded of José Martí, Castro noted that the U.S. intervention confirmed "all the Martí warnings and corroborat[ed] the 'historical fatalism' theory that proclaims that nothing can happen in the region without the permission of the United States."[83]

Also in June 1954, the impassioned speech Castro made in his defense in his Moncada trial was published as a pamphlet, *La Historia Me Absolvera* (History Will Absolve Me). In prison he had recast the text from memory, writing in invisible lemon juice between the lines of letters smuggled out of prison by women who then made the text visible by ironing the letters. He intended the pamphlet as a call to arms, detailing "our program and our ideology." By naming his new rebel movement in remembrance of the attack on July 26, 1953, Castro aimed to turn that disastrous defeat into a moral victory.[84] Castro had justified the Moncada attack by the "right of rebellion against tyranny" that was "at the very roots of Cuba's existence as a nation"— whether the rebellion was against the Spanish or Batista. He also listed "revolutionary laws" that, if the rebels had succeeded, he would have broadcast to the nation: restoration of the constitution of 1940, land reform, profit-sharing for factory workers and planters, and "the confiscation of all holdings and ill-gotten gains of those who had committed frauds."[85]

In February 1957, after his few hours with Castro, Matthews ruled out accusations that Castro was a Communist. "Communism has little to do with the opposition to the regime," he wrote. Matthews insisted that Castro was dedicated to his stated goals of restoring the Cuban constitution and democratic elections.

Matthews's third article framed the rebellion as a turning point in Cuban history. After the coup in 1952, he had despaired of prospects for democracy in Cuba. Extensive poverty and lack of education made democratic elections improbable and led him to the conclusion that Cuba was a republic "without citizens."[86] Five years later, he sensed that a widening spectrum of middle-class Cubans wanted to get rid of Batista and restore democracy. "The old corrupt order in Cuba is being threatened for the first time since the Cuban Republic was proclaimed early in the century." He presented his opinions as fact, as he considered himself an expert witness who "studied Cuban affairs on repeated visits" and had "just spent ten days in Cuba talking to all sorts of conditions of men and women, Cuban and American, in various parts of the island," including Castro himself.[87]

Matthews identified three forces lined up after five years of the dictatorship. There was a middle-class civic resistance formed of "respected political, business and professional groups." In the military, he determined there was "an honest patriotic component of the Army, which is ashamed of the actions of the Government generals." Finally, there were "the youth of Cuba," whom he assumed were all "led by the fighting rebel, Fidel Castro," although the Havana students had said they had their own plans. "At last one gets the feeling that the best elements in Cuban life . . . are getting together to assume power. They have always made up the vast majority of Cubans, but Cubans never had majority rule, least of all since General Batista interrupted a democratic president election in 1952 to take over by force. The Cuban people have never forgiven him for that." Moreover they also blamed Batista for financial mismanagement and worried that "a recession is almost certain." A major debacle was Batista's cherished $350 million public works employment project that had increased the public debt while it created jobs; it was suspect as "an enormous slush fund providing colossal graft." Matthews talked with businessmen who wondered whether Batista should be "got out of the way" immediately so that Cubans could "face the hard times with an honest, orthodox, democratic, patriotic Government."[88]

But regime change was "infinitely harder" because "Washington is backing President Batista," Matthews was told by Cubans with "bitter criticism" of the United States. They mentioned Ambassador Arthur Gardner's frequently expressed "public cordiality and admiration for General Batista" and "the sale of United States arms" to Batista. "While I was there, seven tanks were delivered in a ceremony headed by Ambassador Gardner. Every Cuban I spoke with saw the delivery as arms furnished to General Batista for use in bolstering his regime and for use 'against the Cuban people.'" Some U.S. investors and businessmen were reluctant to change regimes. They "despite their misgivings, naturally want to protect their investments and businesses." As one prominent business leader said, "We all pray every day that nothing happens to Batista." He feared that "the alternative would be much worse, at least in the beginning, perhaps a military junta, perhaps a radical swing to the left, perhaps chaos."[89]

Matthews reported that opposition to Batista was nevertheless evident in civic resistance movements that had formed in major cities. In Santiago, where four youths had been murdered as rebel sympathizers, "business and professional men of the highest type are the leaders. The women of Oriente have cooperated so impressively that for many weeks they have refused to send their children to school. The University of Oriente is closed." In Havana, Matthews also found a "non-violent movement of influential citizens in support of honesty, decency, democracy." He distinguished this movement as far more vigorous than the political parties that had been suppressed under Batista, now "hopelessly divided and discredited." The civic movement hoped to appeal to "the decent patriotic elements in the Army" so that the army "will support them against the regime."[90]

In that third installment, Matthews elaborated on his secret meeting with the five Havana university students. Their urban resistance, members of the "student directorate," had seemed impatient for change. Departing from his practice of keeping sources anonymous, Matthews named one of them: José Antonio Echevarría, a twenty-four-year-old architectural student, "heavy-set, florid, handsome, with a mass of hair in a pompadour prematurely touched with gray." Echevarría was being sought by the police and "therefore has considerable fame in Cuba at the moment." Echevarría had told him students were active in the current civic resistance, "which may or may not have meant they were taking part in the bombings and sabotage." They told him they "had a plan which would put a definitive end to the dictatorship," but they concealed their plan to spark the revolution by attacking the Presidential Palace. Matthews got the impression they were merely "waiting their chance to get into the streets and join a revolution, if there is one. They concede that they are in no position to start one." He was impressed by the revolutionary pedigree of one student, who said his father fought against the dictator Gerardo Machado in 1933 and his grandfather fought against the Spanish in the 1890s.[91]

The students' spirit and courage reminded Matthews of the zeal he found among Republican Loyalists in the Spanish Civil War. Their spirit won people to their cause. "The optimism and the confidence were astounding," he wrote in January 1937. He agreed with the Loyalists that "'Fascism imposed by a foreign army' is worse than anything that can happen to Spain" and with "those who still feel the battle can be won. That was the way I felt in Figueras, talking to the people upon whom the decision lay, and seeing what they were doing or trying to do.... All of us who lived the Spanish Civil War felt deeply emotional about it."[92]

M atthews had guarded his series against any significant changes by *Times* editors. If he was attacked as biased, he defended the bias as necessary and truthful, based on facts on the ground. "I always felt the falseness and hypocrisy of those who claimed to be unbiased and the foolish, if not rank stupidity of editors and readers who demand objectivity or impartiality of correspondents writing about the war," he had declared a decade earlier in *The Education of a Correspondent.* "It was the same old error which readers and editors will always make and which forever continues to plague the chronicler who, being human, must have his feelings and opinions; in condemning bias one rejects the only factors which really matter—honesty, understanding and thoroughness. A reader has a right to ask for all the facts; he has no right to ask that a journalist or historian agree with him."[93]

Honest bias was important and defensible. Matthews contended that "honesty, understanding and thoroughness" required him to make his bias clear, together with all the facts. "True journalism, like true historiography," he asserted, "is not mere chronology—simply to describe the event exactly as it happened—but placing the event in its proper category as a moral act and judging it as such."[94]

As he practiced his creed, born and tested in Europe's wars, Matthews contradicted the profession's adoption of "impartiality" in news reporting. He had been hired by the *Times* in 1923, the same year when the new American Society of Newspaper Editors (ASNE) launched a movement to professionalize journalism aimed at eliminating "subversive partisanship" from news reports. Serious newspapers intended to differentiate themselves from the new sensational and popular tabloid papers by establishing ethical standards. The editors had been prodded to action by President Warren Harding, himself an Ohio newspaper publisher, when in April 1923, he addressed the ASNE, urging them to adopt their proposed code of ethics. The ASNE in turn wanted to avoid any meddling with the free press such as was occurring with controversial Hollywood films that were being criticized and censured. That same year the ASNE approved its Canons of Journalism as "an effort to raise the standards of journalism." One such standard, "impartiality," meant that "news reports should be free from opinion or bias of any kind."[95] Very telling, the ASNE condemned tabloid journalism for "pandering to vicious instincts" and denigrated "selfish or otherwise unworthy purposes" such as accepting bribes.[96]

However, the code did not address reporting from foreign places, although reporting of wars and revolutions was even more problematic than domestic journalism. This was clearly evidenced in 1920 by a scholarly study of the *New York Times's* reporting of the Russian Revolution during and after World War I, 1917 to 1920. The respected journalist-authors, Walter Lippmann and Charles Merz, concluded that "the reporting of the Russian Revolution is nothing short of a disaster" because it misled the nation and national policy.

One of their most telling revelations from studying news reports in more than one thousand issues was that "the news as a whole is dominated *by the hopes* of the men who composed the news organization. . . . In the large, the news about Russia is a case of *seeing not what was, but what men wished to see.*"[97]

This practice of foreign correspondents projecting conclusions in "an environment of hope and fear" continued in the 1930s Soviet Union. The *Times* foreign correspondent Walter Duranty misreported the impact of Josef Stalin's edicts that resulted in widespread famine, relying on inaccurate statistics but rarely warning readers they might be less than the truth. "Duranty was eager for the United States to recognize the Soviet Union," as one historian noted, "which also may have motivated him to explain away the grimmer aspects of the Soviet Union with a long view that foresaw progress."[98]

Nonetheless, foreign correspondents in Matthews's era continued to weave stories from opinion and propaganda. During the war in Spain, Matthews faulted the *Times*'s correspondent assigned to cover Generalissimo Francisco Franco's anti-Loyalist forces for writing a story based wholly on Franco propaganda. Bill Carney, "who was nowhere near the front, not only sent the handout but gave a vivid description of how the citizens of Teruel joyfully received the Insurgent troops, giving them the Fascist salute." By contrast, Matthews had traveled to the front at Teruel and, with firsthand interviews, reported just the opposite. Given the two conflicting stories, the *Times* used both.[99]

During that war, the *Times*'s managing editor, Edwin L. "Jimmy" James, telegraphed Matthews that "ever since there have been wars and war correspondents propaganda has been handed out and sent." But, James assured Matthews, "neither [assistant managing editor] Raymond McCaw nor anyone else here thinks youre [*sic*] sending propaganda in sense you created it."[100]

In Cuba as in Spain, Matthews wrote with the outlook of a veteran foreign correspondent able to discover and explain what was otherwise concealed from foreign eyes. The sheer fact of finding Castro alive gained him the top of the *Times*'s front page by satisfying journalism's "tests" for news value: timeliness, prominence, conflict, proximity, and human interest. Added to that was the self-described heroism of his own daring intrigue, his secretive journey into the Sierra.

But Matthews went even further with his stories. Beyond the basics of foreign reporting, he presented a scenario of heroic youth and honor opposing the might of a corrupt, murderous Latin American dictator. Castro "dominates the Sierra Maestra" against a tyrant whose "horrifying" brutality against his own people was driving them to sympathize with the young Castro. Matthews presented Castro as a formidable force. He declared that the rebel leader was "fighting hard and successfully" against Batista's army. Furthermore, sympathizers in the cities were "lining up" against Batista. "They are against the President to a man: a civic resistance formed of respected political, business and professional groups, and an honest, patriotic component of the Army, which is ashamed of the actions of the Government generals. Together these elements form the hope of Cuba and the threat to General Fulgencio Batista."[101]

Matthews was determined to get to the heart of the Cuban story not only for the *Times*. He saw the conflict worthy of his next book. During two decades as a war correspondent, Matthews acted as a reporter but also thought like an author. Early on, he discovered that books gave him the range and freedom he needed for voicing his perspective. After he covered the Italians at war in Africa, he published *Eyewitness in Abyssinia* (1937); then came *Two Wars and More to Come*, composed as the Spanish Civil War was exploding around him and published in 1938. *The Fruits of Fascism* in 1943 traced Mussolini's promise and betrayal. Next, in 1950, *Assignment to Austerity*, co-authored with his wife, Nancie, told of their life in postwar London. In 1957 he published *The Yoke and the Arrow*—his political assessment of the Franco regime's continuing rule in Spain—just as he was delving into Cuban affairs.

While he used his press credentials to inject himself into the midst of the Cuban revolution, Matthews's outlook was that of a man seeking to characterize the conflict and influence the outcome. After Sunday, February 24, he wrote, "I discovered when I published my interview with Fidel Castro in the Sierra Maestra in 1957 that a journalist can *make* history."[102] He was headed toward becoming an *author* of the revolution.

CHAPTER 3

THE STAGE IS SET

The resurrection of Fidel Castro on the front page of the *New York Times* commanded national and international attention. "The sensational impact of my Sierra Maestra interview," Herbert Matthews self-consciously observed, "set the stage." In the nation's leading "newspaper of record," he had demonstrated the ingenuity of American journalism in confronting the dictatorship's big lie. In newspaper parlance, the story had "legs" and raced across the mediascape. Besides commanding attention, the sensational surprise provoked immediate responses. Newspaper editors and broadcasters with no direct Cuban sources simply recast the story much as the *Times* had presented it. But a few larger newspapers with Latin American specialists scrambled to publish their own stories by getting reactions from Cubans, especially in Havana and Miami.[1]

In Chicago—the metropolis that had been denigrated so recently by the *New Yorker* magazine as the nation's "Second City" after New York[2]—its newspaper of record, the *Daily Tribune,* actually outsold the *New York Times* on both Sundays and weekdays.[3] Also, the *Tribune* had the nation's most prominent Latin American correspondent, Jules Dubois, who was surprised and impressed that he had been scooped on his own beat by an editorial writer.

Since the 1940s, Dubois had been journalism's foremost crusader for press freedom in Latin America. In 1950, as a leader in the Inter-American Press Association (IAPA), Dubois launched and chaired the IAPA's Freedom of Information Committee, and he traveled across the region as both journalist and advocate. With his mobility as a journalist—and with his travel expenses paid by the *Tribune*—he was the IAPA's most active and valued champion of press freedom. In a region "peculiarly prone to dictatorships and authoritarian regimes," as the International Press Institute put it, Dubois's vision of a free press inevitably created friction. In his career, he was put under police surveillance, jailed briefly, and expelled or banned from Latin American countries. At the IAPA meeting in Havana in 1956, police foiled a plot to assassinate him. And in the Dominican Republic, an offended editor challenged him to a duel.[4]

Stunned by Matthews's scoop, Dubois hurriedly organized a response, planning to fly as soon as possible to Havana. Meanwhile, the *Tribune*'s editors could think of no better solution than to reprint Matthews's series after its three-day run in *Times*. Because the two newspapers shared stories on the New York Times–Chicago Tribune Wire Service, the *Tribune* had the right to reprint the series, but the editors shortened it to fit available space; they also spread the three articles over five days and modified Matthews's opinionated prose. Whereas Matthews's first paragraph declared Castro was "fighting hard and successfully," the *Tribune* editors deleted the two contentious words "and successfully." Where Matthews stated that "thousands of men and women are heart and soul" with Castro, they cut the romanticized "heart and soul" and inserted their own judgmental modifier: "fanatically." And where Matthews referred to Castro's "new deal," the *Tribune* preferred "program."[5] They also omitted some commentary, including Matthews's poke at the U.S. Embassy staff in Havana for not knowing Castro was "really in the Sierra Maestra."[6] Then, too, because Matthews's scoop was stirring daily responses in Havana, the *Tribune* inserted some fresh news into the series.

By a coincidence of timing, on February 26, Batista's forty-five-day media censorship decree officially expired. As dictator, he could have extended the decree, but instead he chose to keep his promise, possibly because he still believed reports that his army had killed Castro and suppressed the rebellion.

Taking advantage of the abrupt end of the censorship decree, Havana's newspapers headlined Matthews's interview with Castro. Overnight, Fidel's survival was "becoming a Cuban national issue," seemingly related to reports of a concurrent upsurge in violence and government repression. In one gun battle, Cuban soldiers fought "a band of youths" who authorities claimed were with Castro's revolutionary 26th of July Movement and planned to assassinate military leaders. In response to the violence, on March 2, the Cuban government suspended constitutional guarantees for another forty-five days, but Batista still honored his promise not to reinstate press censorship. So while police were free to make random arrests, editors were technically free to publish antiregime stories, although they remained wary of the dictatorship's possible response.[7]

In Miami, the principal locus for Cuban exiles, Matthews's scoop sent the *Miami Herald* scurrying for its own story to uphold its reputation for Latin

American coverage. The Cuban censorship had handicapped the *Herald*'s own Latin American expert, George Southworth, who tried to write meaningfully from his desk on Miami Avenue. Just a day before the scoop, the *Herald* had published Southworth's confusing story that Castro was dead or perhaps alive—based on unnamed sources who provided "rumors." "Cuban government officials" were reported to be "confident" that most of the revolutionaries "have been wiped out." However, Southworth quoted a "Cuban businessman" who claimed Castro and "hundreds of his followers are still at large," and he also referred to other unnamed sources who told him the rebels had killed "great numbers" of military men. "Most fantastic of all the rumors," Southworth wrote, was that military families were forbidden to go into mourning because the government "doesn't want the people to know the number of the dead."[8]

Southworth did not have Matthews's freedom or good luck, but he was still the *Herald*'s expert because six months earlier Castro had visited him in the newsroom. Castro had left his rebel training ground in Mexico to visit Miami and New York to raise funds; he told Southworth and others his intention to invade Cuba by the end of the year. Looking lawyerly in suit and tie, with a thin, angular mustache, Castro "occasionally would drop into the newsroom" and talk with *Herald* staffers, recalled John McMullen, an assistant managing editor. McMullen thought nobody took Castro's ambitions too seriously, although Castro "declared that he and his men would fight until they die or Batista is overthrown." Now, Castro had repeated this declaration to Matthews. Without a fresh photo, the editors retrieved the one taken at the newspaper's office during Castro's visit, showing him clean-shaven with a narrow mustache and captioned, in part, "Is he winning?"[9]

The *Herald* pieced together a confusing story that included speculations, contradictions, and unnamed sources. It quoted a Cuban "political reporter" who derided Castro as "just a thorn in the side" of the Batista regime. "Batista's biggest headache," the Cuban reporter said, was popular dissatisfaction with "the unstable political situation. . . . The people do not like the bombings—there have been about two dozen in Havana in the last six weeks. . . . Cubans do not believe Fidel Castro and his small band of followers can defeat the powerful Cuban army. That is ridiculous."[10] A "Cuban businessman" quoted by Southworth, however, claimed just the opposite: Castro had been fighting formidably. "There have been many battles between the revolutionaries and the Cuban army in recent weeks, and the rebels have inflicted heavy losses on the government forces." He attributed an exaggerated "several hundred" men to Fidel's troops. Southworth's story also repeated what Castro had told Matthews: "We have [been] fighting for 79 days now and are stronger than ever.... The [army] soldiers are fighting badly. Their morale is low and ours could not be higher. We are killing many."[11]

Across Miami, Castro's surprising survival dominated conversation among Cuban exiles, some of whom had been hoping to overthrow Batista since 1952. By far the most prominent exile was the deposed president Carlos Prío Socarrás, rumored to be funding various invasion plans. Some thought Prío Socarrás in 1956 had given the money for Castro to buy the yacht *Granma* used for the invasion. If now he really had created a base inside Cuba, Fidel Castro was effectively the de facto leader of the opposition, better positioned for power than exiles living hundreds of miles across the water. Eventually the *Miami Herald* would have to get its own interview with Castro.[12]

I n Havana, news of Matthews's interview spread even before the censorship was lifted on February 26. Although censors had busily cut out Matthews's first and second installments, leaving gaping holes in each copy of the *Times*, Cubans learned of the interview from U.S. radio broadcasts and from American tourists. Also, the 26th of July Movement decided to have Matthews's stories mailed to a list of citizens in Havana. To organize that task in New York, Felipe Pazos dispatched Mario Llerena. Llerena was a magazine writer who had sacrificed a faculty position at Duke University to join the revolution after Batista's coup gave him "an unanticipated urge to return to Cuba." In New York, Llerena connected with "several organized groups. All of them were eager to cooperate." His team, equipped with addresses in the Havana telephone directory and the Havana *Social Register,* mailed three to four thousand copies.[13] In Havana, others circulated the stories, and Carlos Franqui, the movement's diarist and publisher, spread the word in hundreds of copies of *Revolución* until police arrested him.

While in New York, Llerena met the famous Herbert Matthews, who introduced him to a CBS television producer. Immediately, the producer hit upon the idea of having Matthews on a CBS program interviewing Llerena about Castro. Matthews refused because, according to Llerena, "he was already too publicly involved with the Castro movement, and a television appearance with me so soon after the publication of his articles might reflect upon his editorial position with the *Times.*"[14]

Llerena then secured a deal to give CBS an inside track to the rebels. During a New York lunch that day, he talked at length with CBS news anchor Robert Taber about the 26th of July Movement, or "M-26," which planned to rid Cuba of the dictator. Enthralled, Taber declared that he wanted to go to Cuba immediately and do an exclusive documentary on Castro. Now that the *New York Times* had focused attention on Castro, a CBS show could draw a national audience. People would want to see and hear Castro. After lunch, Taber's enthusiasm interested Don Hewitt, a rising young network producer.

Imaginative and adventurous, Hewitt became known the "boy genius" of CBS news. One of his early achievements was producing television's first daily evening newscast. Launched on August 15, 1948, "Douglas Edwards with the News" covered the world in fifteen minutes, using film. Six months later, NBC followed suit, on February 16, 1949, with its fifteen-minute evening news show, the "Camel News Caravan" with John Cameron Swayze.[15] Then in November 1951, Hewitt was on the team that converted radio's *Hear It Now* to television's *See It Now*, featuring the network's iconic reporter-narrator Edward R. Murrow. Hewitt also claimed credit for the staging of Murrow's show, in CBS's modern control room amid television monitors showing simultaneous live images from New York and San Francisco. "From the opening seconds," one historian noted, "it was clear that 'See It Now' would be more than televised newsreels or radio with pictures. Images and voices came at the viewer in a shifting kaleidoscope of sight and sound."[16]

In the early 1950s, Hewitt continued to produce shows with political content, and he tried to evade the network's embarrassing love of fluff and celebrities, although this sometimes proved to be impossible. In April of 1956, on a flight home from Europe, Murrow chided Hewitt about his mushy celebrity coverage of the wedding of American actress Grace Kelly and Prince Rainier of Monaco. Stung by the criticism, Hewitt reminded Murrow of his recent "Person to Person" interview with Marilyn Monroe. Murrow had focused on the intimate life of the actress, and Hewitt shot back now with a caustic comment: "The same thing you were doing looking in Marilyn Monroe's closet on 'Person to Person.'"[17]

Although Hewitt was intrigued by the story of Cuban rebels, he was eager to know more. As Mario Llerena recalled, Hewitt "would be interested in sending a reporter to the island if I could offer some assurance that this man—who would try to pass as tourist—would be alerted about upcoming revolutionary events and put in contact with key figures of the underground." Llerena remembered how he felt "practically overwhelmed by these unexpected developments," since he was "fully aware of how vital publicity was for a revolutionary enterprise." Without consulting anyone, he assured Hewitt "that everything could be arranged." Robert Taber immediately scheduled a preliminary reconnaissance trip to Havana for the following week, planning to arrive by March 2.[18]

I n Cuba, after the forty-five-day censorship decree expired on February 26, news had spread that Castro was alive. The regime's response, framed by press adviser Edmund Chester, was delivered by the national defense minister. The statement denied that Matthews had interviewed Castro. As Havana's *Diario de la Marina* reported on its front page, the regime insisted that Matthews had written a "*novela fantastica.*" "The fable interview never took place, nor could it have taken place under the existing conditions," reported the English-language *Times of Havana.* As proof, the government noted that Matthews did not appear in the photograph the *Times* published of Castro. "It seems ingenuous that having had the opportunity to penetrate those mountains and to have held the interview, that he has not had his own picture taken with Castro to confirm his own statements."[19] In response, the *Times* in the second-day installment used a rebel snapshot of Matthews with Castro. That photo was not published earlier, Matthews explained, because it was "not clear enough to be reproduced in a newspaper" though "very clear in glossy print." That second installment was also on the front page of the *Times of Havana,* next to the "fable interview" accusation and with the headline "But Matthews Sticks to His Story."[20]

In New York, Matthews basked in public admiration, as much for his courage as for his scoop. Telegrams and letters poured in from admirers praising his revelations and risky adventure. From the U.S. Information Agency in Havana, Richard G. "Dick" Cushing, a helpful confidant when Matthews was operating secretly, telegraphed congratulations "for a piece of journalism reminiscent of the beats of a bygone age." Because the secret mission had deliberately bypassed the embassy, Cushing advised that "your series caused a lot of seething indignation in high quarters," including those of Ambassador Arthur Gardner.[21] Grayson Kirk, president of Columbia University, Matthews's alma mater, praised the "hazardous exploit," adding, "I cannot tell you how thrilled I was to read your enormously exciting story in last Sunday's Times about ... your successful attempt to make contact with Fidel Castro." Matthews's style was also praised. One reader wrote that the stories read like a novel. A World War II flyer who had been shot down empathized with Matthews's adventure: "It thrilled me no end. Your experience and subsequent story is the height of adventure and reality, as paradoxical as that may seem." An Upper East Side New Yorker wrote eloquently that Matthews's "contribution to the cause for which the Cubans are fighting against a repulsive and sanguinary dictatorship will be forever and ever remembered. Human dignity, liberty and real democracy are forever safe with men like you and a paper like the great New York Times."[22]

Some Cubans found in Matthews a kindred spirit. At *El Mundo* in Havana, the newspaper's editorial director addressed Matthews as "esteemed"— "Estimade Herbert"—and sent him *un fuerte abrazo,* a strong embrace, as a journalist and friend, for his scoop that made "a sensation in Cuba." Also from Havana, the president of the Society of Friends of the Republic telegraphed: "Most appreciative significance your report Cuban political situation as valid contribution toward informed local and world wide opinion." Even Castro's sisters, Lydia and Emma, proclaimed from Mexico that they "bow before you as a reporter for being the first person to tell the world the truth about Cuba."[23]

Matthews's colleagues on the *Times*'s editorial board, however, did not share his enthusiasm for Castro. On the day Matthews's series ended, the board published three paragraphs that merely instructed General Batista "on the evils of censorship," berating him for his "colossal error" of "trying to muzzle the press," and faintly praising the ending of his forty-five-day censorship. Naïvely, the editorial noted that Batista "has realized he made a mistake," but stated that his censorship was also "a warning to the newspapers to watch their step and print nothing to cause trouble." It did note that other constitutional guarantees were still suspended; thus "no Cuban is free and consequently there cannot be complete freedom of the press." Stating that "General Batista has taken a step in the right direction," the editorial simply advised, "He should take more." As for Matthews's alarm about the regime's reign of terror against the rebels, the editorial contradicted Matthews's evidence. The board reasoned that censorship was responsible for exaggerating the current uncertainty in Cuba: "The rumors that go the rounds of Havana and the provincial cities are much worse than the realities." Significantly for Matthews, they ignored what he claimed about Castro's promises.[24]

Realizing that his colleagues were distancing themselves from him, Matthews was "embarrassed" and soon felt the need to disavow any partisanship. Ten days after the first story, he wrote to the newsroom's managing editor, Turner Catledge. He wanted Catledge to know that he had just been doing his job as a journalist. He enclosed some of the adulatory correspondence he had received, describing it as "typical of a problem I have had since we published the Cuban series. Our Latin-American friends always find it difficult to understand the workings of North American journalism" and thus they misunderstood his role. "I am therefore being embarrassed by being hailed as a great champion of Fidel Castor [*sic*, fixed by pen] and have gone to a lot of trouble all along the line to make everybody understand I was simply fulfilling a journalistic duty." If the stories supported Castro's movement, Matthews maintained it was because of the objective realities, not because of subjective partisanship. Apart from that reservation, Matthews admitted to a "special satisfaction" because "the Cuban series has done us a lot of good in Cuba and elsewhere in Latin America. I understand, however, that your dear friend Arthur Gardner was fit to be tied and was planning to issue a statement expressing his feeling. . . . I happen to know that the career staff of the Havana Embassy was delighted with my articles."[25]

J ules Dubois, now in Havana and representing both the *Chicago Tribune* and the IAPA, was granted an interview with Fulgencio Batista on March 6, eleven days after Matthews's scoop. He was accompanied by the most prestigious Cuban newspaper editor, the IAPA's Guillermo Martínez Márques, editor of the Havana daily *El Pais*. Dubois had two missions: he needed a story for the *Tribune* and "assurances" for the IAPA that Batista would not reimpose censorship.[26]

As an ardent IAPA advocate, Dubois had made such appeals to other Latin American dictators, a practice which by now distinguished him as the most prominent U.S. journalist covering Latin America. He was doggedly committed to the IAPA resolution to "condemn any attacks on freedom of expression" in print or broadcast.[27] In Nicaragua in 1955, he succeeded in persuading President Anastacio Somoza García to eliminate censorship. "Everybody insults you in the bars and restaurants," Dubois told him. If he abandoned censorship, he could hear the voices of his opposition. Eight months later, when Dubois returned, Somoza García had ended censorship. But some things had not changed: "Everybody insults me in the bars and restaurants, anyway."[28]

Such aggressive advocacy complicated Dubois's life. In Costa Rica during a military insurgency in 1943 he spent a few days under house arrest. In the Dominican Republic, where Generalissimo Rafael Trujillo had been dictator since 1930, Dubois urged the IAPA to expel two member newspapers owned and controlled by Trujillo because each was an "instrument of a totalitarian regime."[29] Ramón Marrero Aristy, the editor of one of those papers, *La Nación,* in February 1957 declared himself among those "obliged to defend themselves against the insults and slanders of Dubois" and challenged him to a duel.[30] Shortly afterward, Generalissimo Trujillo banned Dubois from the country, labeling him "a continental agitator whose activities constitute a menace against the security of free institutions of the American peoples and against good neighborliness and hemispheric unity." A supportive editorial in Dubois's *Tribune* declared, "We've been thrown out of better places."[31]

Now, meeting with Batista, Dubois and Martínez Márquez were pleased to hear him say he would not reimpose censorship. But, Batista added, "If I do so, then you may be free to say that I have reneged on my word of honor."

Dubois also asked about two American journalists jailed the previous weekend. A reporter, George Prentice, thirty-two, and a photographer, Tony Faletta, thirty-five, on leave from the *Birmingham News,* were arrested while working as freelancers for NBC television. They had been trying to find Castro and were following Matthews's route. Failing to find any rebels, Prentice and Faletta were returning to Havana when they alerted NBC "that they believed they were being shadowed." They were stopped at the airport, stripped of equipment and film, and jailed for two days. After NBC officials notified the State Department and protested to the Cuban Embassy in Washington, the U.S. Embassy in Havana intervened. Batista said, "The men were held because they posed first as miners and then as tourists before admitting they were newsmen after a story." He assured Dubois they were held "only for questioning because several still and movie cameras were found in their baggage, along with revolutionary tracts" and that he would now release their photographs and movie film.[32]

When Dubois mentioned Matthews, "Batista insisted that Herbert Matthews never saw Castro. Even the [*Times*'s] publication of a photograph of Matthews interviewing Castro failed to convince Batista, for he wanted his wish to be the father of his thought." Batista now did concede that Castro was alive in the Sierra Maestra, but "belittled" him and "insisted that Castro does not have more than 10 or 12 men with him."[33]

"Fidel Castro is a Communist," Batista added. Coming straight from Batista, this stark declaration was news to Dubois. Latin American dictators often denigrated insurgents as Communists. Batista's regime in February had stated that Castro, whether dead or alive, was "pro-Communist." Now Batista was calling Castro an outright Communist.

"Is that so? Do you have proof?" Dubois asked.

Batista referred to the *Bogatazo*, a bloody riot in Bogotá in 1948, during a Latin American conference Castro attended as a university student delegate. "Yes. We have proof that he killed six priests in Bogotá during the *Bogatazo*."

"Pardon me, Mr. President. I was in Bogotá at that time and no priest was killed."

"Oh, but we have proof. We have a report from our ambassador there at that time."

"Perhaps you do, but I can assure you the report is not correct. However, if you think you have proof and you care to furnish it to me, I shall be glad to publish it."

That night, Batista sent an aide to Dubois's hotel with a folder. It contained "a spurious manuscript attributed to Castro and an equally spurious varitype publication also attributed to him. There was no proof furnished to substantiate the statement that Castro had killed six priests."

Four days later, on March 10, at a luncheon celebrating the fifth anniversary of his coup against President Carlos Prío Socarrás, Batista vowed to crush Castro's insurrection and publicly accused Castro of acting as a Soviet Communist agent taking orders from Moscow. "He might have persuaded American Ambassador Arthur Gardner to believe this," Dubois mused, "but not an overwhelming majority of the Cuban people, including the Roman Catholic Church."[34]

Increasing publicity about Castro's movement in the Sierra Maestra had attracted American youths in Cuba, as the U.S. Embassy disclosed in early March. After keeping the matter quiet for three weeks, the embassy reported that three sons of American servicemen had sneaked away from the American naval base at Guantánamo on February 17 to join the rebels. They were fifteen-year-old Michael Garvey, and Victor J. Buehlman and Charles E. Ryan, Jr., both seventeen. Having met Cuban students in an exchange program at the Guantánamo high school, they "became enthusiastic over Castro's rebellion." Shortly afterward, the rebels released photographs showing all three in camp wearing rebel uniforms and carrying rifles.[35]

The Cuban underground opposition to Batista erupted into public view in Havana on March 13. Shortly after 3 p.m., about forty men with .45-caliber pistols tucked into their waistbands burst from a nearby building and charged the gates of the Presidential Palace. They planned to assassinate Batista in his second-floor office. All wore open-necked sports shirts and slacks to distinguish them from the coats-and-ties of palace staff. At the Colon Street entrance, the few guards having lunch in the shade of the Spanish portico were caught by surprise.[36]

Sounds of gunfire reverberated across the city. While citizens scurried for cover, Dubois hurried on foot toward the noise a few blocks away, then stopped suddenly in a spot where he "watched the whole operation from behind a thick column that furnished an excellent view of the palace." Soldiers soon arrived from Camp Columbia, and the neighborhood around the palace became a battlefield.

The United Press bureau chief, Francis McCarthy, who in December had written that Castro was dead, reported the ongoing violence from the safety of his office in the Hotel Sevilla-Biltmore. The CBS-TV anchor, Robert Taber, frustrated because he had not yet met Castro insiders as promised by Mario Llerena, now found revolutionaries fighting in full view.[37]

The attackers killed five guards. As UP's McCarthy reported, the gunmen "appeared to have the upper hand until government tanks and troops arrived from headquarters at Columbia Field, eight miles away.... As the battle raged, scores of American tourists and Cubans looked on from the Hotel Parkview and the Hotel Sevilla-Biltmore." In the Toledo Hotel, a Miami travel agent, Charles C. North, said he "started to go out into the street to see what was going on when all of a sudden I heard the rat-tat-tat of a machine gun. I knew what it was right away.... We were told, 'Get back in the hotel and stay there.'" Some were unlucky. Two blocks from the palace, at the San Regis Hotel on Colon Street, a visitor from Clifton, New Jersey, thirty-four-year-old Peter Korenda, stepped onto his third-floor balcony and was killed by a stray bullet, shot in the neck. A companion, too near a window, was wounded. Residents recognized the shooting was related to the revolution. A Minneapolis salesman, Elmer Harris, came back from lunch to his room in the St. Regis and found bullet holes in his suit jacket. Harris said he asked if the hotel was going to buy him a new jacket, but the manager told him "revolutions weren't *his* fault."[38]

Apart from the palace, the insurgents' other primary target was control of a radio transmitter so they could inform and rouse the populace. Just after 3:15 p.m., university students broke into the CMQ radio station to get access to Havana's familiar news and time channel, Radio Reloj. Their leader, José Antonio Echevarría, head of the Directorio Revolucionario and president of the University Students' Federation (FEU), was one of the determined students whom Herbert Matthews had met in February and mentioned in his third installment. Now over the airwaves they announced their revolution.

"Radio Reloj reporting. . . . Radio Reloj reporting. . . . At this moment, armed citizens are attacking the Presidential Palace! Radio Reloj reporting—President Batista has been struck down by bullets in the Presidential Palace!"[39]

They also announced the arrest of the other key power holders, the high-ranking army officers, notably General Francisco Tabernilla, the army chief of staff (and closest to Batista), who was said to have been rewarded for tortures of political prisoners, summary executions, and reprisal killings of civilians.

Then Echevarría delivered a formal proclamation: "People of Havana! The revolution is in progress. The Presidential Palace has been taken by our forces, and the dictator has been executed in his den."

Suddenly his voice was cut off. A switch had been thrown in the transmitting plant. Now police were arriving. Bullets fired at the station scattered the students, who fled in two cars.[40]

Minutes later, Echevarría lay dead on the street. A passenger in a car, Arno Raag, a twenty-three-year-old Chrysler engineer from Detroit, later told how the body was "lying in a huddled-up position in the street. We could see he was riddled with bullets. . . . There were machine gun and rifle bullets all over the pavement. . . . The chauffeur stepped on the gas and we got out of there fast!"[41]

The report of Batista's assassination was false. American correspondents pieced together the failed plot. Forty men had died in two hours, five palace guards and thirty-five attackers. Dubois wrote that some of the revolutionaries were members of the university students' Directorio Revolucionario, but other conspirators were linked to exiled president Prío Socarrás. Four students had reached the president's second-floor office, but Batista, using a secret passage, had gone earlier to have lunch with his wife and son in their third-floor apartment.

CBS's Robert Taber, thrilled at last to have some overt revolutionary action, learned that those who reached the second floor "had been provided with a detailed floor map"—possibly supplied by Prío Socarrás—indicating "a secret passage . . . to his residential quarters. . . . No such passage could be found." Upstairs, out of reach, Batista now took the offensive, giving the public appearance of a defiant general as he directed a counterattack from his window. "Grabbing a pistol and crouching below window level," as *Time* magazine framed him, "he phoned army and navy forts for help." The *Miami News* portrayed the president to disappointed Cuban exiles as holding "a pistol in one hand, a telephone in the other."[42]

By nightfall, as anxious tourists waited, the army reopened the airport. Although order was restored, the attack had altered Cuba's political life. What Dubois termed "the forces of rebellion" had surfaced with violence and produced martyrs. He expected that Batista could now justify retaliation against those behind the attack as "pro-Communists." Dubois disputed such a claim, explaining to his readers that the attackers were not Communists, but a mix of students and "partisans of ex-President Prío Socarrás who was overthrown by Batista five years ago" and "sympathizers of Fidel Castro, rebel leader who is holed up in the Sierra Maestra. . . . The young men who took part in the revolt are mostly sons of families who resented Batista's seizure of power in 1952 and who believe his election to the presidency in 1954 was rigged. Many Cubans are openly bitter about what they call the president's military dictatorship and they call his army supporters corrupt." Already the regime was taking "stern repressive measures. . . . Cars were halted and occupants searched while wholesale arrests were made."[43]

Dubois framed Batista's retaliation as a "reign of terror." Hours after the palace attack, three of Batista's political opponents were killed, most notably the popular former senator Pelayo Cuervo Navarro. Police tracked him down hiding at a friend's house. He was last seen alive getting into the police car. Cuervo Navarro's body was found "riddled by bullets," Dubois wrote. "Two other oppositionists were found hanged. Scores were arrested. . . . Persons questioned by this reporter about Cuervo's death quickly responded, 'They have killed a great man.'" Dubois knew Cuervo Navarro as an "honest, respected and courageous lawyer" and president of the opposition Ortodoxo Party, who single-handedly had dared to sue former president Ramón Grau, accusing him of stealing $170 million from the national treasury.[44]

Batista now resorted to partial censorship, this time banning Cuban television from showing any of the fighting and casualties. However, he allowed the press to print what Dubois called "an abundance of gory photographs of dead and wounded." Dubois chose to focus on Cuervo Navarro's assassination, which might rally the opposition even more than the students' deaths would. "Cuervo's secretary disappeared yesterday afternoon. It was reported he was tortured by intelligence personnel. Relatives and friends said they believed Cuervo's whereabouts were extracted from his secretary under torture." The senator's widow, Rosana Galano de Cuervo, declared that "Batista and his dictatorship killed my husband." Dubois told her that the chief of the investigation bureau said the police had always given Cuervo Navarro protection. "What protection?" his widow scoffed. "They protected so well that they killed him."[45]

Cuervo Navarro's funeral served to convene the regime's opponents, stunned by his murder and by the deaths of so many young men. Mourners "vowed at his grave," Dubois reported, "that they will fight President Batista until the people regain their republican freedoms." Elsewhere, "reaction against Batista was general. Cuban editors said they were convinced there can be no peace in Cuba while he remains president." Cuervo Navarro's Ortodoxo Party committee of forty-one men and women charged that the senator had been "vilely assassinated by the Batista dictatorship" because of his staunch opposition, and they pledged to "combat the sinister regime that bleeds the country." On the same day, Batista tried to placate the opposition by promising to hold a general election in 1958. But, Dubois noted, "the announcement stirred no enthusiasm among the public."[46]

Given his reputation as an insider, Dubois merited a personal opinion column in the *Tribune*. Now he used that platform to frame the significance of the violence in Cuba. The "forces of rebellion" were "moving fast." Fervent sentiment against Batista that Matthews had found a month earlier had now erupted into violence. After the murder of Senator Cuervo, Dubois wrote, "passions are inflamed" across a spectrum of society—among political foes, "younger officers of the army," and students determined to "avenge the slaying" of Echevarría, who "was cornered alone by the police as he drove away from the radio station here after he announced the rebellion.... The shooting of Pelayo Cuervo has created a situation which Batista probably never anticipated." Batista's brutal retaliation united his opponents, driving them to greater secrecy and conspiracy. Dubois forecast the specter of other "suicide squads" that possessed "caches of arms and ammunition scattered throughout the country as well as hidden in Havana."[47]

Comparing the situation to earlier insurgencies in Cuba and Argentina, Dubois projected Batista's eventual demise. Cuba's dictator in 1933, Gerardo Machado, had been forced to flee to Miami Beach after his brutality against opponents "carried Cuba into a blood bath." In Argentina in 1955, after dictator Juan Perón narrowly escaped assassination, he too retaliated with terror. "He ordered the churches burned. That finished him. It was then only a question of 12 weeks before he was out." Now, Dubois wrote, Batista had "escaped and won the battle" but "lost the war." Even Batista's military and civilian allies contemplated seizing power. "Batista's friends are reported to be planning a palace coup to keep control of the government and the treasury. If they should succeed, they will take over the government and establish a military dictatorship."[48]

For days, Dubois monitored Batista's "reign of terror" and the opposition's response. On March 17, he concluded that "Batista is living a precarious life. Some of his countrymen have marked him for death." Dubois quoted Batista's foes who said, "Political peace can be restored only if Batista grants the people complete freedom.... He must empty the jails of political prisoners and allow all exiles to return home." Hundreds had been jailed since the assault on the palace. "Other thousands have been imprisoned for months. Many prisoners have been tortured for two or more years. Their mutilated bodies have been tossed into fields or suddenly found dead."[49]

The Batista regime, supported by army officers, had turned into a ghastly enterprise characterized by terror and murder, reminiscent of other Latin American dictatorships. Persuaded that Batista would eventually fall, Dubois decided he was well situated to document the whole Cuban saga. No journalist better understood from experience the characteristics of Latin American dictatorships.

President-General Batista fit precisely Dubois's stereotype:

The Latin-American dictator is an egomaniac, a man of greed and at times a sadist. He is determined to enrich himself from the income of the national treasury and considers the entire nation is his personal domain.... He acquires a personal fortune by devious means.... He crushes everyone who is an obstacle in his path.... He orders persecution, torture, assassination and exile of political, military and commercial obstructionists.... He operates a police state with mail, telephone, telegraph, press, radio and television censorship and limitless spies. He restricts freedom of assembly for opposition political parties or bans adverse political activity.... He eradicates the independent press and radio and television by bribery, threat, intimidation, legislation, confiscation, destruction and seldom by purchase.... He forbids the citizens to read newspapers or magazines published abroad or to listen to radio broadcasts from abroad. He denies to the people the right to dissent.... He converts the labor bosses into docile political tools of his regime or bars unions. He professes to be anti-Communist but gives the Communists a free rein to operate so he can undermine and destroy his political and labor opposition. He always brands his critics and opponents as Communists—in order to ingratiate himself with the State Department and the American public—when an overwhelming majority of them are the contrary.

Dubois could explain how Cuba had moved from democracy to dictatorship during the terms of its three elected presidents from 1940 to 1952. Concerning "presidents who are not dictators," Dubois noted, they "also enrich themselves in a fabulous and scandalous manner, while they do nothing to check poverty and misery" and thus "perform a devastating disservice to the forces of freedom. They create an atmosphere that is made to order for ambitious military men who, taking advantage of the moral decomposition of the regime, can perpetrate a successful coup and destroy constitutional government. A disillusioned people, who have been mesmerized into a state of helplessness, refuse immediately to take up arms in defense of the grafters."[50]

Having witnessed the rise and fall of regimes, Dubois also described the life cycle of Latin American revolutions. The typical Latin American revolution involved rearranging of loyalties and allegiances among contenders for power—usually involving military officers and rising politicians. But the winners typically agreed to make no fundamental change in the organization of power sharing in the regime; any such changes could lead to another realignment of loyalties. "The 'typical' Latin American revolution," one scholar noted at the time, "does not demolish the previous structure of power relationships, but adds to it that of the revolutionaries" who have "demonstrated a power capability that other power contenders had found it advisable or necessary to recognize and accommodate into the power structure of society." By contrast, a "real" revolution, as Fidel Castro with his own armed force seemed to want, would conceivably alter the roles of both the army and the president. In that case, Castro could be free to do as he pledged and restore the democracy. Yet Dubois wondered if Castro could "degenerate into a dictator himself."[51]

Dubois planned to expand the scope of his reporting to at least three factions. He needed to develop a channel to Castro as well as one to the insurgents in Havana and one to the anti-Batista Cuban exiles in Miami, led by Carlos Prío Socarrás. The political strife offered an excellent Latin American test case for human rights, matching his own personal crusade for freedom of the press. However this turned out, Dubois envisioned a monumental story, a book that only he, as the ultimate insider, could write.

After the palace attack, Batista—true to Dubois's stereotype—initiated a public relations campaign to improve his image in the media. Advised by his public relations counselor, Edmund Chester, Batista agreed to controlled interviews during which he portrayed himself as fearless, tough, and clever. He claimed he had anticipated the attack and used it as a trap. "I knew they wanted to attack the palace," Batista stated in a ninety-minute interview with a *Miami News* correspondent. "I decided to use myself as bait to draw them in here rather than fight in the middle of the city." He described the attackers as ex-convicts, smugglers, and Communists friendly to Castro and employed by exiled former president Prío. He derided Castro as having as few as three or four men and thus posing no threat to the government. Among Miami's exiles, one businessman thought the attack strengthened Batista's hold on the government. "An uprising by a group of hot-headed university students won't weaken his position. If anything it will cause him to become tougher."[52]

"In Cuba," reminded one Miami columnist, "the man with the guns on his side is the man to be reckoned with." The phrase had been heard before. In fact, Herbert Matthews had used it in a 1952 article noting how Batista had seized power.[53]

Amid the terror and with no hope of an honest election, some Cubans now looked to Castro for a solution. *Time* magazine reported that "wearing away at his regime is the tiny guerrilla uprising under Rebel Fidel Castro in eastern Cuba's rugged mountains."[54] From the Sierra Maestra, Castro criticized the palace attack as misguided. Although his 26th of July Movement had a general pact with the Directorio Revolucionario, the "assault had not been co-ordinated with the Castro underground movement," Dubois wrote. Castro "was opposed to Batista's assassination. Castro preferred to get his hands on him and try him." An assassination that removed the dictator likely would lead to the familiar Latin American solution for a power vacuum: a quasi-legal military junta.[55]

Meanwhile, Castro benefited materially from the failed attack. Urban insurgents recognized that Castro's armed rebels were more likely to succeed against an army whose generals stayed loyal. Although Batista "branded" Castro as a "Communist agent," Dubois noted, "the public refused to shudder. The most responsible editor of a Havana newspaper denies Castro is a Communist."[56]

In late March, Herbert Matthews, watching from the quiet of the ninth floor of the *Times* building, addressed one of his editorial columns to "anyone with a feeling for Cuba and the Cubans." He was hoping for a way to avoid the worst case, "a blood bath and chaos too dreadful to contemplate." But there was not "much reason for optimism," he concluded, because the "brutal counter-terrorism of the Batista Government" had gone almost too far with the murder of Senator Palayo Cuervo Navarro, "one of the most distinguished lawyers and respected citizens of Cuba.... It was not only a terrible crime; it was a terrible mistake." Whether it was at Batista's order or not, "this foul deed has aroused Cubans much more than anything that has happened in years." Abruptly, Matthews ended with a note of optimism for a political solution that "must come soon with the announcement of fair and free elections, of the restoration of constitutional guarantees and true freedom of the press." It was as though he were whistling past the graveyard.[57]

By April, Castro was planning his next American media interview in the Sierra Maestra. Although the Cuban censorship had been suspended, army patrols still blocked access to the mountains and not even the most enterprising Cuban editors dared to publish much about the rebels. "Little is heard about Fidel Castro's activities in the Sierra Maestra," Dubois wrote on March 24, eleven days after the palace attack, "because the government won't let local newspapers send correspondents to the 'front.'" A Cuban journalist would be risking capture, jail, torture, and death. Also influential in suppressing news about Castro was systemic bribery—the practice of supplementing many journalists' paychecks in exchange for loyalty to the regime, including silence about Castro.

Castro's strategy in the wake of the palace disaster required breaking that media silence. The best way was through the U.S. media. The *New York Times* and Herbert Matthews had established Fidel as a living and formidable force, but now Castro needed continuous attention and, for the sake of credibility, it would be better to have other voices in addition to Matthews's. This time Castro aimed to reach Americans and his own Cubans through U.S. television—the very idea that Mario Llerena had brought from New York. The rebel camp was awaiting the arrival of CBS's Robert Taber.[58]

CHAPTER 4

CUBA'S JUNGLE FIGHTERS

H aving returned from Cuba, Robert Taber needed CBS approval to go forward with the Cuban story. Specifically, Taber had to persuade Don Hewitt that the rebellion was worth what Taber wanted—a half-hour documentary across the CBS national network. Taber's sole advantage was in knowing that Hewitt was ambitious and adventuresome. But Taber had failed in his main objective, to interview Fidel Castro or any rebels directly allied with Castro. So the proposed focus for the half-hour was expressed in general terms: the seething insurgency in America's Caribbean vacation spot ninety miles from Key West. Taber knew that story was weak, too conceptual, and hardly better than the news reports that had already been on the air. For the network documentary, this had to be one helluva story—an exclusive, timely, important, and dramatic story. That was television's mantra: *It's the story.*

What Taber had so far seen and collected was not the story, but the background for the story. He had the frame for a thriller: students' blood spilled in the streets, the triumph of the dictator. The attack at the Presidential Palace certainly took the story beyond where Herbert Matthews had left it. While Batista sounded jubilant, his enemies had multiplied, retreated, and regrouped. Castro's armed rebels had emerged as the opposition's best hope. The story now had blood and death and a sharper focus on Señor Fidel Castro. Taber needed to go back to Cuba, this time with a cameraman. He would take the CBS audience into the rebels' hideout in the jungle. They would see and hear Castro.

The headlines from Cuba seemed to justify the network's investment. After the palace attack, the U.S. media had made Americans more aware of the turmoil and elevated President-General Batista's political profile. With the cunning that had kept him atop Cuban politics for more than twenty years, Batista used the attack as leverage to strengthen his regime. As a U.S. ally in the Cold War, he emphasized the need to send more arms and military trainers to guard against the Soviet Communist menace in the Caribbean. In the frame of the Cold War, Batista addressed two key factors shaping America's Cold War foreign policy—fear and power. The intense U.S.-Soviet competition for allegiances left the Third World with what one historian called "wreckage spread far and wide, in toppled governments, loathsome dictators." Batista's anti-Communist stance led the U.S. State Department to accept the collateral damage caused by his wreckage of the Cuban democracy. So long as he was staunchly anti-Communist, he had U.S. support, including military supplies and training, ostensibly for "defense of the hemisphere."[1]

Taber now set about to persuade Hewitt and his bosses to send him back to Cuba. He had much of the evidence he needed in his "reporter's note-book." On arriving in Havana on March 2, Taber noted that he visited the U.S. Embassy—something Herbert Matthews had avoided because he distrusted Ambassador Arthur Gardner, who had been "simply furious" about the *Times*'s scoop.[2] At the embassy, a staffer told Taber that anti-Batista groups respected the viability of Castro's movement but distrusted its motives. "With regard to Batista's opposition, the oppositionists are divided among them-selves principally by fear of the political demands that Fidel Castro might make, were he to emerge as the hero of a popular revolution. They don't want him on their team; they feel that he's too young, fiery, militaristic, anti-Yanqui; in their opinion, a potential dictator worse than the present one."[3]

The rivals for power, Taber was told, would likely "race" to fill the power vacuum if Batista fell. One opposition group, supported by exiles in Miami, hoped to restore the ousted president, Carlos Prío Socarrás. "In this connec-tion," Taber noted on March 2, "my source in the Embassy agrees with Cu-ban contacts that Prío's people here in Havana probably do have a big cache of arms and are sitting on it, not so much for revolutionary purposes, as to use in exploiting the chaos that would be attendant on a popular uprising sparked by Fidel Castro. That is, if Batista were to fall, the arms would be used in the resulting race to beat Fidel to the presidential palace."[4]

During his stay in Havana in March, Taber remarked on the Batista re-gime's pattern of issuing statements that were soon revealed as false. On March 1, the government had declared that the army had made the Sierra Maestra "practically normal." Taber contrasted that with a published report from Oriente "of clashes between rebel and army forces . . . in no fewer than seven separate areas in the foothills of the Sierra . . . using artillery against Fidel's forces. . . . A short while later, it was further disclosed that the army was airlifting twelve hundred troops into the Oriente . . . to reinforce the sol-diers already there." The regime's duplicity was revealed repeatedly. "The fact was that the government was trying desperately to do two things at once—to stamp out the insurrection and at the same time to persuade the public that it had already done so. It failed in both efforts." By March, Taber surmised, "Fidel was secure, but he did not yet have the means of posing a serious threat outside of the Sierra. The army could accomplish nothing by entering, in whatever force. The situation was, in a word, static."[5]

The political situation changed dramatically on March 13 when so many Cuban youths became martyrs in the attack on the Presidential Palace. Taber regarded Batista's subsequent optimism as theatrical, another big lie. "Newspaper pictures of Batista made immediately after the abortive attempt on his life show him wearing an assured grin, his hands clasped overhead in the triumphant gesture of a veteran boxer who has won yet another in a long series of ring victories." While a *New York Times* editorial, probably written by Matthews, asserted that the attempted assassination cast "a lurid light on a dark and unhappy situation," Taber probed the wisdom of the attack. "One can easily imagine what success would have meant. At worst, a slaughter of opposition elements by the army, a mad scramble for power within the Cuban military establishment, and a succession of military juntas . . . prolonging the revolution indefinitely. And at best, perhaps, restoration of the political circumstances of the pre-Batista era, i.e., renewal of the very conditions that had created Batista in the first place."[6]

Taber concluded that "the various insurgent groups in rivalry with the *fidelistas* had felt the need to 'do something' if only as a matter of saving face." The "sensation produced by the Matthews report was having its effect not only on the government and the populace, but on revolutionary factions which may be considered to have been, to varying degrees, *rivals* of the 26th of July organization" even though "some of them were also collaborators" with Castro. Taber identified three urban insurgent groups. The first attackers, mostly students, were led by Carlos Gutiérrez Menoyo, who was killed at the palace, while nearly thirty of their men were stuck in a Fast Delivery truck blocked in traffic by a bus. The second group of university students, led by José Echevarría, who also was killed, seized the radio station. The third group, led by Ignacio González, a *priísta*—a follower of Prío Socarrás—was to have made a "second wave" assault but apparently never reached the palace, so the "first wave had been entirely unsupported."[7]

Confident of his findings, Taber in New York on April 1 wrote a lengthy "report" to the CBS news directors predicting the "downfall" of the Batista regime and confirming Matthews's assessment of the insurgents. "The revolution which Herbert Matthews sees in progress in Cuba does indeed exist, in the sense that a great many Cubans are at work in one way or another, gnawing away at the foundations of the existing government. The Batista regime will owe its downfall in large measure to the self-contradictory policy of denying the existence of any real opposition, while at the same time clandestinely employing the most brutal and unintelligent methods—and men—to suppress it. The very corruption of the regime is enough to insure its eventual overthrow."[8]

Taber passed along what he learned at the U.S. Embassy. "At the moment, the anti-Batista forces lack two important elements of success: (1) a generally acceptable leader, (2) a mutually agreed-upon program. There is no real collaboration among these forces. Each bides its time, hoping to exploit the recklessness of the other. The opposition groups contain a number of diverse elements with totally opposed philosophies." Given such divisiveness, "it would seem the outlook for a popular, general uprising is remote. The revolutionaries are intelligent enough to see that. They say their hope is to keep the spark alive, to keep the country in a state of emergency which will undermine the government by damaging its economic and diplomatic arrangements, so as to create a climate in which the Batista regime must ultimately strangle and collapse of its own weight."

So far, that plan had not been effective. In Havana, "the underground is disorganized, inefficient; in the half-boast, half-apology of some of its members it is made up of 'a lot of amateurs.'" Since Castro's arrival, the Batista regime had become "confused, disorganized, inefficient, and, what is more, frightened. Thus, although the government has the great advantage of being in, and solidly entrenched, time works against it. Fidel Castro serves a vital purpose in keeping the insurrection alive, in the public press and in the minds of the people."[9]

The Cuban press played a key role favoring Castro. Although banned from visiting the rebel camps, Cuban journalists were permitted to write about the capture and killing of rebels, such as those in the Presidential Palace attack. While the Batista regime figured that such stories discouraged other insurrectionists, Taber thought just the opposite: "Each time the government captures or kills a young rebel courier, or jails or murders an elder statesman, or spends another five thousand dollars for information leading to the discovery of another arms cache, there is another newspaper headline, and another hundred Cubans enlisted on the side of the rebels."[10]

The end was in sight, Taber concluded. "Sooner or later, economic support, diplomatic support must be withdrawn from Batista. The funds to subsidize public works will dwindle. Popular clamor will interfere with the free flow of graft. Police terrorism will reach an excess which will demand re-forms even within the police state. The agents of that state will begin to look out for their own skins and investment. And the end will be at hand."[11]

Apart from the report, Taber noted how the military moves benefited Cas-tro. First, the Cuban Army had withdrawn from fruitless attacks in the jungle and mountains, now favoring a strategy of "confinement" by encircling rebel territory. Second, that strategy conceded territory to Fidel, an apparently "impregnable citadel" in the Sierra Maestra. Third, Castro's movement—its cause (*la causa*) and its struggle (*la lucha*)—now received a flow of reinforce-ments and support in the form of everything from goods to weapons. These came from Cubans across social classes, from people in cities as well as the countryside. Finally, the attack on the Presidential Palace, though a disas-ter, was an unforgettable statement by Cubans across classes. "The failure of the assault on the presidential palace left the underground groups which had participated in the attack rudderless and demoralized. Influential and wealthy Cubans, who had in a manner of speaking, placed their bets on one or another of these groups, now looked reluctantly toward Oriente."[12]

Apart from his thorough research, Taber could cite the need to beat the competition at the National Broadcasting Company (NBC). That network was already seeking Castro, as evidenced by their sending two freelancers from Alabama who were jailed after wandering around Santiago de Cuba. Taber's network, CBS, of course, would want to be first. Its younger corporate culture encouraged leadership, and it stressed imagination and speed. In the mid-1930s CBS had become a news leader, breaking from dependence on news agencies, developing the first radio news team. Led by the genius of Edward R. Murrow and the cash of CBS's founder, William S. Paley, the network offered radio's best news and commentary. Its timing was fortunate. During the rise of Nazi Germany, Murrow went to Europe and hired and managed a team of journalists to give weekly radio reports from Berlin and Paris, while he him-self covered London. "Murrow's Boys" included William Shirer and Howard K. Smith in Berlin; Eric Sevareid in Paris; as well as Charles Collingwood, Larry LeSueur, and Winston Burdett, plus an energetic broadcaster Murrow recruited in Texas, Charles Shaw. Together they pioneered broadcasting be-fore and during the World War. When the German planes bombed London, Murrow daringly broadcast from a London rooftop, backgrounded by the sounds of explosions of modern, total warfare. After the war, Murrow led CBS's transition to television, creating on-air opportunities for seasoned broadcasters with "faces for television" and jobs for young inventive producers behind cameras. The most enterprising producer was the man who converted Murrow's *Hear It Now* to *See It Now*, Don Hewitt, and it was Hewitt now who would decide if Taber should go forward.

Despite the competition and such thorough reporting, Taber still had no assurance that he could interview Fidel Castro. After the weeks in Havana and Santiago, he had returned home with no arrangement for an interview, not even one with a key contact within Castro's 26th of July Movement. His only link was with Mario Llerena, the former Duke University professor being used as the movement's courier between Havana and New York. Llerena blamed himself as "indirectly responsible" for luring Taber to Cuba for an "apparently useless trip," noting that "Taber decided he was wasting his time in Havana and went back to New York." But Llerena promised to contact Taber "at the first sign that something was about to develop."[13]

In fact something propitious was developing in Havana. At about the same time as Taber wrote that CBS memo, the prospect of his usefulness to the 26th of July Movement, the M-26, was discussed in a secret meeting attended by Llerena. Havana's M-26 secretary, Armando Hart, had just returned from the Sierra Maestra with messages from Castro. In the wake of the palace disaster, Castro wanted to shift revolutionary support from the city to the Sierra Maestra. Also, he was insisting on arranging more interviews with American journalists. Hart "mentioned the tremendous impact of Matthews's articles," and Llerena immediately suggested they should bring back Matthews.

"No," Hart said. "Fidel preferred to have some other reporters this time." Hart said that Castro had a theory about how the news reporting could more effective as propaganda. "Both Matthews and the *New York Times* could be considered practically in our pockets, so it was better to keep them in reserve for the future. Good publicity required an impression of absolute impartiality in the reporting."[14]

Llerena then proposed Taber at CBS television.

"Hart was enthusiastic about the idea," Llerena wrote, "so much so that he rejected the telephone or cable procedure in favor of sending someone to New York personally. I argued that that was not really necessary, but he insisted, and all the others agreed.... Who should go? This did not take them too long to decide, either—who else? I knew Taber. I spoke the language. I had a ready visa. Money for the round trip and expenses was produced immediately—the 26th of July leaders always seemed to have substantial amounts of cash at their disposal—and the next day I was once again on a plane to New York."

In New York, Llerena phoned Taber.

Taber was elated. "This seems to be it, doesn't it?"

"His enthusiasm was greater than his surprise," Llerena recalled.[15]

The next morning over breakfast in Taber's Manhattan apartment, he and Llerena worked on the plan. By 2 p.m. they were at CBS and persuaded Hewitt to take the next step. For the all-important cameraman, Hewitt wanted the talented Wendell Hoffman, whose journalistic instincts matched his technical skills. Hoffman was out of town on assignment when he got the message. Hoffman recalled that CBS's Jack Bush "located me in Nebraska and tells me, frenzied, to fly to New York for 'a special job.'"[16]

For this secret mission, Llerena told the journalists they would enter Cuba as Christian missionaries. He knew that Presbyterian sympathizers in Havana would vouch that Taber and Hoffman were "American missionaries on a field trip to inspect and photograph the Presbyterian schools in Cuba." At the Havana airport, Llerena arranged for the two to be greeted by the pastor of the First Presbyterian Church, who was also in the M-26 underground. Late at night, Taber and Hoffman passed through security and customs "without the slightest difficulty." After midnight, their station wagon stopped in front of the Presbyterian Church on Calle Salud in downtown Havana, where another two cars were waiting. Everybody spoke in whispers. Any noise or disturbance at that hour could attract the attention of a police patrol. With extreme care they transferred the Americans' cameras and recording equipment from the station wagon to the cars. Llerena, whispering good-bye, handed them off to "two other 26th of July militants, armed with pistols and submachine guns." The rebels would escort the Americans to Oriente Province. "When everything was ready, the two cars left for their long journey to Santiago," Llerena wrote, evidently relieved that his plan had worked. "My part in the mission was over."[17]

For the six-hundred-mile journey to the Sierra Maestra by way of Santiago, they were to be escorted past army roadblocks by two M-26 men also posing as missionaries and calling themselves Marcos and Nicaragua.[18] On reaching Oriente Province, they met three more rebels, a man posing as Lalo Sardiñas, a commercial traveler, and the movement's two most important women. One was Haydée Santamaría, Armando Hart's wife, who had been with Castro's revolt since the attack in 1953 on the Moncada fortress. The other was Castro's personal assistant, Celia Sánchez, code-named La Paloma, the Dove, whom Che Guevara regarded as "our constant reminder that the angels are on our side."[19]

In the foothills of the Sierra Maestra, Taber and Hoffman, weighted down by cameras and recording equipment, glanced at Castro's mountain and braced for the climb. It would be far more arduous than Matthews's trek. In February Castro had been so eager to meet the American journalist that he risked danger by coming down from the heights. Since then, Fidel had moved his camp farther up in the mountains, near the highest peak in the range, Pico Turquino. The change was for security but also, as Guevara noted, "to impress the journalists." Forewarned, Hoffman lightened his load, leaving behind "some things that are not absolutely necessary. I abandoned boxes, tripods, some clothes. Even so, I was overloaded." A photograph showed the journalists trudging up the "roughness" of the Sierra—on the rocks, amid tropical jungle growth. They climbed with no clear path, just one rocky or rain-slicked foothold after another. On April 23, they reached Castro's camp and found themselves received as celebrities. "All of the rebels who were hiding in the Sierra were hanging on the arrival of the two American journalists," Hoffman recalled. He was told that "the rebels had avoided all encounters with the enemy for 20 days in order not to put our lives in danger."[20]

After his weeks of planning, Taber had reached his goal. Castro welcomed the two warmly and soon started talking about his revolution. Hoffman, a writer as well as a photographer, noted that he was "surprised to encounter a man so sensible," as he stated in his article for Cuba's popular *Bohemia* magazine. Fidel, speaking of his enemy, told them, "I don't bear a grudge against the soldiers that fight against us." Such a philosophical attitude could not win a war, Hoffman thought. But as Castro continued, Hoffman recognized a killer instinct. "Later I could understand that this discreet Doctor Castro is capable of giving the order to kill when circumstances require it."[21]

Before the filmed interview with Castro, Hoffman ranged around the rebel camp taking photographs. Castro's men posed for him, some peering from behind trees in the forest—the "jungle," as Taber called it. Such was the habitat of the "jungle fighters." Hoffman photographed one rebel at rest who was nevertheless ready for the enemy "with rifle in hand, tobacco in the mouth and cartridge belt" across his chest. Raúl Castro posed handling a rifle and showing off its telescopic sight, indicating the rebels' ability to pick off distant targets.[22]

Taber and Hoffman also became the first to photograph and interview the three teenagers who had run away from the Guantánamo Naval Base. The eldest, seventeen-year-old Charles E. Ryan, Jr., asked Hoffman for any news from Hungary since the October 1956 revolution. "Chuck Ryan asked me eagerly, 'What has happened in Hungary?' Days later, speaking with this young man, I discovered why he was in unity with the [Cuban] rebels. Because it was impossible to go to fight in Hungary."[23]

For the centerpiece of the CBS project, the interview with Castro, Taber and Hoffman were told they had to lug their equipment still higher up in the mountains. As Guevara noted, Castro had chosen as a symbolic backdrop a memorial to José Martí. It was a bronze bust of Martí made by Cuban sculptor Jilma Madera to commemorate the centennial in 1953 of Martí's birth. It was one of hundreds of Martí memorials Cubans had erected since 1905, but this one had the distinction of its situation at the summit of the tallest peak in the Sierra Maestra. The site at Pico Turquino had a personal connection as well. In 1953, in the year of the Moncada attack, Dr. Manuel Sánchez Silveira and his daughter, Celia Sánchez, now Castro's confidante and aide, had climbed to the peak, more than 6,500 feet above sea level, to put the monument in place.[24]

In choosing the site, Fidel Castro wanted viewers to associate his struggle, *la lucha,* with José Martí's martyrdom in 1895 in the war for independence from Spain. Since then, identification with Martí and his legacy of resistance and hope had become a common practice for Cuban patriots and politicians using "his image for their political agendas," as one historian noted. In 1905, Cubans unveiled the grand statue of José Martí in Havana's Central Park. The date of Martí's death in 1895, May 19, was made a national day of mourning. And in 1921, the legislature's "Law That Glorifies the Apostle" decreed that Martí's birthday, January 28, would be a national holiday and mandated organized celebrations. The glorification required municipalities to erect public memorials; these might be as grand as a statue or column or bust—or as modest as a bronze plaque or stone tablet. By law, the memorials were to be focal sites for annual celebrations, including those of all the schoolchildren honoring his memory "with a flower on their breast" and reciting verses and singing hymns.[25]

Seated in front of the José Martí memorial on Pico Turquino, Castro looked directly at Hoffman's camera, addressing his American audience. As the film rolled, Hoffman squinted into the viewfinder, closely framing Castro and Taber as they sat side by side. Fidel wore military fatigues and a cap, his beard now thicker than the "scraggly" growth Matthews had seen in February. A photograph of the occasion showed Taber, with a slight beard of his own, holding the microphone with his right hand while his left hand held his lit cigarette from which he took a few drags off camera. From time to time, Taber glanced at the tape recorder to make sure his reels were still rolling.

Castro, leader of the revolution, presented his message to the CBS audience: the rebels were invincible. At one point, he surprised Taber—and possibly charmed the TV audience—with his unexpected sense of humor in ridiculing the failure of the mighty army to defeat his small band of rebels. "At this time," Castro said in his broken but understandable English, "there's not a one to admit that he's incapable of defeating us. He hopes to obtain *by liar* that which he cannot get by force of arms. Sometimes he says that *I am dead.* Another time he says that *there's nobody in Sierra Maestra.* But he won't let anyone to come here to Sierra Maestra. And when the solders are killed in battle, he says that they were *died in accident.* Eh. There have been a *great deal of accidents* here in Sierra Maestra last month."[26]

Taber, catching Castro's humor, grinned slightly, but was more concerned with recording it. Castro's understatement—"a great deal of accidents"—communicated his talent for speaking English with Cuban characteristics. In his own voice, then, he was delivering what he said was the truth: despite the great Cuban Army, the rebels were gaining strength while Batista hid reality by telling lies and banning Cuban journalists from trying to find the truth.

After three weeks in the Sierra Maestra, Hoffman departed for New York, carrying the film, audiotape, and photographs. Taber had decided to stay longer to do a radio broadcast from the mountain range. Back in New York, Hoffman told a *Bohemia* correspondent that "Robert Taber and I spoke a long time with Fidel Castro." Castro had told them, "This is only the beginning. The last battle will be in the capital." On that prediction, Hoffman said, Castro added emphatically: "You can be sure that this will be so." The *Bohemia* interview ended abruptly when its correspondent wanted to know more about M-26 involvement in arranging their journey and departure. "No more," said Hoffman. "I am not going to talk about the return. Now I am here, in CBS, in New York, and I feel happy in having done this work." He reserved the rest of his story for his own article in *Bohemia.*[27]

From Castro's camp, Taber broadcast a report on CBS radio in early May, establishing his own scoop while publicizing Castro's ascendancy. "Within a very short time," Taber stated, "the rebel band headed by Fidel Castro, which invaded Cuba in December and has since grown considerably in strength, will take the offensive in Cuba's eastern province of Oriente, outside of the mountain range called Sierra Maestra." Despite government propaganda, "Castro's mountain guerrillas" were not "figments of subversive imagination. ... After three weeks with Fidel Castro, this reporter can assert with confidence that, if fiction is being written, it is in the presidential palace in Havana."[28]

The government's fiction, Taber stated, extended to its army. Despite having three thousand soldiers in the Sierra Maestra, the Cuban Army had failed "in all attempts to crush Castro's force." The generals had ordered the bulk of those troops to withdraw from those mountains because, the government announced, "no problem existed there." Taber contested that claim, saying the troops were withdrawn "at least in part to defend the towns which lie on the plain outside of the Sierra. City garrisons are being reinforced in fear of imminent attack. And despite the disparity which exists in the relative strength of the opposing forces, the fear is justified."[29]

When Taber left the Sierra Maestra, two of the runaway Guantánamo teenagers went with him. Michael Garvey and Victor J. Buehlman said long good-byes to the rebels and their friend Chuck Ryan. With rebel escorts, they made it safely back to their families. A brief story appeared in *Life* magazine, with Taber's photographs of the two who left with him. His photos showed both boys with beards—Garvey with cigar in his mouth and Buehlman wearing a "26 Julio" armband saying good-bye to Castro and his "chieftain," Camilo Cienfuegos. "The sputtering Cuban civil war went grimly on," read the text in *Life*. "The realities of the war proved too much for some spirited American youths who had joined the rebels." Chuck Ryan decided to stay, he told Taber, because "I figure the fight in Cuba is for the kind of ideals on which the U.S. was set up." Then, Taber said, Ryan burst into tears.[30]

As Taber was leaving the Sierra Maestra, he observed the rebels celebrating the arrival of a cache of weapons from insurgents in Havana. "When I parted from Fidel Castro," Taber wrote, "he was on his way to receive a shipment of arms—heavy machine guns and bazookas." Taber heard that these weapons came from revolutionaries in Havana after the disastrous attack on the Presidential Palace. "The arms," he learned, "had been held in readiness for the attack on the palace, in trucks which were to have sped to the scene, to support the planned 'second wave' under Ignacio González—the wave which had failed to materialize because those responsible for the delivery of the weapons had failed to give the necessary orders."[31] Now the guns had been smuggled to Santiago, where the M-26 underground kept half of them and sent the other half by schooner along the coast, with the weapons hidden in sealed oil drums. Fishermen brought the drums ashore and local lumbermen took them up the wooded slopes to Castro's men. Che Guevara counted "10 machine guns, 11 Johnson guns, and 6 short carbines."[32] Taber's inventory was mostly correct: there was no bazooka, and the rebels now also had thousands of rounds of ammunition. In the larger scope, the transfer of the arsenal was de facto recognition by the benefactors that Castro, by surviving while others failed, was now the best bet to defeat Batista.

That shipment of weapons from the urban insurgents "formed the basis" of Taber's general prediction. Having spent weeks in rebel territory—in contrast to Matthews's few brief hours one morning in February—Taber confidently asserted that "the revolutionary spirit is running high in Oriente. In a mountainous area of some five thousand square miles, the people are ready to support the rebels against whatever force may be dispatched from the capital." Others were coming up into the mountains to join the rebels and were especially welcome if they brought their own weapons. "On my way out of the mountains I met twenty-eight volunteers.... In the first village I reached, I spoke with a dozen men who told me: 'We pray that Fidel will come here. If he came today the entire village would rise as one man to join him in his march on the capital or Oriente.'"[33]

In New York, Don Hewitt took charge of producing the show. It would be based almost completely on Taber's interview and Hoffman's film. Hewitt and others at CBS endorsed Taber's credibility in portraying Castro as a genuine threat to the dictatorship. The CBS network scheduled the documentary for a prominent slot, on Sunday evening, May 19, which happened to be the Cuban holiday honoring Martí's death. As the film began, with dramatic music, the narrator likewise dramatically announced: "Rebels of the Sierra Maestra: The Story of Cuba's Jungle Fighters. This is their story. This is the Sierra Maestra. 200 miles of jungle." As if seeking to establish verisimilitude with a jungle context, Hewitt used film in which rebels rose from behind bushes, as they had posed for Hoffman.[34] Rebels peered through gaps in large-leaf growth. Rifle barrels protruded menacingly from behind bushes. One man suddenly spun from behind a tree and pointed his rifle directly at viewers. In groups, rebels lifted their rifles and waved them, cheering jubilantly. Fidel Castro was seen as the leader among his rifle-wielding rebels in the jungle. When he was not speaking about the revolution, he was seen acting his part, aiming and firing a pistol.[35]

The documentary introduced a confident Castro in good humor, and it allowed him to appeal for a major rebel objective. In a lawyerly manner, he argued that the United States should end arms shipments to Cuba on the legal grounds that the regime used the weapons against Cuba's people instead of as intended, for hemispheric defense against communism. It was an appeal that some in Congress might begin to take seriously if Batista could be shown to be an unsupportable dictator.

The documentary was treated as a news scoop and made headlines in the U.S. press and in Havana. A critic underscored the program's imbalance favoring Castro. "Critical commentary," one historian wrote, "was limited to Taber's concerns about the careless way the men handled their firearms, which resulted in one of them accidentally shooting himself in the hand while Taber was there."[36] In Havana the next day, because of a lapse between the regime's censorship decrees, the United Press story out of New York was published in Spanish and English newspapers. On its front page, Havana's Spanish-language *Diario de la Marina* focused on Castro's assertion that Batista could not defeat him and that "the last battle for Cuban freedom" would take place in Havana. "Robert Taber and the *camarographer* Wendell Hoffman from CBS cross by foot about 25 kilometers at night, through the jungle. ... Castro and his men, boasting about their dominion over the region, conducted the representatives of the CBS to Pico Turquino, the highest mountain in Cuba . . . where correspondent Taber made the extensive televised interview." The United Press noted that the documentary "ended with the insurgents singing the Cuban national anthem, on the top of Turquino." The English-language *Times of Havana* ran the story on page 3 with a headline that "Fidel Castro 'Stars' on Television Program," together with a photograph showing Castro "and several members of his mountain force let[ting] out a rousing cheer somewhere in the Sierra Maestra." They credited the photo to a member of the CBS "team which penetrated the mountains to interview the rebel leader."[37]

In Miami, a special preview of the CBS documentary was attended by deposed Cuban president Carlos Prío Socarrás and about two hundred others. They were invited to a "closed circuit" transmission because Miami's network CBS affiliate, WTVJ, had scheduled the documentary for broadcast the following Sunday, May 26. Prío Socarrás, who was then planning his own anti-Batista militant insurgency, realized more than ever that the Miami exiles had to act soon to challenge Castro, who in the documentary asserted that "all towns of Sierra supports us [*sic*]. We have demonstrated that the people will always fight for freedom and we have won many victories over Batista's soldiers. There are thousands that would want to join us, but we need more armaments." In publicizing the need for "more armaments," Castro, like Prío Socarrás, affirmed that only a military effort—not political negotiations—could dislodge the dictator.[38]

In Washington, on Monday, May 20, the day after the broadcast, a group of anti-Batista Cubans responding to the television publicity demonstrated and marched outside the White House. For background on Castro's movement, the press quoted its Washington spokesperson, Ernesto F. Betancourt, an economist who was resourceful in conducting demonstrations and raising money. Betancourt was quoted as saying that the protest was an attempt to convince the U.S. government to abstain from sending weapons to the Batista government—precisely Castro's appeal in the CBS documentary.[39]

Thus in the beginning of 1957, four U.S. correspondents—Herbert Matthews, Jules Dubois, Robert Taber, and Wendell Hoffman—had projected a positive image of Fidel Castro in the American media. First in nationally circulated newspapers and then on network television, they presented Castro as a freedom-loving young attorney who gave up the comforts of life to struggle against great odds for a cause: the end of a dictatorship and the restoration of democracy and free elections in his country. Negative accusations—notably that Castro was a Communist—lacked credibility and traction, mainly because Castro's detractors were associated with the dictatorship, notably Edmund Chester, the former CBS television executive serving as Batista's press agent.

Matthews had led, or "set the stage." He could take credit for elevating Castro to the news agenda of the American media, while basically reporting straight from Castro's script. Essentially, Matthews played the role of an ardent, faithful coauthor with Castro, communicating Castro's statements, ideas, aspirations, and promises. Dubois, Taber, and Hoffman followed on the "stage" with Castro's elaborations.

That cohort of correspondents in early 1957 created Castro's persona in the media marketplace where, as with repetitive advertising, repetition helped to sell it. By May, Dubois, in his dual roles as Latin American correspondent and chairman of the IAPA Freedom of the Press Committee, was devoting continuous attention to Castro's story. Then the CBS television script allowed Castro to speak earnestly and directly, making him an instant news-film personality.

Dubois thought Taber and Hoffman's telecast, because it also featured the teenage American runaways from Guantánamo, "awakened the imagination and desire for adventure of many another young American throughout the United States. Volunteer after volunteer tried to establish contact with the rebels. Many wrote letters to me, and I always replied that Castro did not need manpower since there were several million Cubans ready to fight under him if they could get their hands on the guns and the bullets that he needed."[40]

CHAPTER 5

MARCHING WITH CASTRO

obert Taber's departure from Castro's camp was welcome news for the impatient freelance adventure writer from New York who had been kept waiting in Santiago de Cuba. Andras Szentgyorgyi—who wrote under his Anglicized name, Andrew St. George—had imagined this opportunity since that Sunday in February when he read Herbert Matthews's spectacular adventure. That scoop struck him with envy because it was the very sort of story he could have written. His wife, Jean Szentgyorgyi, recalled that he "came out of the bathroom, with a towel wrapped around his waist—he had been shaving—waving a copy of the *New York Times* with Herbert Matthews' article about Fidel in the Sierra. He was so excited, and kept saying, 'I wish I had done this!'"[1]

Inspired by Matthews, St. George wrote a proposal for a Cuban adventure story and sold the idea to editors at the men's "Action and Adventure" magazine *Cavalier*. With an assignment in hand, he made the necessary connections with Castro's 26th of July Movement in New York. His timing fortunately coincided with Castro's demand that his movement leaders send him more U.S. correspondents. Crossing Cuba and arriving in Santiago in April, St. George was frustrated to learn that the CBS crew had beaten him to Castro and was still in the rebel camp. Taber had been told about St. George and Castro gave the order to stall him. "They kept him waiting in Santiago," St. George's wife recalled. "Then Taber left and he went in."[2]

One disadvantage for St. George was that he was not an accredited journalist and belonged to no significant media organization. Since coming to the United States in 1952 at age twenty-eight, he had been trying to make a living as a freelance writer. He specialized in the genre of espionage that he knew firsthand, having worked in the Hungarian underground during the Nazi occupation in World War II and afterward, in the Cold War, against the Communist regime.

St. George found the American magazine market eager for true war and spy stories. *Real*, the self-described "exciting magazine for Men," published his thriller "We Counter-Snatched Russia's Most Dangerous Spy" (by Clyde

Benton as told to St. George). In an introductory note, *Real*'s editor praised St. George's expertise and admitted he had underestimated "little Andy." "The first time we saw 5 7½" Andrew St. George we had our doubts that he could punch his way out of the proverbial paper bag. But little Andy, who authored REAL's spyne-tingler ... is as tough a hombre as you'll ever find. At the age of 17, he tangled with his first intelligence assignment, and by the time he was 20 he'd had a stretch in the famed [Budapest's] Margitkorut Military Prison, a caravansary run by the Gestapo." When totalitarian Communists supplanted the Nazis in Hungary, St. George found employment as a secret agent for the United States. "Andy," as *Real*'s editor noted, "has worked as a field operative for U.S. Army Intelligence in every capital from Ankara to London. A Hungarian by birth, he's now waiting to become an American citizen and is studying psychology on the side."[3]

St. George sought other magazines with hopefully bigger paychecks. The men's magazine *Argosy* published his piece on "The Cold War's Hottest Kidnapping" (August 1955) and in 1956 bought four more stories, including "The Spy Who Out-Swindled the Kremlin" (April) and his two-part series on the Dominican Republic's dictator, Rafael Trujillo—"The Case of the Missing Professor" (September) and "The League of Condemned Men" (October). In 1957, at age thirty-three, St. George turned his attention to Fidel Castro and to another publisher of true adventures.

At *Cavalier*, St. George presented the Castro story as a thriller within a thriller. First, shadowing Matthews's hero's journey, he planned to lead readers on his own perilous Cuban revolutionary adventure as he made underworld connections and slipped past the dictator's secret police and the army patrols. Then, bettering Matthews, St. George would do more than visit Castro for a few hours. Instead, he would live for weeks among the rebels, or as long as was needed, sharing dangers and exploits. It was an American scenario, rooted in swashbuckling nineteenth-century journalism, as when in 1871 the *New York Herald* sent Henry Morton Stanley to Africa to find the presumably lost Scottish missionary-explorer David Livingston, or when Richard Harding Davis famously went to Cuba to report the drama of the Spanish-American War.[4]

St. George's scenario was right down *Cavalier*'s editorial fairway. It promised to be as alluring as *Cavalier*'s April lineup of personal exploits: "Jimmy Doolittle: Boldest Hero of Them All" and "Amazing Dr. Reich and His Fantastic Sex Machine."[5] St. George's Hungarian accent may have sealed the deal. "It was a dream come true for him," his wife, Jean, recalled. "He got the assignment because the editor at *Cavalier* magazine knew he had an accent and they thought it was Spanish. He didn't then speak a word of Spanish. He spoke French."[6] He would be paid $1,000 to $1,500 for the story and photographs, a significant sum for a man who had submitted to IQ testing at Columbia University to earn a mere $25.[7] The fact that he had to cover his expenses to Cuba posed a problem. The cost of travel depleted the household budget, requiring Jean and their 3-year-old son Thomas to move in with her parents.[8]

St. George's enthusiasm was impressive. "I think," Jean Syentgyorgyi said, "he was just so excited and fascinated." The *Cavalier* editors regarded him as "the ideal man to send behind-the-lines to Fidel Castro." His raw wartime experience satisfied the editors that he could convert the idea into pure suspense. They gushed over his sleuthing with military intelligence during World War II "and afterwards as a civilian War Crimes Investigator for Hungary." When the Soviets occupied Hungary and established a Stalinist regime, St. George fled first to Austria and "put in six years with the U.S. Counter-Intelligence Corps, rescuing people from behind the Iron Curtain. He needed all his knowledge of intelligence tactics for this assignment, which was as dangerous as any in his career."[9]

St. George had envied Herbert Matthews's scoop for its novelty and shock, for Matthews's raw experience and Castro's revelations. But for *Cavalier*, St. George could do better. He would take the reader deeper into the reality and danger of the world of spies and war. While Matthews as an opinion writer had taken liberties with journalistic practice to express his own opinions, St. George had even more freedom as a writer of "true adventure." There would be his own cloaked search for Castro, and the peril shared by the hunted rebels. He knew: *There must be fear.* The reader must share nerve-wracking suspense. And he knew: *There must be blood.* Here would be men bleeding and dying for a cause. In such a world, Fidel Castro himself would be revealed.

By April, when St. George arrived in Havana, President-General Fulgencio Batista seemed securely in power, encouraged by confirmed and renewed U.S. support. Yet after four months of trying, the dictator's mighty army had not disposed of the rebels in the Sierra. Since Matthews's articles in February had proved that Castro had not been killed, the elusive leader had become the subject of general conversation and stories. Though Cuban journalists were banned from traveling in the Sierra, the mere mention of Fidel sold newspapers and magazines. In Havana, St. George found Castro's name "emblazoned on every front page on the newsstand. . . . The invisible Castro has now become a hero and a symbol of resistance to millions of Cubans weary of the dictatorial regime of General Batista." Cubans seemed to assume that what the regime forbade them to see was all the more believable and that somewhere in those mountains was a formidable force outwitting the army.[10]

News of the rebellion meanwhile was attracting other foreign writers who found Cuba's concoction of conflict and culture worthy of fiction. Two were distinguished and prominent British novelists, both veterans of British intelligence during World War II, Norman Lewis and Graham Greene. Lewis was also unsurpassed as a literary travel writer; his interest in the ongoing Algerian war for independence from France led him to the Cuban Revolution. Graham Greene regarded Lewis as "one of the best writers, not of any particular decade, but of our century."[11] In Lewis's novel *Cuban Passage,* he portrayed "the glittering façade of Batista's Havana." His opening scene was peaceful, set in a seaside café looking out upon the Malecón seawall and broad esplanade, the Avenida de Maceo, named for Antonio Maceo, the famous black revolutionary commander killed by the Spanish in the War for Independence. "Visiting the harbour café in the first cool of the evening had become a social habit of the city," says Lewis's narrator. "People sat there to calm and steady their vision with a pacific vista of ships, and to catch a little of the emotions of travel, the gaiety of arriving and the melancholy of departure. . . . There was no better place in Havana, Hollingdale believed, to introduce a newcomer to the rich and complex flavours of local life."

As one foreigner to another, Hollingdale was briefing a newcomer, Sanger, on Cuban culture. "You'll find them easy to like, amiable, shallow and profoundly superstitious. This must be the only capital city in the world where Woolworth's have a counter stacked with charms and voodoo paraphernalia. One of the ministers in the present government is said to belong to an African cult practicing human sacrifice. Presidents start off as starry-eyed idealists and finish as monsters. They still have a law on the statute book giving a woman the right to be present when her husband is tortured!"

> "What about the rebellion?" Sanger asked.
> "Eighty-two zealots bent on changing the face and destiny of this incorrigible land started it off in Oriente. . . . They were ready and willing to throw away their lives and most of them did."

"But the thing keeps going?"

"It's dead," Hollingdale said, "but it won't lie down."

Sanger had heard that the rebellion was "an invention of the press."

"That's not quite true," Hollingdale said, "but it's been blown up by the newspapers out of all proportion to its significance. After all, it sells papers."

"But you think it will come to nothing?"

"It *has* come to nothing. Quite shortly now it will either be suffocated—or even more probably it will simply peter out. What can you expect? A couple of hundred crack-brained university dropouts and middle-class unemployables led by a bearded and bespectacled lawyer taking the best equipment and best-trained army in Latin America, with the US at its back? In one year from now it will be forgotten."

"That's a comfort."

"Leave it to me to worry about the rebellion. It's my job. If there's anything turns up I feel you should know I'll be the first to tell you. Otherwise don't let it bother you."

"I won't."[12]

Meanwhile, Graham Greene was writing a spoof on the British Intelligence Service. He made the main character in *Our Man in Havana* a vacuum cleaner salesman, hired as a secret agent, who then completely fools his spy bosses, the agency superiors in London. With his World War II experience in Britain's MI6 spy agency, Greene constructed in Cuba a perfect tableau of conspiracy and danger. In *Our Man in Havana,* wrote Greene's biographer, "we come to *know* Havana—the beauty of the women, the nightclubs, the wild weather streaming in from the Atlantic—our increasing knowledge running in tandem with the increasing danger being unearthed. . . . He would report on what he observed, attitudes of mind: he would criticize the British government in the press; would rightly vilify the corrupt Batista government," exemplified by the lecherous policeman Captain Segura.[13]

These same elements of conspiracy and danger were what St. George was seeking in April as he arrived at José Martí International Airport. Following specific instructions from the 26th of July Movement contacts in Miami, he posed as a "businessman" and claimed his tape recorder was a business "*diktafon.*" He cleared immigration and went straight to the Hotel Siboney, one of the lesser hotels along Havana's wide, tree-lined Paseo de Prado. There he was to wait. "To see Castro was not going to be easy," he noted, "and we started with wartime intelligence tactics. We used a pair of common match folders. As an added identifying mark, I scribbled the office phone of *Cavalier* on the inside cover of each." In the Siboney's lobby, St. George did as he was told. *Buy a tobacco. Keep it where one can see but do not light it. Do not talk to anyone.* He waited and watched men come and go. For "two stiff, sweaty hours" he sat beneath "an open-armed girlie poster . . . beckoning tourists to 'See ALL of Exciting Cuba!'" Then he noticed that "a lanky fellow in a loose *guayabera* swung in from the blazing noon sidewalk and swept the lobby with a searching look." *This was it.* "I saw him peer at the unlit stogie clenched between my teeth. Slowly he ambled over and slumped into the chair next to me, fumbling with a brown Trinidad cigarette and a folder of matches, Kelly-green U.S. paper matches."

Despite all his experience in the Hungarian underground, St. George felt his throat tense.

"Got a light?" I asked.

"Maybe, friend."

My tall neighbor palmed his match folder and held it toward me. I could see a phone number scrawled on the inside cover. It was my own handwriting. The matches seemed damp with sweat. No spark.

"Hold on a minute," I said. "I might have some left after all."

From his shirt pocket, St. George withdrew his own matchbook, "the twin of my neighbor's folder." St. George opened it, as if to strike a light, allowing the stranger to see the code inside, the phone number of the Manhattan office of *Cavalier.*

The stranger dragged deeply on his smoke.

"You have a room here, my friend?" he asked St. George.[14]

They rode up to the room without speaking. Suddenly, St. George experienced "that old, almost-forgotten wartime feeling of tautness in my knees. I locked the door."

"Give me those matches," the man told St. George, then flushed both folders down the toilet and squatted on the edge of the bathtub and grinned. "If we are arrested together and they find the same matches on us it would look funny, no?" He said his name was Aurelio but friends called him Jojo. "I come from Fidel," he said. He carried a gun. St. George noticed "the round potato-like outline of a gun butt visible under Jojo's loose shirt."

St. George "had to fight off an attack of fear.... I realized something I had not foreseen—that if trouble came, my Cuban companions would shoot it out rather than risk capture and torture. And that meant I, too, would catch it before I could unhinge my jaw to shout 'Me reporter!'" Just the day before, about five hundred miles southeast of Havana near Santiago de Cuba—St. George's next destination—two corpses had been found in a ditch "full of government-issue .45 slugs." The bodies were identified as two newsmen who had been nosing around, a magazine reporter, Juan Bautista Rey, and his cameraman. "General Tamayo's threat to nosy newsmen had been plainly more than empty bluster."[15]

The next morning St. George did as told. He arranged for a taxi trip to the airport, then changed to a taxi to the less suspicious train station. There he caught the 7 a.m. express to the city that was the center of the insurgency, Santiago de Cuba. When he arrived, he learned that the CBS crew was with the rebels, had been there for weeks, and planned to stay longer. This shattered his exclusive. Even worse, he worried about the timing—no doubt CBS would air its show long before St. George's story was published. *Cavalier* had scheduled it for October. The solution seemed obvious: He had to discover what his competition missed, or misunderstood. He had in mind the larger question raised by Herbert Matthews: How could these few defeat the Cuban Army?

Meanwhile, the rebels guided St. George out of Santiago and into the Sierra Maestra, to a rearguard camp well below Castro's headquarters. Here he was turned over to the care of the camp's Argentine doctor, Ernesto Guevara de la Serma, called "Che" by the Cubans during their training in Mexico. Language proved to be the bond between the Argentine and the Hungarian. "Since I was the only person in the column who spoke French," Che Guevara recorded in his diary, "I was chosen to look out for him." The arrangement served St. George well because Guevara translated into Spanish the interview questions for Castro. St. George used the time to take photographs that showed the rebels camped and rested, with loaded rifles within reach. One photograph depicted the thick forest growth being parted as a rebel marched through, returning from lookout duty. He photographed Che standing relaxed with his weapon slung from his shoulder. Speaking as the doctor, Guevara told him that he "tries to get to [the] wounded before [the] Cuban army, which kills them."[16] And he photographed Castro's second-in-command, Lt. Universo Sandoz, with his shirt displaying the 26th of July insignia. He found the rebels "fun-hungry" as they "listen happily to the twang of Cuban guitar."

Their one luxury was a supply of cigars. One day, a group of "volunteers from [the] countryside" came to offer money and arms.[17]

Even after Robert Taber left Castro's camp, St. George was held back. Guevara told him that Castro was in a foul mood and was avoiding correspondents. That was not the whole story. Guevara suspected St. George's motives, partly because of the way he had been cleared to come to the Sierra. The agents in the United States had expedited his passage, spurred on by Castro's urgent demand for U.S. correspondents. They had hardly questioned his Hungarian background. Guevara thought St. George "showed only one of his faces—the less bad one—that of a Yankee journalist." Eventually he concluded that St. George was "an FBI agent with a touch of journalistic ambition in his heart."[18]

During the delay, St. George experienced more of the rebels' hardships as they constantly trekked, avoiding army patrols, usually changing camp daily. "We were moving around Pino del Agua toward the source of the Peladero River," Guevara noted. "These were rugged areas and we all carried heavy packs." St. George recorded how the "guerrilla army moves at least once every 24 hours. To do away with permanent headquarters it carries every last bullet and bean on its groaning back. There are no beds, no tents." The men slung hammocks in the trees, or slept on the ground, where countless *macagüera* horseflies left infected bites on legs, wrists, and necks. "Daily jungle marches of 10 to 20 mountain miles, with field packs—burlap sacks with makeshift shoulder straps—weighing between 65 to 75 pounds, plus a firearm and full ammo supply—these speak of physical feats not easily believed until you happen to have seen them yourself, as I have. Yet the forest fighters have learned the hard way that such endurance is essential. Whenever they've slowed up or let down, they've taken a trouncing."[19]

Occasionally, they entered a sparsely settled area with "a few peasant villages." There Guevara impressed St. George with a fundamental political aspect of the revolution that had eluded Herbert Matthews because he had not done the trek. As Guevara explained, the rebels were "establishing a kind of extralegal revolutionary state, leaving sympathizers charged with informing us of anything that happened, including the movements of the enemy army." In a region plagued by robbers and rapists, the rebels introduced law and order and enforced it, on occasion, by capital punishment. Grateful peasants also assisted the rebels with supplies, paid for in cash. Peasant support was not only helpful but absolutely necessary. With it, Castro slowly expanded rebel-controlled territory—which he now claimed as his liberated "Free Cuba."[20]

After two weeks in lower elevation, St. George was told Castro would meet him. He was led up through the forest to that day's command post, in an old shack. Inside, St. George found so many men that he didn't spot Castro until Castro "shouldered his way through the crowd to shake hands. He was munching a small green banana. Instead of a welcoming speech he dug into his jacket and handed me one."[21]

In the two months since he was photographed with Matthews, Castro had grown a fuller beard. St. George thought he saw a resemblance to a Civil War photograph of the Confederate general Stonewall Jackson, a "tall, thick-shouldered, heavy-faced man with an Old Testament beard that is actually a neat, natural combination of two mutton chops and a spade." Castro had just been cheered by two radio news bulletins. One reported that his 26th of July Movement leader in Santiago, Frank País, had been released from jail. Before joining Castro, País, Faustino Pérez, and Mario Llerena (the go-between for CBS's Taber and Hoffman) had all been members of the same anti-Batista group, Movimiento National Revolucionario (MNR). Afterward, País formed his own armed resistance group, Acción National Revolucionario (ANR). In April, País sent Castro fifty-six urban recruits, probably from his ANR ranks.[22]

The other good news by radio was that a Court of Appeals judge in Santiago had made a surprising declaration that revolutionary action against tyranny had a legal basis in the Cuban constitution. During the trial of some of the Movement's members, the judge concluded that "it was not a crime to organize armed forces against the regime" that had seized power and abrogated the constitution; revolutionary action against the regime was "rather something perfectly legal under the spirit and letter of the Constitution and the laws." Such a remarkable declaration, Castro said, "exalted the name of the Constitution." Judge Manuel Urrutia Lleo instantly became one of Castro's favorites. Urrutia Lleo, however, was overruled by the other two judges, who sentenced the defendants to prison.[23]

Prison, Castro told St. George, was probably safer than freedom. The freeing of his comrades would have unleashed "the brutality of the regime." They could have been re-arrested and murdered, after torture. That specter of an agonizing death was "always on their minds," St. George stressed, because of "the Cuban Army's habit of killing its prisoners, as often as not by slow torture." Their constant readiness was evidenced at the headquarters shack, where two men "never quite took their hands from their weapons. The .45 Thompson Tommygun of Manuel Majardo, Castro's broad, button-eyed bodyguard, was always on 'Full Auto,' never on 'Safe.'"

St. George noted the organizational details of Castro's military. "Around Castro I could see several men with the shield-shaped officer's patch on their shoulders (a single patch for lieutenants, patches on both shoulders for captains). The captains carried .30-06 scope-fitted rifles of Belgian or Swedish make. The lieutenants were equipped with automatic or sporting guns of every imaginable variety." Castro—"a legendary marksman"—carried a Swedish .30-06. Castro told St. George (as he had told Matthews) that in the forest their scopes enabled them to shoot with accuracy from a distance.[24]

For the tape-recorded interview, St. George determined to let Castro speak without interruption, expecting value from every word on tape. If the subjects discussed were too tame for *Cavalier*'s appetite for adventure, they would certainly interest editors elsewhere. He seriously wanted to see this entire story with photographs in the prestige mass media.

St. George's service in the Hungarian underground made him appreciate organization and economy. He was duly impressed by the attention Castro paid to details of ordnance. "Bullets come by vintages, like wine, especially in Latino countries," Castro said. "Mexican cartridges made in 1955 are very good. That was a good year. But they shoot very differently from, say, 1952 Mexicans. Once I am zeroed in, I like to use the same kind of rounds. After all, sometimes we are sniping at 800, 900, yards." For the size of the rebel force, Matthews had accepted Castro's numbers. St. George did likewise. "Castro soon told me that his main force consists of approximately 300 combat effectives. Couriers, outriders and detached small squads bring the troops on active duty to over 400. The bulk of this force is organized into five *pelotons* or platoons, each commanded by a captain. Every platoon has three to five *escuadras* (squads) of six to 14 men under a lieutenant."[25]

It was getting dark. Outside the hut, two men guarded the open side, "keeping a lookout for movement on the surrounding hillsides or the gorge below." No camp could be considered safe for more than a day. Undisturbed, Castro kept talking. His every statement made him stand out as one of the most remarkable men St. George had ever met. To reveal the man and authenticate the adventure, the journalist determined to present Castro's distinct speech patterns, enhanced by his dictionary English. He thought, *this will be real*. "As Castro talked about his early days in voluble English he'd acquired by memorizing a dictionary in jail, I let the tape run."

It started in the spring of 1953. President Batista was in power for about a year then. A very ugly dictator. Before Batista, we have no dictatorship here in Cuba for many years. We had democracy with voting, congress, police—very polite—standing on the street corners touching their caps. But Batista came in March 1952. A strong man; an ex-sergeant; and he seized the power with army help. He changed Cuba into a dictatorship. My friends and I, we decided to push Batista from the power.

Castro spoke in "proud tones" about launching the revolution in Oriente Province in eastern Cuba, the region since 1868 at the heart of Cuba's wars against Spain.[26]

Well, I was born in this province, Oriente. Oriente Province for us Cubans, that is like Texas for you Americans. This is the biggest province in Cuba. We do the most work here in Oriente, we make the most rum and sugar. We make the most money, too. People here are independent. They hate dictators. So we decided to make a revolution here in Oriente first. We knew the people here would fight with us against Batista.

Here was the rebel leader himself narrating the birth of his revolution, based on moral opposition to dictatorship. He expected the morality of his cause to raise the population into resistance. As he spoke, St. George glanced aside occasionally to make sure the tape reel was turning. Castro was telling how he organized the first attack on the army barracks at the Moncada fortress:

My friends voted me *comandante* of the action. I don't see why. I was a lawyer then, not a military man. Most of my clients were poor people. But when I was voted *comandante*, I went out and I collected 120 guns. I collected them one by one, so the police would not notice. Half were shotguns, the others mostly .22 repeaters.

I smuggled these guns 700 miles away, to the other end of Cuba, to Pinar del Río. I wanted to organize an attack on the biggest army fortress in Oriente Province, the Fort Moncada. To be safe, I wanted to organize it as far away as I could. In Pinar del Río I recruited 150 young men. That was my first troop, my first army. I gave each of them a job as we trained together a little. In July 1953 we filtered back to Oriente, one by one, with our guns hidden in rice sacks or in raincoats.

On July 26, the force split up. "Thirty men went off to attack another town, Bayamo," Castro said.

The rest of us put on army uniforms. For camouflage. We shook hands, embraced each other. I felt very strange, because I am a Catholic and I have never thought of killing anybody. But now we would have to kill.

The vanguard went forward in two cars. Their job was to take the guardhouse of the fort by surprise. Then came our main force in 13 cars. I was in the first, in the front seat.

At five o'clock in the morning we were before the big yellow fort. I could see the cars of vanguard speed very fast, crashing through the barrier. I could see them run into the guardhouse with their shotguns. They did their job very well.[27]

The attack failed, as Castro told it, not because he and the others were amateurs at war—which they admittedly were—but because of bad timing.

My car was four blocks away from main gate of the fort, the other cars behind me, moving very slowly. I told the driver to speed up and drive through the gate, into the fort. The time had come. And then a jeep patrol of soldiers came around the corner and stopped there.

I could see that they were looking at our uniforms very suspiciously. A sergeant got out of the jeep and started walking toward my car. I couldn't wait for him to come up to us; we had uniforms but no papers. So I jumped out the car and aimed my shotgun and shot the sergeant.

The advantage of surprise was lost. Inside the fort, alarmed soldiers—a regiment with tanks—responded.

Then I saw that all 13 cars had stopped behind me and all the boys were getting out and firing their guns. You see, I had told them to watch me and do what I did, because I hadn't counted on that patrol jeep. But now we were all out of the cars and shooting, and in the fort the soldiers had time to wake up.

We kept firing till our bullets were gone, but never took the fort. We were all captured within a week, except five men from the vanguard who got into the barbershop of the guardhouse and were shot to death in there by the soldiers.[28]

St. George did not interrupt the running of the tape to ask Castro what happened after he fled. In the days immediately after Moncada, according to credible accounts, there was a concerted effort to save Castro's life. While Fidel was a fugitive, his wife, Mirta Díaz Balart, sought help from the archbishop of Havana, Manuel Cardinal Arteaga y Betancourt, a longtime family friend; the archbishop telephoned Santiago's bishop, Monsignor Enrique Pérez Serantes, who asked the Moncada comandante, Colonel Ríos Chaviano, to spare Castro's life. Meanwhile in the hills, an army patrol found Castro asleep in a peasant hut. By chance, the patrol leader, Lt. Pedro Sarría, recognized Castro from the University of Havana. Lieutenant Sarría countermanded the shoot-to-kill order.

"Don't shoot," Lieutenant Sarría told his men.

He told Castro, "Don't say your name."

Lieutenant Sarría ordered him taken to the police station, not to the Moncada fortress, where, Castro later told his high school teacher, a Brazilian priest, Frei Betto, the soldiers would have "made mincemeat of us."[29]

In fact, inside the Moncada fortress, Cuban soldiers, whether on their own or by directive from Havana, ignored the rules of war for treatment of prisoners of armed conflict. The rebels' fear of torture had been mentioned in Matthews's *New York Times* series. But Matthews had given no details such as readers of *Cavalier* would expect. *This must be real. There must be blood.* St. George presented Castro's account of mutilations.[30]

When we attacked, the soldiers got very scared, so afterwards they got very ugly. They smashed the prisoners' faces against the wall, kicked them in the body. They took about 10 of our boys down into the butchershop of the fort and sent the butchers home. Then they tied the prisoners on meathooks and castrated them with their bayonets and watched them die.

There was a girl captured with us, Maria, that girl there [Castro gestured to a quiet, brownhaired woman perched on a tree-trunk, perhaps 10 feet away]. The soldiers found out she was engaged to marry one of the prisoners. They took her down and tortured them together and then castrated her fiancé before her eyes. When we were put on trial, there were only 50 of us. The soldiers had tortured 65 of our companions to death.[31]

Then, at the trial, St. George wrote, "Castro startled everyone present by appearing in the double capacity of chief defendant and chief defense counsel." He described Castro's four-hour statement as a "blistering defense summation that became a Latin American political classic" after Castro, in prison, revised it for a pamphlet—*La Historia Me Absolverá* (History Will Absolve

Me). Fidel was sentenced to fifteen years in solitary confinement, and his brother Raúl to seven years, starting in October 1953 in Cuba's newest military prison on the Isle of Pines, off Cuba's southern coast. Fidel Castro told St. George that the torture he experienced in prison was by beatings, and that he was repeatedly beaten:

> Each time we got a beating, we learned something, and we improved. Third beating we got was not so bad as the second beating. Second beating was a lot easier than the first beating. The first beating was very ugly. I learned very much from that. That first beating we took was the worst. But in prison I think about it and I discover that I have learned much.[32]

Years later, Castro's published prison letters barely mentioned abuse, but he described his solitary cell as infested with ants, flies, mosquitoes, and spiders. He mentioned some favors—receiving cigars and special foods, and many books. He said he spent ten to fourteen hours a day reading Dostoevsky and Balzac, Freud, Marx and Lenin. In that cell he founded the 26th of July Movement, urging his followers that "the 26th of July must be commemorated with dignity." To one female Moncada prisoner, released in 1954, Castro stressed the importance of publishing and circulating *La Historia Me Absolverá*—the "pamphlet whose ideological thrust and unbelievable accusations will have decisive importance. I want you to read it carefully.... Our propaganda must not let up for one minute because it is the heart of the struggle."[33]

In May 1955, President-General Fulgencio Batista decreed an amnesty, freeing the Castro brothers and their compatriots. In February Batista had been officially inaugurated for a four-year term as president. He had won an uncontested election after his main opponent, former president Ramón Grau San Martín, withdrew, claiming the election was rigged. Flush with victory and the appearance of legitimacy, Batista agreed to the amnesty as a sign of good will. Photographs taken on May 15, 1955, showed the sequence of transition from prison to freedom: Fidel Castro carrying a duffle bag as he, Raúl Castro, and other prisoners descended the steps from the Isle of Pines Military Prison; Fidel waving from aboard the ferry to the mainland; and finally, Fidel arriving in Havana, and being carried from a railroad train while holding aloft the Cuban flag.[34]

St. George charted Fidel's movements between prison and the invasion in December 1956. "Immediately, he set about putting his lessons to use." Instead of returning to Oriente he went to the United States, where he began gathering Cuban exiles who shared his sentiments about Batista. In October 1955, Castro visited Miami and New York, seeking funds for the 26th of July Movement. "Castro, long known as an untiring organizer, emerged as a magnetic orator whose ability to inspire his audiences has been compared to the personal magic of the young Franklin D. Roosevelt. Citizens of substance rallied to him, not merely from Cuba but other Latin countries, and fat contributions began to roll in." When the Batista regime protested, U.S. immigration authorities cut his visit short and canceled his visa for future visits. Then he "moved to Mexico, gathered a small corps of young Cuban exiles about him and began planning the most daring political coup of the decade."[35]

The rebels who had attacked Moncada in 1953 had little training—a deficiency Castro planned to correct in Mexico. He rented farmland in a secluded, mountainous area suitable for simulating conditions in the Sierra Maestra. And he "dug up a weathered colonel of the Spanish civil war," as St. George described him, "and coaxed him into taking over as head instructor." That colonel was Alberto Bayo, who had lived in exile since Franco's victory. Castro had met him in Havana late in the fall of 1955 when a friend took him to the colonel's home at 67 Avenida Country Club. Colonel Bayo, born in Cuba of Spanish parents, had graduated from the Infantry Academy of Madrid, then served in the Spanish Foreign Legion in guerrilla war operations in Africa. During the Spanish Civil War he had commanded Republican troops fighting Franco. When he met Castro in 1955 he was sixty-three years old and stocky, with a distinguished Van Dyke beard. He had settled in Havana and owned a furniture company. Yet Castro persuaded him to sell the furniture business and leave straightaway for Mexico.[36] There, Colonel Bayo—the "hard-driving old man"—was joined by some junior U.S. trainers with experience in the early 1950s in the Korean War. Over the months, they taught guerrilla warfare: "the tactical advantages of mountains; the military potential of a moonless night; the importance of not being too earnest about survival; and the care and field-stripping of warlike hardware."[37]

Castro told St. George that he wanted his army to be disciplined but also "a different army, an army of gentlemen. Not the rich or educated kind. I wanted *hidalgos*, natural gentlemen." Castro said he dismissed recruits without the proper personality: "I spent many nights watching them. It is the way you do *little* things that really tells. When one of the boys would curse, or shout in anger, fail to obey the quiet word, I sent him home."[38]

The invasion day drew near when Castro bought the *Granma*,[39] which he described as "a low smoke-gray, 60-foot yacht packing twin Diesels." But the plan to make extensive repairs had to be canceled after Mexican undercover agents arrested some of Castro's men. When the Mexicans wanted to know where the Cubans stored their guns, Castro knew there was a traitor in his camp. The invasion plan was saved by old-fashioned bribery. "Though Castro got his men sprung (and the traitor identified) by dispensing crisp persuaders of a particularly high denomination," St. George wrote, "it was plainly time to go." At the harbor, Castro gave "some last-minute bribes to port officials who considered the weather foul" and the *Granma* "wholly unseaworthy." Castro and his eighty-one men crowded onto the yacht for the 1,200-mile voyage, leaving behind as many as fifty trainees. On the afternoon of November 26, 1956, as the creaky boat left the harbor of Tuxpan, the "sea was running high" and one hour out of port, the overweighted boat began taking on water.[40]

Days later on the southeast coast of Cuba, the *Granma* ran aground and the Cuban Navy discovered it. Wading ashore and running for cover, all but twelve of Castro's men were killed or captured in the next several days. "For 19 days," Castro told St. George, "I hid in the bush with two men and lived off sugar cane. Our revolutionary troop, our citizen army was destroyed. We had to start from the beginning again. But why not? We were home in Cuba and many of us were still free."[41]

Now, in the spring of 1957, two months after Herbert Matthews's stories, St. George found the rebels still outwitting the army and obviously stronger in numbers and public support in Oriente Province. "Despite ferocious government persecution, the 26th of July Movement gained hundreds of civilian recruits in every township. Oriente Province adopted Castro as its favorite son; there were gifts, collections, even a 'secret war bond issue' for the jungle fighters. Under the noses of the furious constabulary, the bonds were taken by some of the country's wealthiest citizens."

> We have no big problems now, only one: weapons. We get weapons, a *few* weapons through the volunteers. But for *real* arms, a whole shipload, we need a road to the sea. Then everything will change. We will be a real army. You are lucky to be here now. You can come and see us make a way to the sea.

"After 50 years of political drought," St. George wrote, "Cuba had found itself a national hero."[42]

St. George was ready to leave camp and so he was pleased when Castro invited him to join the trek down to the coast. From there he could get a boat to Santiago and then fly to Havana and home. But the opportunity to leave had come suddenly when Castro learned that smugglers with a load of weapons for him would soon be arriving at a drop point on the coast. Castro told St. George that the timing was fortunate for his departure. "Luck, of course is a relative thing," St. George wrote, feeling his physical reality, that he had not slept at all the previous day and, with blistered feet, was not in shape for the march.[43]

That same day, Che Guevara noted that St. George's mood sank when the rebels "heard that the film Bob Taber made about the Sierra Maestra had been shown [on Sunday, May 19] with great success. The news cheered everyone except Andrew St. George," who "had his petty journalist's pride, and felt somewhat cheated of glory. The day after learning the bad news, he left." By then, Guevara believed the speculation that St. George was an FBI secret agent.[44]

As it turned out, the trek to the sea furnished St. George with the real danger, terror, and death that his story so far lacked. At 3 a.m., with Castro in the lead, they started into the jungle in the rain. St. George's legs "were creaking stilts of pain, my socks stiff with the dried blood of a half-dozen blisters, my arms raw with the lattice cuts of jungle thorns." For days, they wound cautiously through the mountain forest "where the rainy season melted rotting leaves and earth into a sucking ooze. . . . The jungle that will hide you will hide a hundred dangers." As scouts went ahead, one man near the rear had a horrid fall. St. George noted the strange feeling:

> Picking your way down a steep slope, you hear the man behind you slip, tumble, and then you hear his choking groans: the weight of his pack has impaled him on a jagged, daggerlike root. The root had entered the man's back just above the kidney, but as he lies there, twitching like a beetle on a pin, the root tip breaks through the skin below his ribs. It had gone through his entire body.[45]

On an afternoon when they had been marching for several hours and were walking along a narrow ridge, they were ambushed. Suddenly St. George was in the midst of war.

> I heard the submachine guns open up ahead with loud, spiteful banging. I squatted down in the grass and listened.
>
> Then all hell broke loose. Captain Almeida's scout squad on the right flank had raised an army patrol. The soldiers were perhaps 50 or 60 strong.

On any other day it would have gone badly for them. Now the rebel column was strung out thinly for 500 yards.

I found myself carried backward by a running rebel squad . . . and as I watched them, I frog-hopped left and knelt among the thick, leathery underhang of a sea-grape tree. There was an explosion of gunfire over us, the bullets thwacking across the tree-trunk with a ripping sound or raising tiny spouts of red mud around our feet.

The soldiers seemed afraid to close in; their fire was receding rather than advancing. . . . Then suddenly there was a lull. Somebody must have spotted the rebel guard, wheeling back in a wide semi-circle to cut them off, and the soldiers took to their heels. . . . Four soldiers were dead, but we had lost a man too.[46]

St. George now had an experience that bested those of Matthews, Taber, and Hoffman. His story was sealed by the battle, fear, courage, and blood. As though a partisan, he wrote in the collective "we." "We—our side—had lost a man" in the fire fight. The man, Guillermo Dominguez, had become a friend, the "tall, melancholy lieutenant who was the rebels' official photographer." The soldiers had tortured him before killing him, the practice so often mentioned. Now St. George witnessed the body of Lieutenant Dominguez, who while still alive had been subjected to the torture of repeated bayonetting.

They had done to him what they usually do to rebel prisoners, except when there is a Red Cross commission around. They tied his hands with his own belt and stabbed him fourteen or fifteen times with a bayonet, opening bloody little mouths in his neck, and chest and thighs. This was torture that seemed to give the soldiers special pleasure. Then they took his own weapon, an automatic shotgun, and blew off the rear of Guillermo's head.[47]

"We stood around," St. George wrote, "none of us really crying, none of us knowing what to say, till Castro came."

"He was a good man," Castro said. "Bury him now."

The battle was even more costly, as Castro quietly told St. George. "That was not a good fight. Now the soldiers know we are near the coast. Now we must go fast."

For the next two days, they moved relentlessly. Their "path-cutting machetes worked like windmills" while the scouts "kept going at a dogtrot, darting back to the column with their chests pumping wildly, their eyes feverish with exhaustion." The forced march left St. George "too drained to eat."

> On the third day we tumbled down a steep canyon wall and into the shielded gorge of a small stream. A small group of red-faced, sombrero-shaded campesinos were squatting silently on their heels around a small inlet. When Castro got near enough, he tore off his cap and waved exuberantly. These were his weapon smugglers, and they made it to the meeting all right.[48]

They feasted that night on a cow the smugglers had led up from the coast along a road that, according to a "short, wrinkled man," was clear and safe. "Tonight," he said, "the weapons are coming." The weapons came as promised. "Toward midnight, sitting with Castro halfway up the canyon slope," intrepid St. George verified what Taber had only alluded to:

> We heard the panting of the bearer train moving down a hidden path directly behind us. It took another minute to spot them in the darkness. There were over 30 men, rugged mountaineers, and from the straw-wound rolls they dumped with a grunt emerged the barleycorn barrel sights of .315 Madsen machineguns, Garrand butts, brick-shaped ammo cartons. Castro had especially hoped for mortars; though they turned out to be World War II PIATS, British bazookas, they could be used as mortars and were, in truth, the next best thing.[49]

Even more anxious to get home, St. George left the rebels and followed the smugglers. They led him down the steep misty paths to the sea. On board a tiny, rusted banana freighter headed for Santiago, he stuffed his notes, tapes, and film into a rice sack to be held for him in a safe house in Santiago. Those precautions soon paid off. A Cuban gunboat stopped them, and soldiers came on board armed with cocked tommy guns. They escorted the boat to a nearby port and seized St. George for questioning. "They propped a deck chair for me topside, and the sailors stood around staring at me and making sawing motions across their Adams' apples to let me know what to expect." He had to improvise a new story. He could no longer masquerade as a businessman. In high boots and mud-soaked pants, the only business he might have had was suspect. So he identified himself as a reporter who had been looking unsuccessfully for signs of a civil war. "As for Castro, I pretended to be hard put to even recognize his name."[50]

In Santiago, the soldiers took him to the Moncada fortress, which scared him as nothing else. He had wound up too far inside his story. He was in the place where in 1953 Castro's rebels had been executed. This Hungarian immigrant was waiting, perhaps looking at his executioners. At least an hour passed while a "half-dozen coatless, greasy-haired bruisers were playing dominos around a scarred table."

"Journalist?" one asked.

"Yes," I said.

"Where are your films?"

"They got wet," I lied desperately. "All wet. I threw them away," adding a Spanish word I thought meant truth: *"vero."*

"No films," said a fleshy, lumpy-faced fellow. "That is bad."

St. George watched him open a locker and pull out "a long oxgut whip" which he threateningly "began to flick."

"I was sitting, literally, in Cuba's worst spot. How many men had died on this linoleum floor?" St. George could imagine his fate: after beating him, they would dispose of his body. One Hungarian of little note would simply have disappeared.

Hours passed. They neither tortured nor killed him. He later told his readers he was rescued by something like a miracle. Someone, probably at the fort, sent word of his arrest to Castro's supporters in Santiago, and they alerted the American consulate. But it was at night so nothing would normally be done. But somehow the assistant U.S. consul Robert Weicha did intervene. "And then, wondrously, the telephone tinkled. It was the American consulate, and they knew with polite certainty that I was up in the fort. Castro's courier had sounded the alarm just in time. That saved the situation; I was dismissed in a few minutes." Thankfully retrieving the rice sack with his notes, tapes, and film intact, St. George left Cuba, and two days later he was back in New York.[51]

At home, St. George learned who else was behind the miracle of his deliverance from Moncada. When he had not called home as his wife Jean expected, she telephoned for help. "I didn't know what was going on," Jean recalled. "I called my cousin Mary, who was a CIA person."

"What happened to him?" Jean had asked.

"I'll see if I can get somebody to find out," Mary said.

"They went in and got him out in Santiago," Jean recalled. "They had to leave a party that the ambassador was giving to go in and get him out of jail. We didn't find out until the 1990s that she had sent somebody in. The CIA actually saved him from Batista, from killing him. . . . He was arrested. . . . My cousin got him out."[52]

After spending much of the spring with the rebels, in July St. George settled down to write. The editors at *Cavalier* were pleased. He had everything an adventure story needed. It even filled in the background of the 26th of July Movement. But, like Herbert Matthews and Robert Taber, St. George probed little into the years before Moncada.

Who was Castro, really? After his background research, St. George conceded that "hard facts known about Fidel Castro are still skimpy. Five years ago he had been an apprentice attorney in Havana, struggling to make his way in a city historically overstocked with legal talent. Four years ago, Castro, then a revolutionary, was in jail. Less than a year ago, his troubles seemed over: it was officially announced that he was dead, killed in a pitched battle with government troops on the eastern coast of Cuba." Then Matthews "emerged from the interior with the front-page report" that Castro had "successfully invaded Cuba with a small band of guerrillas, and, far from being dead, he and his private army were doing fine in the rugged mountains of eastern Cuba."[53]

CHAPTER 6

THE TWO HAVANAS

J ules Dubois was kept busy during the spring of 1957 minding troubles in Cuba and elsewhere, including his own. Personal problems could be expected as he crusaded for press freedom in countries ruled by military dictators, *caudillos*. In Argentina, he had already been branded as the "No. 1 Gangster of U.S. Journalism" by Juan Perón, who had risen from colonel to president. Now Dubois found himself formally banned from two countries— from Colombia for his role as a diehard reporter, and from the Dominican Republic for his IAPA agitation for press freedom. In April, the Dominican Republic's *caudillo*, Generalissimo Rafael Leonidas Trujillo, issued a dictatorial decree banning Dubois from re-entering the country. That newsworthy action merited attention in *Time* magazine's "Press" section, which described Dubois's adventuresome career since the 1940s, noting that he had been "pistol-whipped, jailed and shot in the course of covering revolutions in ten Latin American countries. During Costa Rica's 1948 revolt against its pro-Communist government, six Red goons worked Dubois over with rifle butts. A month later, while covering a revolution in Colombia . . . to get his own and fellow newsmen's copy to a cable office, Dubois ran a gauntlet of machine-gun fire." Evidently fearless, Dubois had simply bought unbreakable spectacles.[1]

Then in May, Dubois was in trouble inside Colombia. Its *caudillo*, President-General Gustavo Rojas Pinella, on May 10 ordered Dubois to "leave the country immediately." As Colombians were rioting and clamoring for Rojas Pinella to resign, Dubois infuriated the dictator by estimating the riot death toll at fifty—ten times more than his government claimed. One day later, however, other generals deposed Rojas Pinella, sending him packing with his family to Miami via Panama, and allowed Dubois to stay. His clash with Rojas Pinella was a featured story on the front page of his *Chicago Tribune*, accompanied by a photo of the triumphant journalist, smiling. His managing editor at the *Tribune*, Don Maxwell, concluded that Dubois was fearless, "absolutely unafraid. He scares us with the situations he gets into."[2]

To Dubois, who took seriously his role as chair of the Inter-American Press Association's Freedom of the Press Committee, Colombian journalists had gained nothing. Gone was the *caudillo*, immediately replaced by Latin America's characteristic solution for maintaining law and order—a gang of generals—a military junta. The hemisphere continued to be cursed by generals and dictators who resented that the IAPA publicly branded their regimes as authoritarian and their press as subservient and censored.

In Havana since the Presidential Palace attack, there had been a peaceful lull giving the impression of business as usual in the streets, sugar exchange, and casinos. By the first of May, fighting between the Cuban Army and insurgents "seemed to have died out," *Newsweek* reported. "The procession of bombing episodes and sabotage which had kept the island on edge since November had subsided. The last of a big sugar crop was coming in, bringing millions in hard cash to the island."[3] Peaceful weeks calmed Cuban and American businessmen who had told Herbert Matthews that, while they worried about Batista's regime, they worried still more about the rebels who wanted to take his place.

Cuba's *caudillo*, President-General Fulgencio Batista, cleverly kept his grip on power, while appearing to loosen the reins. Advised by his publicist, Ed Chester, the dictator restored civil rights and a degree of press freedom that had been suspended for forty-five days. He also pulled back to Havana most of the 560 soldiers who had been assigned to fight Castro. However, not totally optimistic, Batista made some precautionary moves, *Newsweek* noted. He fortified his Presidential Palace with fifty armed police, chains on the doors, and sandbags on the stairs. He extended the closing of the University of Havana—a "traditional spawning ground of student revolt" since the 1930s insurgency that had deposed President Gerardo Machado. Meanwhile, military intelligence agents arrested and interrogated "suspected revolutionaries" and "secret police continued to patrol Havana's streets."[4]

Suddenly in the last week of May the insurgency flared on three fronts. In Havana, saboteurs damaged the business district; on the northeast coast, exiles from Miami landed a guerrilla force; and in the southeast, Castro's rebels came down from the Sierra Maestra and boldly ambushed an army post and seized weapons. Back in Havana, Dubois conferred with Cuba's newspaper editors and then wrote that a "terroristic campaign" had struck Havana and other cities across the island. Sabotage and bombing focused on economic targets and was particularly disturbing in Havana, where saboteurs using bottles of flaming gasoline torched a mattress factory; others cut telegraph and telephone wires, shutting down communication between Havana and the eastern provinces. A week later, Dubois reported, an underground dynamite explosion that blew up a gas main and electricity lines in Havana's old sector "paralyzed" the city's business and hotel district. Without power, no morning newspapers were published, and power was expected to be off for two days. Police blamed an electrical worker who they said "rented an apartment eight blocks from the capital building" and "dug a tunnel under the house to blast telephone lines, power cables, and gas mains."[5]

During the chaos, Dubois managed to find and interview the 26th of July leader in the city, Armando Hart. In one of his hideouts, "Hart told me that the sabotage operation in the heart of Havana had cost the rebels only $600. Hart's wife, Haydee Santamaria, fighting with Castro, came to fetch him to transfer to another hiding place for both of them for that night. He was the most wanted man in Havana."[6]

Not since the revolution of 1933 ended the dictatorship of Gerardo Machado had Cubans been so plagued by sabotage. Young men of that generation in the Abecedarios, the ABC resistance—including University of Havana student Carlos Prío Socarrás—had become proficient in assembling homemade bombs.[7] The chaos strategy helped depose Machado and empower the army, meanwhile enabling Batista's ascent to power from corporal to general. A generation later, saboteurs aimed to rid the country of Batista. Outside Havana, in Pinar del Río, in the far southwest, two bombs damaged a church and adjacent houses and a town councilman's home and nearby buildings. In the southeast, in Santiago de Cuba, the center of greatest opposition to Batista, bombs exploded in a residential section and a gasoline fire damaged a railway warehouse. Electrical service was interrupted, and restoration was delayed by organized absenteeism at the Cuban Electric Company, which served the entire island. In a massive response, Batista's army and secret police herded hundreds of "oppositionists" to jails. Two youths, for instance, were accused of having three thousand copies of a weekly letter allegedly distributed by the Communist Party.[8]

The Miami exiles' invasion on the northeast coast was quickly suppressed. In the last week of May, the Cuban Army reported that five hundred of its troops had captured five invaders and surrounded another twenty-two. They had come ashore on May 24 from the yacht *Corinthia*, which the army traced to Miami. The invasion and the ongoing sabotage sparked dark rumors about Batista's demise. Amid the confusion, Dubois wrote that Batista was "reported ready to decree martial law throughout the island in an attempt to halt the growing insurrection." Others speculated that "a military junta would replace Batista."[9]

Before the fate of the south Florida expeditionaries was known in Miami, the exiled former president Carlos Prío Socarrás publicly offered Batista a way to end the strife through a political settlement. Prío Socarrás's proposal acknowledged for the first time that Castro's armed rebels were a significant factor. Naïvely, he proposed "negotiations to permit Fidel Castro and his rebels to lay down their arms."[10] Dubois reasoned that Batista, who did not respond to the offer, wanted to keep the proposal on the table to "buy enough time to prevent the insurrection from reaching a stage that would cause his downfall." Days later, Prío Socarrás learned about the army ambush and that nearly all the invaders from the *Corinthia* had been killed or captured. Eventually Dubois found out that the army had been warned, and that Prío Socarrás's group thought that Batista had a spy planted among them. The trail would at last lead to a woman no one suspected; she had been right at the center of the exile community.[11]

The *Corinthia* expedition's disastrous end benefited Castro's 26th of July Movement for the same reason he gained from the Presidential Palace attack. His success, one historian observed, "depended in part on the defeats suffered by the other opposition movements."[12] Castro rose as others fell; he succeeded by surviving.

The failed invasion, together with Prío Socarrás's political activity, shifted Dubois's attention from Havana to Miami, where he had his home in the tree-lined suburb of Coral Gables near the University of Miami. He soon was making the rounds of the Cuban community centered among the coffee shops and restaurants along Miami's Southwest Eighth Street, Calle Ocho—but also in the plush houses on or near Miami Beach, including the residence of Prío Socarrás. There, the ousted president, who had managed to maintain some wealth and self-respect, continued to be a focal point for Cuban patriotism and pride. He claimed to have been the best president of Cuba, despite the corruption and political gangsterism during the terms—limited to four years—of Batista (1940–44), Ramón Grau San Martín (1944–48), and Prío Socarrás (1948–52).[13] "Grau's rule," one historian concluded, "drew to an end after four years of deception and disappointment. Trampling on the expectations of the many people who placed faith in his promise, he did a great disservice to the cause of democratic reform." Such was the graft that Grau San Martín's old friend José Manuel Alemán, after serving only two years as minister of education, moved to Miami in 1948 with $20 million in cash, in addition to Cuban land holdings, sugar mills, companies, and houses.[14]

On taking office as Grau San Martín's successor in 1948, Prío Socarrás was forty-five, handsome, and *simpatico*—nice, likeable, friendly, agreeable—and supportive of social democratic movements. As a leader of the Auténtico Party, he had campaigned to end labor strife and diminish Communist influence in labor issues. One campaign poster declared he aimed to "secure the peace": "Asegure La Paz Con Prío Socarrás." As Grau San Martín's minister of labor, Prío Socarrás had manipulated the Communists "from their position of power" in the unions. The poster depicted Prío Socarrás, in suit and tie, with one arm around a laborer holding a wrench and the other arm pushing aside a foreigner with hammer and sickle.[15] But as president, he made one absolute mistake, which was to ignore Grau San Martín's warning not to permit Fulgencio Batista to return from Daytona Beach after he was elected *in absentia* as a senator. As was warned, Batista seized power, later explaining that people who asked for his help claimed that Prío Socarrás would not relinquish the presidency if the opposition Ortodoxo Party won.[16] Prío Socarrás's exit into exile, along with two cabinet ministers, his wife, and two small daughters, ended that generation's struggle to maintain a constitutional democracy.[17]

Prío Socarrás did not accept as permanent the status of exile, *el exilio*. To him *el elixio* meant displacement from his people and culture. Other Cuban exiles to different degrees shared that uneasy existence, a condition that the Cuban novelist Leonardo Padura Fuentes called "a terrible condemnation." The exiled Cuban writer Reinaldo Arenas, who has lived in *el exilio* in London and New York, told an interviewer, "Everyone who lives outside his context is always a bit of a ghost, because I am here, but at the same time I remember a person who walked those streets, who is there, and that same person is me. So sometimes I really don't know if I am here or there. And at times the longing to be there is greater than the necessity to be here."[18]

Florida had been a logical staging area for Cuban revolutions. The exiled José Martí had raised money among the Cuban tobacco workers in Key West and Tampa, and in 1894 he attempted to raise an invasion force in Florida.[19] The exiled Fidel Castro had come to Miami in 1955 to raise money for his 26th of July Movement, and supposedly he got enough from Carlos Prío Socarrás to buy the aging yacht *Granma*. Now two years later, Prío Socarrás found himself in an awkward legal position. He was plotting against both Castro and Batista while trying to conceal his activities to avoid deportation. In 1956, when Prío Socarrás was permitted to remain in Miami, immigration authorities had "admonished" him not to engage in subversive activities against any government recognized by the United States—specifically Cuba.

Jules Dubois, now back at home in Miami, pieced together the story behind Prío Socarrás's sudden proposal to Batista and the disastrous *Corinthia* expedition. To Dubois, the two actions together revealed the Miami exiles' desperation to act quickly and decisively against Batista to counter Castro's rebels, who were gaining recognition and strength. It seemed to be the same pattern of desperation that, two months earlier, had led the student insurgents with the Directorio Revolutionario to attack the Presidential Palace. That disaster, said one survivor, "nearly destroyed them." By April the police in Havana eliminated most of the student leaders, tracking the last group to an apartment and shooting them as they fled.[20] By May in Miami, Cubans *in exilio* understood that Castro, simply by surviving on the island, had gained the upper hand. Even those who hated Castro—Prío Socarrás considered him a social and political pariah—nonetheless had to concede his political ingenuity. After all, Castro was *inside* the country, not *outside* it in south Florida. Furthermore, his rebels had so far eluded the army. When Batista fell—as everyone expected he would—Castro could be positioned to influence whatever came next. Thus elites among Miami's exiles had determined to invade and open their second front.

So important was the *Corinthia* expedition that its loss shocked and disheartened the exile community. As Dubois learned, Prío Socarrás had not only "financed and outfitted" the *Corinthia* but also paid for training the men in guerrilla warfare. For that job Prío Socarrás chose a proven expert, the same veteran soldier who had trained Castro's invasion force in Mexico—Alberto Bayo, the former Spanish army and air force colonel who had fought against Franco in the Spanish Civil War. Prío Socarrás tracked him down in New York where he had been working for Castro's 26th of July Movement, circulating anti-Batista propaganda. "I was not tied down to one group or to one party in this fight for Cuban liberation from dictatorship," Bayo told Dubois. "I was friendly with Castro, friendly with Prío and friendly with Aureliano Sanchez Arango's Triple-A group that had become antagonistic to Prío. I was also friendly with the Directorio Revolutionario. I maintained contacts with all."[21]

The man Colonel Alberto Bayo trained to lead the *Corinthia* force, Calixto Sanchez White, had no experience in guerrilla warfare. Before he fled Cuba, Sanchez White had conspired with the anti-Batista underground in Havana to help in the March 13 attack on the palace. As head of the Airport Workers

Union, he was conducting smuggling operations through José Martí Airport. Sanchez White told Dubois that intelligence agents "discovered he was smuggling weapons into Cuba by air freight, especially in the interior of refrigerators." That discovery foiled Sanchez White's plan to aid the palace attack. He was supposed to take control of the airport, and his failure, Dubois wrote, "preyed on his mind. He wished to vindicate himself, and the [*Corinthia*] expedition . . . was the way he hoped to clear his name."[22]

Aboard the *Corinthia*, Sanchez White and his twenty-six men with their cargo of arms and ammunition had sailed surreptitiously down the Miami River and across the Florida Straits to Cuba's north coast. As Dubois learned, the expeditionaries had no problem until they were marching into the hills. There they were ambushed. "They didn't pay attention to my recommendations," Colonel Bayo told Dubois. Bayo had warned them: *Trust no one*. The colonel learned from the survivors that they had forgotten his warnings and made two major mistakes, one after the other. Bayo said that "while they were marching, some of Batista's soldiers, dressed as *guajiros*, approached them, shouting: 'Viva Fidel Castro! Viva Fidel Castro!'" Fooled, they fell into the trap. "Then more than a dozen of them surrounded Calixto Sanchez and his men. Whereupon they announced: 'You are surrounded by 3,500 soldiers. There is no possible escape for you. Surrender and we will guarantee you will not be killed.'" Then they made the second mistake. "Our men," Bayo said, "were so foolish that, ignoring my recommendations, they surrendered. Seventeen of them were vilely assassinated by Colonel Fermin Cowley's men." Ten escaped into the hills "from where they entered the cities to work in the . . . underground."[23]

The *Corinthia* episode confirmed President-General Batista's hold on power and his uncanny ability to anticipate his enemies. In Cuba, his police worked the cities, especially in Havana and Santiago; in the countryside, his army surrounded and contained Castro in the Sierra. In Miami's "Little Havana," Batista had expanded his payroll for informants to keep closer surveillance on Prío Socarrás and other exiles. Dubois learned that a spy close to Prío Socarrás had sent a message to Havana alerting Batista about the *Corinthia* expedition, information enabling the ambush. Also, with that information Batista publicly accused Prío Socarrás of financing the attack. In fact, Batista could have had him deported for violation of his immigration status. But when Prío Socarrás denied the accusation, he prevailed because, as Dubois noted, Batista chose to protect his spies rather than reveal the source of his information.[24]

Eventually, four months later, the spy ring was exposed. In September 1957, Prío Socarrás's group trapped one of President-General Batista's most valuable spies. Rather belatedly, as Dubois noted, they had become "suspicious of the leaks that were torpedoing every plan of theirs." They suspected Cuba's consul general in Miami, Eduardo Hernandez, and in September set a trap for him at Miami International Airport. Three men arranged to steal his briefcase as he was departing on one of his occasional flights to Havana, Dubois learned. "One of them tripped him as he walked toward the gate. The briefcase fell from his hands, and two of them fled from the terminal with it." The contents included reports from various Cubans in Miami "who were in Batista's pay as spies operating under the direction of Consul Hernandez. . . . There was also a notebook listing the names of the spies and their code names."[25]

The exiles realized they had been amateurs at conspiracy, unable to keep even the biggest secret. In the *Corinthia* expedition, they had not followed Colonel Bayo's admonition to trust no one. In Mexico with Castro, Bayo had admonished the rebel for publicly announcing he would invade Cuba before the end of 1956: "Don't you know that a cardinal military principle is to keep your intentions secret from your enemy?" It did not matter to Colonel Bayo that Castro made that announcement to inspire a coordinated uprising in Santiago.[26]

One spy's report in Consul Hernandez's briefcase astonished everyone, even the suspicious Colonel Bayo. The author of the report was a prominent Cuban woman whom the exile leadership trusted implicitly. Marisol Alba, a former star on Cuban television, now lived in a luxurious house on an island along the Venetian Causeway between Miami and Miami Beach. It was assumed that her wealth came from her television career. She was gregarious and befriended numerous exiles, even inviting some who had no base in Miami to live at her house. Colonel Bayo, fresh from New York to lead the *Corinthia* training, had stayed in her house and held secret planning meetings there. Her hospitality charmed the colonel into disregarding his "cardinal military principle."

Alba's house guests also included Bayo's aviator son, also Alberto Bayo, and a veteran arms smuggler, Candido de la Torre. Since 1953, De la Torre had sailed frequently from Mexico to Cuba, delivering tons of contraband weapons and ammunition to rebel groups. At Alba's house, De la Torre and Colonel Bayo planned another voyage for the summer of 1957. That venture ended abruptly when Mexican authorities caught the crew, having been tipped off, Dubois learned, "most probably, according to de la Torre himself and Bayo, because of the reports furnished to Batista by Marisol Alba."[27]

Dubois traced one other debacle to Alba. In September, days before the Miami exiles tripped Consul Hernandez and snatched his briefcase, Batista crushed a planned navy rebellion at Cuba's southern coastal port at Cienfuegos. Before the uprising, one of the conspirators, Manuel Antonio de Varona, had visited Miami. "Varona talked freely in Miami," Dubois wrote, "especially in the presence of Marisol Alba, who was very friendly with Prío. Soon Batista had all the details of the ramifications of the Cienfuegos naval uprising and there was a complete shake-up in the motorized division of the police force in Havana which, Varona had reported, was involved in the conspiracy."[28]

The revelations of spying stunned and horrified the militant Cubans, who reacted with anger and retribution. Alba, according to Dubois, "became known as the 'Mata Hari' of the Cuban Revolution." In secrecy, he was told, some of the accused "were brutally beaten by irate Cubans." Alba and others were "tried before drumhead courts-martial in Miami, convicted and sentenced to death upon [the exiles'] return to Cuba, on the ground that their espionage work for Batista caused the death of many of their countrymen."[29]

In late May, soon after the *Corinthia* disaster, Castro's rebels came out of hiding for their first major combat mission after four months of trekking in the wilderness. Freshly supplied with weapons, including a Madsen machine gun, the rebels now had as many as one hundred men, armed variously with shotguns and .22 caliber rifles. Their target was one of the garrisons used by the Cuban Army to surround the Sierra Maestra; this one, at El Ubero, had sixty soldiers, most with automatic arms.[30]

Reports of the battle reached Havana but were sanitized by the army for release to Dubois and to the Cuban press. The army chief of staff, Major General Francisco Tabernilla, said merely that in a "clash between rebel forces and the Cuban army ... there were casualties on both sides." The army did not reveal that the rebels ambushed the post and forced the troops to surrender.[31] As rebel sources later reported, at the first light of day they surprised the garrison with a barrage from shotguns, .22-caliber rifles, and two machine guns, the new one handled by Che Guevara's four-man crew.

Robert Taber, in New York, understood the advantage of surprise, noting that the rebels "penetrated past eight sentry posts before the Ubero [sic] garrison was aware of what was happening." Castro lauded his men's courage when the defenders resisted. "In many cases, combat was a matter of man-to-man action," he wrote, noting with pride the impact of his machine guns. "Finally, the barracks, where sixteen men were still holding out, surrendered under the cross-fire of two .30-caliber tripod-mounted machine guns, which never stopped firing and answered every enemy shot with a hail of bullets. The field of El Ubero was covered with corpses of enemy soldiers and rebels."[32]

The army reported eleven soldiers dead and more than twenty wounded. The rebels lost eight men, and so many were wounded that Guevara wrote, "We spent the whole month of June 1957 nursing our compañeros." But the victory benefited morale and added weapons to their armory. In a convoy of four trucks belonging to a local timber merchant, Castro's men drove off with forty-six rifles, two machine guns, and six thousand rounds of ammunition, plus food, medicine, radio and telegraphic equipment, and twenty-five prisoners, whom they later released. Before evacuating, Castro ordered Guevara and his medical team to attend to the army's wounded. It was a policy of humane treatment to wounded and captive soldiers that the rebels followed throughout the war, usually releasing prisoners shortly after their capture. That was in complete contrast to the army's continued practice of torturing, then shooting captives. The rebels evacuated El Ubero shortly before a Cuban Navy gunboat closed in offshore and shelled the fort.[33]

Castro preferred the early morning surprise attacks that "began to soften up the enemy," he wrote in June. "You know what it's like: a troop of 350 men beside the sea, delighted with themselves, and then . . . a hailstorm of bullets from nowhere! Fire away! Because all our shooting took place at two in the morning, or at two-thirty or at one; no one could sleep. When night fell, the shooting began. This kind of thing lowered their morale; they really respected us."[34] Now that the rebels had brazenly attacked an army fort, hope for the insurrection shifted even more toward Castro. As Taber noted, "until [El Ubero] there had been no word of aggressive action on Fidel's part to sustain this propaganda coup." The surrender of the army post was "the opening of a new phase in the Oriente campaign," which was "both an embarrassment to the government and a source of considerable anxiety to the army high command." With the student insurrection in March and the exiles' invasion in May both defeated, Cubans on the island would now look increasingly for ways to aid Castro's rebels.[35]

By the end of May, Dubois could imagine the end of Batista's dictatorship. Alone among U.S. journalists covering the insurgents, Dubois had developed continuous access to all key factions—President-General Batista, the army,

Fidel Castro, Carlos Prío Socarrás and other exiles in Miami, as well as insurgents in Havana and Santiago de Cuba. "Sabotage is widespread," Dubois wrote. Santiago was "seething with rebellion ever since Fidel Castro landed with a rebel force from Mexico six months ago." On June 1, three days after the battle at El Ubero, Dubois reported that thirty-one church and civic leaders in Santiago demanded that President Batista end a "reign of terror" in the city after four boys were found shot to death, "allegedly murdered by Batista's forces."[36] The next day, Batista's military intensified attacks on the rebels, announcing they would burn the rebels out of the mountains dropping napalm bombs, a warning also to every peasant who lived there and gave aid to the rebels.[37]

Prío Socarrás now attacked Castro, claiming he was doing more harm than good. In Miami, he told Dubois that Cubans, especially the citizens of Santiago, were suffering solely "because of their sympathy towards Fidel Castro." At the same time, Prío Socarrás worried that he might be deported for supporting violence against the Cuban regime, so he cloaked his personal involvement with the *Corinthia* expedition and with recent rioting by anti-Batista exiles in Miami. He disclaimed any connection, saying any "revolutionary action is the personal initiative of innumerable Cubans inspired only by love for liberty."[38] But in late June, in a political move to undermine Castro, Prío Socarrás supported an alliance of five anti-Batista groups in Miami and "emerged from the meeting as an even more powerful foe of the Cuban dictator." Yet constantly he was overshadowed by the attention to Castro, who was obviously absent. "Castro's name," the *Miami Herald* noted, "was mentioned by almost every speaker, and invariably the crowd went wild with applause."[39]

By midyear, Dubois's connections with such a wide range of sources made him the most informed journalist covering the revolution. His frequent references to Castro in almost every story from Cuba or Miami had kept the rebels competing well for space in the *Tribune*, balanced somewhat by statements from President-General Batista. In July 1957, the rebels fed Dubois a story that scooped the *Miami Herald* correspondents who, since the *Corinthia* invasion in May, had started going to Cuba more frequently.

Dubois had been recommended to Castro by a supporter named Justo Carrillo. In a letter to "Alejandro," code name for Fidel, Carrillo stated that he had tested and now trusted "the highly qualified Jules Dubois."[40] On August 29, this trust led the rebels to invite Dubois to a clandestine rendezvous with, as he put it, "five bearded rebels," *barbudos*, from Castro's hideout. At night,

Dubois was driven circuitously to a safe house. The security arrangements resembled the method by which Herbert Matthews had been delivered to Castro. Like Matthews, Dubois obeyed the clandestine plan, as he was driven first to one house and then to another. At last Dubois met the five *barbudos* whose safe arrival in the city "proved that in nine months Batista has not been able to crush Castro's force or destroy his lines of communication."[41]

Dubois had a scoop worthy of his reputation in the region. Other journalists had satisfied the public appetite for news that Castro as a rebel was alive and fighting. Now Dubois presented Castro as a *political* leader. His story asserted that Castro's movement had gained converts among Cuba's solid professional middle class—even members of Prío Socarrás's own political party, the Partido Auténtico. The story revealed that the esteemed former president of the National Bank of Cuba, the economist Felipe Pazos, "has joined the rebel forces of Fidel Castro in the Sierra Maestra mountains.... He has long been a member of the rebel underground." In the same story, Dubois said the rebels were considering setting up a governmental "advisory board" chaired by Castro and including Pazos and Raúl Chibás, a leading political convert from Partido Auténtico who had recently come to the mountains. The board's mission was to plan for the post-Batista government. Dubois also reported that Castro now had four hundred men with him and another hundred near Santiago.[42] In giving this story to Dubois, Castro was testing him as both a confidant and a conduit for major propaganda statements.

CHAPTER 7

THIS IS ABSOLUTELY FALSE

Andrew St. George handed *Cavalier* a page turner. He made the deadline, with his wife, Jean, converting his work into typed pages, feeling that his fascination "with the whole experience... probably came through as he was writing the story."[1] The thousands of words flowed more through the scenes and conversations revealing the heroic qualities of two main characters, Fidel Castro and St. George.

Cavalier liked the way St. George wrote himself into the center of the intrigue—beginning, middle, and end. At the start he is an intrepid sleuth in the underworld of a Caribbean island, trusting secretive strangers to lead him to the hideout of the rebel chieftain. After weeks of living with the rebels, he leaves the mountains with a story to tell. But he is captured by the army and threatened with torture; then he surprisingly is rescued. *Cavalier's* editor congratulated himself for hiring "the ideal man to send behind-the-lines to Fidel Castro" and raved about how "*Cavalier's* reporter made a perilous trip behind Cuban Army lines to bring back this story of the rebel who threatens to take over Cuba."[2]

Like Herbert Matthews and Robert Taber, St. George brought Castro's story out of Cuba to an attentive public. But far more than Matthews and Taber, St. George revealed his own sympathy with the revolutionaries. As a "true adventure" writer, he was not bound by American journalistic conventions and "red line" cautions against crossing the border into partiality, advocacy, and activism. He followed his own ethical codes, tested and shaped in the Hungarian underground while fighting tyranny, first against the Nazis and then against the Reds. Those ordeals informed his discernment of the good and the true.

Cavalier published his Cuban saga as scheduled in the October 1957 issue. The narrative of St. George's "perilous trip" ran for ten pages, illustrated with seven of his photographs. The first page featured a photo of St. George standing alone against the terrain, wearing his broad-brimmed hat and looking into the distance, with the caption: "CAVALIER'S reporter as he looked in the jungle with Castro." Sharing the first page was a frontal photograph of Fidel

Castro, gripping his rifle with the telescopic sight that, as he had stressed to Matthews, gave him the advantage of being a sniper in the forest. A photo caption alluded to Castro's growing legend: "Castro listens intently to reports of enemy movements. A superb general, he is also a legendary shot with his .30-06 rifle." St. George was disappointed that *Cavalier*'s cover did not mention his story. Instead, the editors promoted Erskine Caldwell's new short story, "Nannette," and a freakish tale: "Strange Story: The Horse That Talked to People."[3]

In any case, St. George had not waited for the October publication in *Cavalier* to make his next move. During the summer of 1957 he was angling to return to the Sierra Maestra, this time for a larger magazine, a bigger paycheck, and expenses up front. The *Cavalier* story gave him credibility and, meanwhile, Castro was becoming increasingly newsworthy. St. George's access to Castro increased in value as newspapers and magazines focused more on the Cuban drama.

St. George now aimed for New York's two rival photography magazines, *Life* and *Look*, both with more than 5 million readers in the late 1950s.[4] *Life*'s editors already recognized that the Cuban rebels warranted attention. On May 27, *Life* had published Taber's photographs of Castro with the teenage runaways from Guantánamo.[5] Now *Look* was in the market for something about the rebels, but more substantial, and St. George offered them a chance to trump *Life*.

Given their mission as a picture magazine, *Look*'s editors were less interested in a hero's adventure, though they still needed St. George's personal saga to document the mission's clandestine intrigue. For authenticity, they wanted a taped interview with the "rebel chieftain." But those two pieces would be supportive of the main goal: first-class photography. *Look* planned for a visual spread of several photos depicting how Castro and his rebels survived day-to-day—an intimate, photographic, *authentic* view inside Castro's mysterious "mountain hideout."[6] The editors wanted a multitude of pictures from which to choose, something of everything and everybody. With a variety of subjects and expository captions, *Look* could construct a semblance of reality in a state-of-the-art photo essay.

Look had adopted the photo essay shortly after *Life* pioneered it in the 1930s. *Life*'s innovative photographic director from 1937 to 1950, Wilson Hicks, developed the photo essay format as he expanded his staff from four to forty photographers.[7] For *Life*'s first issue on November 23, 1936, publisher Henry Luce (also publisher of *Time* in 1923 and *Fortune* in 1930) dispatched his favorite photographer to the West to document construction of the world's greatest earth-filled dam. There, in a Depression-era boomtown—named New Deal after President Franklin Roosevelt's New Deal—Margaret Bourke-White took hundreds of candid and posed photos. By day, she focused on capturing the monumental structure of the Fort Peck Dam, the picture eventually chosen for *Life*'s cover. By night, she mingled among the men and women gathered to drink and dance in the settlement's only entertainment spot, a place named the BarX. For better reproductions of the photographs, *Life* used glossy paper and adopted the more costly, higher-quality rotogravure process, which it explained in an early issue.[8] Within a year, *Life*'s circulation rocketed past 1 million.[9]

Within months of *Life*'s launch, *Look* was on the newsstands in February 1937. Its publishers, Gardner Cowles and John Cowles, based in Des Moines, Iowa, adopted the photo essay and the rotogravure process. In short time, *Look* also reached a million in circulation, prompting its publishers to move the office to New York. Both magazines thrived, engaging a generation of professional "photojournalists" who documented domestic life and, during World War II, carried 35mm cameras into combat. By the mid-1950s, *Look* had a circulation of more than 3 million.[10]

Contracting with St. George for the project, *Look*'s editors shared some basic Cold War concerns. Was Castro, as President-General Batista had declared, leading a band of "crypto communists"? Was Castro a Communist? Or did he have Communists in his movement? Although St. George thought otherwise—as did Matthews and Taber—*Look*'s editors wanted additional assurances. They wanted St. George to deal squarely with the Communist question. From the editors' point of view, they were planning to feature this rebel chieftain who had been called a Communist by the man the United States recognized as the legitimate president of Cuba. With this daring leap, their foreign editor would be able to claim that *Look* was "one of the first U.S. publications to take Castro's rebellion seriously." On the other hand, the editors had to wonder why *Life* had not paid more attention to Fidel Castro.[11]

With the lucrative *Look* assignment in hand, St. George also contracted to freelance for a second magazine, one not competing with *Look*. *Coronet*, an artsy celebrity magazine started by the publisher of the men's magazine *Esquire*, had a circulation approaching 3 million.[12] Its editors also worried about Communists among the rebels. Amid Castro's obscurity, U.S. press reports in 1957 identified him with various shorthand descriptors: he might be "a bearded bandit" or a "screwball" or a "Robin Hood figure in the hills." To clarify Castro's identity, *Coronet* wanted Fidel to write his own story, "for the first time in his own words." They offered to publish his treatise or manifesto uncensored. St. George's part would give the background and document the journey. For illustrations, *Coronet*'s art staff would use St. George's photographs to sketch some drawings, depicting Castro writing his personal story in the mountain environs, with his now notable telescopic rifle close by.[13]

By the fall of 1957, American news editors were publishing stories about Cuba more frequently. Occasional stories about the lingering rebellion focused on President-General Batista, who consistently dismissed the rebels as an insignificant force of hardly more than twenty persons. Nonetheless, the political outlook there seemed murky. There seemed to be a wider rebellion, notably when bombs were detonated in Havana, or when word reached Havana about battles in the eastern provinces around the Sierra Maestra, where Castro was obviously still operating. Added to that, the 26th of July Movement's agents in New York issued press releases accusing the Batista regime of brutal tortures and murders.

In U.S. newsrooms, the handling of news from Cuba depended on the judgments of editors, most of whom had no reporters on the island, depending instead on news agencies.[14] In the months after Matthews's scoop, the *New York Times* editors had questioned their own coverage of Castro. By mid-1957, the *Times*'s news editors declined Matthews's offer to write more stories for the news pages. Some news editors already worried about the attention he had given Castro. The fact remained that Matthews had crossed a line established to keep opinion in the editorial pages, out of the news sections. Deferring to that journalistic convention to protect the integrity of the *Times,* the chain of command in the newsroom generally concurred that Matthews was too personally involved with Castro to report the news impartially. According to the *Times*'s managing editor, Turner Catledge, Matthews was "politically committed and concerned, given to deep emotional involvement in the stories he wrote." Privately, though, Catledge agreed with Matthews's assessment that Castro "stood a good chance of overturning the Batista dictatorship." Later, in his own book, Catledge conceded, "I was in sympathy with Castro's revolution, as I am in sympathy with most revolutions." The news editors' decision disturbed Matthews. As his biographer noted, he "felt like a martyr, sacrificed because of his beliefs." Matthews insisted that he had presented the news "deeply and expertly and in a true framework of Cuban history and politics—and this is what should count."[15]

★ ★ ★

On reflection, such a "true framework" had often been lacking in America's foreign correspondents' reports, especially in the coverage of revolution. The research published in 1920 by press critics Walter Lippmann and Charles Merz concluded that the *Times*'s coverage of the Russian Revolution had been "a disaster" because correspondents had written without a foundation of facts. But "most of all," the stories from 1917 to 1920 were subjectively skewed "by the hopes and fears of reporters and editors themselves who saw in the Bolsheviks what they wanted to see." Influenced by "organized propaganda," fear of a "Red Peril," and using unidentified sources, the *Times* assured readers on ninety-one occasions that the revolutionary regime was near collapse. The critics cautioned in 1920, "Certain correspondents are totally untrustworthy because their sympathies are too deeply engaged." Ultimately, the "core of journalism's corruption [was] in its own smug assurance of knowledge and its eagerness to assert opinion rather than provide facts."[16]

In faulting the press, Lippmann and Merz argued that the United States, as a new world power, required better journalism, emphasizing the same argument made seventeen years earlier by Joseph Pulitzer, publisher of the *New York World*. Departing from the yellow journalism of the 1890s that had diminished the trustworthiness of newspapers, Pulitzer published a thirty-nine-page manifesto declaring that only smarter, college-educated journalists could match wits with twentieth-century political and business leaders. He rejected traditional on-the-job training as grossly insufficient. "Nobody in a newspaper office has the time or the inclination to teach a raw reporter the things he ought to know before taking up even the humblest work of the journalist." Journalists should consider themselves professionals, like doctors and lawyers, requiring higher education. So, he bequeathed $2 million to fund annual prizes and to establish a college of journalism at Columbia University.[17] By 1920, Lippmann agreed that "no amount of money or effort spent in fitting the right men for this work could possibly be wasted, for the health of society depends upon the quality of the information it receives." The nation, he stated, needed "professional training in journalism in which the ideal of objective testimony is cardinal."[18]

Then in 1923, the American Society of Newspaper Editors (ASNE) approved its voluntary national code of ethics, its "Canons of Journalism." This was an effort to raise standards but also to avoid government meddling with First Amendment freedoms. The canons condemned wayward newspapermen. "A journalist who uses his power for any selfish or otherwise unworthy purpose is faithless to a high trust. . . . Promotion of any private interest contrary to the general welfare, for whatever reason, is not compatible with honest journalism. . . . Partisanship, in editorial comment which knowingly departs from the truth, does violence to the best spirit of American journalism; in the news columns it is subversive of a fundamental principle of the profession." In the code, impartiality meant that news reports "should be free from opinion or bias of any kind"—the essence of which became identified with the value of *objectivity*.[19]

However, the Canons of Journalism did not consider the special role of foreign correspondents, although by 1923 American correspondents had covered numerous wars in Europe, Asia, and Latin America. Even after World War II, the Overseas Press Club had promulgated no such canons for foreign correspondents. The conclusion by one scholar of the press was that the "code of objectivity appears to be operative only within the geographical limit of the United States."[20]

In war, the line between reporting and advocacy blurred, especially when combat prevented the correspondent from reporting from more than one side. "Fair play" and "impartiality" or objectivity often became irrelevant. Instead, correspondents acted on their own principles, frequently with guidance from reporters who had traveled the same territory before them.[21] Sending home hard-gotten information, often raw, sometimes analyzed, a correspondent passed the responsibility to the home office. Editors, without firsthand knowledge, usually published the stories. If the correspondent was too sympathetic with one side, editors made revisions, as the *Times* editors did in 1937 when Herbert Matthews's reports from the Spanish Civil War seemed to favor the Loyalists defending against Generalissimo Franco's forces.[22]

The news from Cuba during 1957 presented U.S. editors with an ethical problem. The increasing focus on Castro's rebels constituted unbalanced coverage. Yet in the offices of U.S. print and broadcast media—from the *New York Times* to CBS to *Life, Look,* and *Coronet*—the coverage of the rebels could be justified as giving attention to the "other side" of the story suppressed by the Batista regime's censorship.

As the insurgency persisted into late 1957, U.S. correspondents focused even more on Castro and his "ragtag" rebels in the "jungle" as the main actors in the Cuban drama. With each story, the rebels gained in stature in opposition to the dictator who had seized power illegitimately. Matthews, explaining later why he and Dubois focused on Castro, dismissed the journalistic canon of impartiality as irrelevant in a revolution: "There can be no such thing as an 'unbiased,' 'impartial' study because no one can write intelligently about the revolution unless he was somehow identified with it."[23]

St. George was also disinclined toward fair play, impartiality, or objectivity. Given his experience in Hungary, St. George appreciated the freedom of expression he found in the American press, especially in the magazines, where he felt no constraints for balance and objectivity. He focused solely on the "story" and more or less ignored the regime and any other voices that contradicted heartfelt values of truth and justice. More than Matthews, Dubois, or Taber, St. George admired Castro's rebellion against a brutal dictator. Having fought authoritarian rule, he identified with the Cubans giving their lives to the resistance. St. George had found in the New World a place where he could slay more dragons.

By the end of 1957, St. George's investment in the rebels was paying off. The longer Castro survived—it was nearly a year since the invasion—the more valuable he became as a commodity. Now St. George headed back to the Sierra Maestra with better press credentials, representing *Look* and *Coronet*. In early October, he connected with the rebel underground in Havana. "The Hungarian-Yankee reporter Andrew is with us again," René Ramos Latour wrote to Castro on October 4. "He is definitely thinking of going to the Sierra as a war correspondent. We'll keep him here until we have your opinion about him." Latour, now a Movement leader in Havana, knew Castro wanted to meet more journalists, but Latour's immediate concern was hiding from the police; he was on the run. "This letter was interrupted yesterday by a tremendous search they made of the block. Fortunately we were able to get out in time, and we've been going from one place to another since last night and have still not found a safe place. The circle is getting smaller by the minute."

Havana was more dangerous than the Sierra Maestra, but Latour was generally optimistic: "As far as the organization is concerned, I can say that it is constantly improving. The new structure we've given the Action units has increased the effectiveness in this sphere. Both sabotage and action are on the increase, and it is likely that Plan No. 4, already in effect, will work more efficiently than the previous ones. To date, Oriente, Camagüey, Santa Clara, and Pinar del Río provinces are well organized. In spite of the efforts of Maria [Haydee Santamaria] and the doctor [Faustino Perez], Havana has not reached the level of the remaining provinces (except for Matanzas, where there is still much to do)."[24]

In October 1957, President-General Batista resumed censorship of the Cuban and foreign press and suspension of civil liberties. On October 9 he refused appeals by the Inter-American Press Association and the Cuban Press Association to lift the censorship. He claimed that the rebels' propaganda was spreading dangerously. "Since it is known to all of Cuba, I do not believe I have to try to demonstrate how the agitation has operated and the extent of the influence of the propaganda emanating from reports on organized terrorism." Circulation and recirculation had spread "dangerous" distortions. "The frequent publication of certain acts and certain names has given these dimensions which in reality they did not have." He reasoned that censorship protected the Cuban press from error. "The press itself has at times been caught unaware in dangerous rumors, and has been unable to avoid this because of the rapidity with which news has to circulate." The nation's economy was also at stake. Distortions were "threatening to be detrimental to the good name of Cuba, our economy, and even the prestige and culture of our people in the eyes of the world."[25]

Amid such concerns, the army ordered closer surveillance of even weekend casino tourists. Arriving in October at Havana's airport, St. George thought he was "a marked man." He had heard that his *Cavalier* article "dangerously displeased General Batista." It had been four months since he had been in Cuba, and he now noticed more "gun-bulging plainclothesmen" looking at everyone suspiciously—"their marbled moist eyes following you silently." Afterward, he could boast how he slipped past Cuban security men and then fooled Cuban customs officers by posing as a golfer. He stuffed film, cameras, and recording equipment "into a pair of expensive golf bags which fairly screamed 'tourist!'"[26]

St. George described "the gauntlet I had to run in order to get to Fidel Castro." For most of the time, the Movement smoothed his way. St. George noted how the rebels eluded police and soldiers, causing him to conclude that "no blockade is impregnable." His guides hid his equipment "in spare tires, secret under-the-chassis compartments." Then he was handed off to "a short, broad, smiling engineering student who shepherded me down to Santiago." There, he met Castro's "chief blockade runner."

Sharing the details of going undercover, St. George wrote how they all "donned coveralls, cloth caps, gloves. We were ostensibly going 'crop-dusting.' A small farm truck picked us up, dodged innocently through the rumbling military traffic, and dropped us again deep among green rice fields. A jeep was pulled up by the roadside, its engine running; we swung aboard and darted along a back road to a small rice farm. We sat down in a bedroom, drank Criolla café and waited while my equipment arrived in several installments."[27]

In the countryside, at town squares and village crossroads, St. George observed the enemy everywhere—the "khaki-clad gendarmes of the Guardia Rural with their machetes and swinging, long-nosed pistols." At one point, his blockade runner pulled out a pistol, a .38 automatic, as they passed through the prohibited area, with "zone of death" checkpoints manned by "stiff-faced army troopers, their tommy guns tensely cocked, their orders: 'Shoot on suspicion.'" Then, safely at the foot of the Sierra Maestra, St. George climbed for fourteen hours "straight up the mountainside, and through the thick of the jungle. I remembered little about my walk except for the burning orange blur of exhaustion before my eyes and the incredibly voluptuous feeling of finally taking the load off my mangled feet." After another three days' climb, they reached Castro's camp.[28]

On his reunion with Castro, St. George found him "a free man and a triumphant one." St. George soon saw that Castro's rebel force had grown to "over a thousand strong." Furthermore, they were "well armed—mostly with U.S. weapons captured from Cuban government troops—their morale is high, their guerrilla tactics well learned," and they had expanded Castro's "Free Cuba." "Castro rules a 'liberated zone' of 1,500 square miles populated by 50,000 civilians." And beyond the zone, St. George added, "one newspaper recently estimated that 90 percent of the Cuban population supports Castro."[29]

With a leap of imagination, St. George speculated that Castro's feat had earned him respect across Latin America and beyond. "And above all, Fidel Castro's name has become a lodestar of hope throughout restless Latin America.... The world has known few revolutionary leaders quite like Fidel Castro."[30]

But was Castro a Communist? St. George said no. He based his opinion on his Eastern European experience with Communists and on the views of Fidel's supporters, including well-placed Cubans whose numbers he multiplied, writing that President-General Batista's were rejected by "thousands of staid, solid middle-class citizens [who] work for him at the risk of their lives." If editors at *Look* or *Coronet* still had doubts, St. George reminded them that the new U.S. ambassador in Cuba, Earl E. T. Smith, replacing Arthur Gardner, had been asked whether the State Department had any proof of Castro's alleged Communist connections. At his first press conference in the summer of 1957, Ambassador Smith "answered firmly that the U.S. had no such evidence."[31]

Coronet in its February issue printed St. George's sketch of Castro's past, with the early years briefly summarized. The mini-biography swept over Fidel's childhood as the second of three sons in a "vast, vigorous, wealthy, landowning family." The school years involved "the customary education of a rich cane-planter's son: Jesuit fathers, then Havana University," where he "found time to qualify for not one, but three degrees: law, international law and social sciences." A classmate was quoted as recalling Castro's "near-photographic memory that never let him down.... Before exams, Fidel would prop himself up with a textbook and go through it carefully—once. When he got to the bottom of page, he'd tear it out and toss it into the wastebasket. 'We won't need this anymore,' he'd mutter."[32]

St. George's sketch of Castro's University of Havana years did not probe the extent of his political involvement, his Communist friends, and his "leftist perspective." Nor did St. George depict the Castro who carried a loaded revolver out of fear that political gangs would assassinate him as they had done other political opponents. And, too, it did not mention allegations that Castro had killed a man.[33]

Instead, St. George traced Castro's opposition to authority to his brief practice as a lawyer defending the poor. Castro "specialized in low-fee cases, defending the everyday sort of people who have been long abused in Cuba." Castro, St. George wrote, "recalls those early ebullient days with relish." Fidel told him that in 1951 during the Prío Socarrás administration, he defended people evicted by a corrupt landlord who bribed a building inspector to get his tenements condemned. He then dispossessed all his tenants and readmitted them to their wretched lodgings at double the former rent. Castro took the tenants' case and won a reduction of rents.

"The landlords," Castro said, "used to scream: 'What? These miserable people can afford a *lawyer* now?'

"And I would shout back at them, 'Yes, these miserable people can afford a lawyer—me!'"[34]

In 1952, Castro ran for Congress in the Ortodoxo Party, whose members voiced a devotion to the ideals of José Martí. Castro was "a top-notch campaigner," St. George wrote, "a tall, forceful young orator with a dignified Roman face and great personal magnetism." To promote his campaign, Castro started a program on the "Voice of the Air" radio station that attracted as many as fifty thousand listeners.[35] But on March 10, Fulgencio Batista and army officers engineered the barracks coup, then canceled elections. "Castro found that the national emergency called for stiffer measures," St. George wrote, and on July 26, 1953, he led the attack on the Moncada fortress. Although he survived, sixty of his men "were killed by the army in an orgy of sadism and revenge—most by castration" in the fort where St. George himself had been held.[36] St. George summarized the aftermath of Moncada—Castro's defense, his "fiery, unrepentant summation against tyranny that became a Latin American political classic," then the prison sentence, amnesty, and journey to Mexico to train his force, the invasion, and his amazing survival despite the loss of seventy of his eighty-two men. To St. George, Castro's escapes signified heroic deliverance.

In December 1957, after a full year in the Sierra Maestra, the rebels had gained supporters simply by surviving. "Unable to kill Castro or to check the tidal rise of his popularity," St. George wrote, "General Batista has fought back with the flailing ferocity which overcomes declining dictators." Militarily, Batista "doubled the size of his army within a year" to fourteen thousand, by drafting prisoners, St. George wrote, and stationing them in forts surrounding the eastern mountains. In the cities, especially in Santiago, the army and the police increased attacks on civilian sympathizers. Officers with reputations for "sadistic outrages against political prisoners" had been placed in charge of a new military task force to subdue Santiago and other "rebellious" towns. All this was failing, St. George noted, because Batista had driven his enemies into the mountains to which there now was such a steady stream of supplies that Castro seldom lacked anything, including boxes of cigars.[37]

St. George related the thoughts of a "wealthy Cuban" in Santiago who saw Castro as the only hope for Cuba's classes, the one everyone had been waiting for. "We need Castro because we need a change. And we will never change from corruption, lethargy and military brutality unless we have a leader—and Castro is the only leader we have. . . . But remember, Castro has done what the middle classes, the intellectuals, the young people have been waiting for, all the way from Venezuela to Argentina—he has defied the military might of a dictator, and he has won his gamble. He has won it if he does nothing but stay alive."[38]

St. George's introduction set the table for *Coronet*'s main course: Castro's uncensored personal statement titled, "Why We Fight." Robert Taber had given him a few minutes on CBS in May 1957, but now he had several pages in which to explain the "aims, plans and aspirations" of the 26th of July Movement—space enough to justify and legitimize the revolution. Writing as a lawyer making a closing argument, he aimed to sway an American jury. "In obtaining and publishing this exclusive article—the only first-person story written by me since we landed in Cuba on December 2, 1956—Coronet Magazine has given us the opportunity to state our aims and to correct the many errors and distortions circulating about our revolutionary struggle." An "iron censorship" and a "military blockade around the combat zone" prevented any such articles in the Cuban media. "Batista can point to a single successful achievement: he has effectively muzzled all public communication in our country, silenced TV, radio and the press, and so intimidated our news publisher that not a single Cuban reporter has ever been assigned to *our* side of what is, in effect, a spreading civil war."[39]

He was fighting the war against a "great many evils" bred by "dictatorship, ignorance, military rule and police oppression." But "all these evils have a common root: the lack of liberty. The single word most expressive of our aim and spirit is simply—freedom. First of all and most of all, we are fighting to do away with dictatorship in Cuba and to establish the foundations of genuine representative government." Castro stressed that his movement aimed to dismantle the dictatorship and restore elections "within twelve months." First, they must "eject" Batista and all his cabinet officers and "impeach them before special revolutionary tribunals," set up a provisional government to be "nominated by special convention," consisting of delegates of "our various civic organizations," with the "chief task... to prepare and conduct truly honest general elections within twelve months."[40]

Castro denied allegations that he would become the president. He said he was ineligible. "The truth is that, quite apart from personal reluctance to enter the presidential competition so soon, our Constitution, as it now stands, would prohibit it. Under its age requirements, I am, at 31, far too young to be eligible for the presidency and will remain so for another ten years."[41]

However, he listed seven "program points" or signifiers, which "might serve as a basis for action by the provisional government."

1. Grant immediate "freedom for all political prisoners, civil and military." Batista "has imprisoned dozens of officers and hundreds of enlisted men from his own armed forces who have shown revulsion or resistance to his bloody suppression of political discontent."

2. Give "full and untrammeled freedom" of public information for all communication media. "Arbitrary censorship and systematic corruption of journalists has long been one of the festering sores of our nation."

3. Re-establish personal and political rights. Castro pledged to restore "our much-ignored Constitution" under which since 1940 Cuba had elected three presidents for four-year terms.

4. "Wipe out corruption in Cuban public life." A career civil service, such as in the United States, could attack the problem of "venal policemen, thieving tax collectors, rapacious army bosses." Employees should be "paid enough to be able to live without having to accept bribes."

5. Sponsor "an intensive campaign against illiteracy." Through literacy, people can learn to protect their health and feed their families "a wholesome diet" rather than "roots and rice," and farmers can learn to use irrigation.

6. Push for "land reform bills adjusting the uncertain owner-tenant relations that are a peculiar blight of rural Cuba. Hundreds of thousands of small farmers occupy parcels which they do not own under the law. Thousands of absentee owners claim title to properties they've hardly ever seen. ... We will support no land reform bill, however, which does not provide for just compensation of expropriated owners."

7. Support speedy industrialization and raise employment levels.[42]

Rumors, Castro said, had spread a "distortion" that the Movement's reforms would nationalize property. "We have no plans for the expropriation or nationalization of foreign investments. . . . I personally have come to feel that nationalization is, at best, a cumbersome instrument. It does not seem to make the state any stronger, yet it enfeebles private enterprise." Further, "foreign investments will always be welcome and secure here."[43]

Castro justified the rebels' new strategy of burning the sugarcane crop, which President-General Batista had denounced as "terrorism and insurrection" and reason enough to continue press censorship to prevent "the inevitable publicity... which has served their ends." In the *Coronet* manifesto, Castro admitted that it was a "terrible decision" to burn Cuba's "entire sugar cane crop," but civil war justified it as legitimate economic warfare. The destruction of Cuba's money crops—in sugarcane fields and tobacco warehouses—reduced the regime's tax base; sugarcane alone accounted for as much as a third of the national income. "If the cane goes up in flames, the army will grind to a standstill; the police will have to disband, for none of them will get paid; and the Batista regime will have to capitulate. Once the tyranny has gone up in smoke, we will see the way to a decent, democratic future." The message was clear: As long as Batista rules, profits will suffer.[44] Although

Castro did not mention it, the sugarcane burning achieved another of his strategic aims—to grab attention in the American press.

St. George accompanied Castro's men on the first sugarcane raid, and his photographs of the burning were featured in *Look*'s photo essay, published in February of 1958 (as was the article for *Coronet*). From hundreds of photos, *Look*'s editors chose sixteen—four on the sugarcane sabotage. The caption with the pictures read: "Three hundred men who had lived for months in the rain forest of Cuba's highest mountains moved down by night, for the first time on the perilous open plains." Curiously, *Look* credited St. George only as the photographer, although he provided not only the caption information but also the taped question-and-answer session with Castro:

> **Q.** You say you will burn Cuba's entire sugar crop. The island's economic life depends on it. What can you gain by this?

> **A.** Our intent is to burn the harvest to the last stalk, including my own family's large sugar-cane farm here in Oriente Province. It is a hard step. But it is a legitimate act of war. From sugar taxes, Batista buys bombs and arms, pays his newly doubled army. Only their bayonets now keep him in power. Once before, Cubans burned their cane, razed their very towns, to wrest freedom from Spain. During your revolution, didn't the American colonists throw tea into Boston Harbor as a legitimate defense measure?[45]

During the first cane-field raid in November, St. George's first picture showed the men on the march, captioned: "Carrying weapons largely captured from Cuban Army, rebels invade open country for first time." A few sentences summed up the background:

> Edgy, tense, they listened to a pep talk by Castro. Then they split up into combat teams of 50, ready for stiff fight with government troops. A regiment of 1,200 Cuban soldiers was stationed only a half hour from them. All day the "Fidelistas" fired huge stands of harvest. By dusk, the skyline billowed with smoke and flamed with a purple neonlike glow. Late in the afternoon, army planes strafed open roads, and the troops never showed. Streaking back to the foothills in commandeered buses and cars, the rebels celebrated by singing their favorite Pancho Villa revolutionary song, "Cama de Piedro" ("Of stone will be the pillow of the woman who loves me").[46]

Another St. George photo showed one rifleman on guard as another set the fire. In the clipped language of caption writing, the editor explained: "Using ordinary match rebel fires dry, ripe cane. Government has decreed that anyone found at any time in cane field with match is to be shot." The third photo gave a view of the blazing field with the caption: "Cuba's chief crop burns briskly in the dark. To counter such moves, Batista has doubled the army's size." That day, none of Batista's army appeared. The fourth picture showed the rebels leaving the fields in vehicles they seized. "Rebels speed back to safety of foothills in cars and buses commandeered from startled drivers."[47]

Look's editors were also impressed with the fact that the rebels enforced civil laws, held "court" trials, and conducted executions. *Look* published a sequence of seven photos showing the progress of an execution, captioned: "The rebels mete out stern jungle justice.... Bandit gangs spring up wherever the government troops withdraw. These outlaw 'wolf packs' are Castro's biggest headache. Unpoliced, they pillage helpless villages for money, weapons, women. 'If we don't keep order in our liberated zone,' says Castro, 'the people suffer. Our revolution is tarnished.' Prisoners shown here were bandit chiefs, captured after a week of relentless tracking by rebels. From dawn to dusk, for 12 days, the trials went on. The tribunal of five included lawyer Castro, Celia Sánchez, top rebel political organizer, and Humberto Sori, an ex-vice-president of the Inter-American Bar Association. The jungle has no prisons. The penalty for extreme crimes was death."[48]

That executed man was identified as Carlos Ramirez. Castro and his men questioned Ramirez and heard witnesses' testimony, then convicted him and sentenced him to death. Castro's brother, Raúl, led the execution squad. The sequence of captions in the photo series read: "Stoically, Carlos Ramirez awaits execution for multiple rape, robbery and murder.... He headed a 22-man gang. Thirty farmers testified against Ramirez in a three-day trial.... Tied to execution tree, Ramirez hears last words of comfort from Father Varese, Catholic chaplain who marches with rebels.... Shouts of '*Fuego!*' (Fire!) still ring in his ears as he is smashed by bullets of a six-man execution squad. ...End of a man—a final bullet in the head.... Still wearing his campaign cap, he is untied from the tree. To mountain people and puritanical Castro molestation of honest women is an intolerable crime."[49]

St. George photographed everyday camp life. *Look* used his photographs of a sixteen-year-old girl cook, an armed sentry smoking a pipe, a "fighter" who like the others "serves without pay," and a rebel catching one of the snakes which "skinned and eaten" were "great delicacies" in a diet of "rice, yucca roots and cattle purchased from local farmers." The main photo of Castro was a profile and showed him looking into the distance, captioned: "Bearded Castro spent 22 months in prisons, gave up law practice and family farm to take to hills." Another showed the leader in action, "wearing rumpled U.S. Army fatigue uniform" as he "listens to scout's report and plots final strategy with top lieutenants. Peasants in the Sierra Mountains serve as intelligence and supply corps for the rebels."[50]

St. George again raised the Communist question during the second half of *Look's* taped interview. Castro had emphasized his army's growth from "a dozen men in the bush" after the invasion in December 1956 to "now, one thousand strong... small, mobile and combative." He had also described his democratic post-Batista plan for a "provisional government, whose heads are to be elected by some 60 Cuban civic bodies, like the Lions, Rotarians, groups of lawyers and doctors, religious organizations." And he had laid out his economic plan to "root out the fearful corruption that has plagued Cuba, wage a war against illiteracy... speed industrialization, and thus create new jobs."

Q. Charges have been made that your movement is Communist-inspired. What about this?

A. This is absolutely false. Every American newsman who has come here at great personal peril—Herbert Matthews of the *New York Times,* two CBS reporters and yourself—has said this is false. Our Cuban support comes from all classes of society. The middle class is strongly united in its support of our movement. We even have many wealthy sympathizers. Merchants, industrial executives, young people, workers are sick of the gangsterism that rules Cuba. Actually, the Cuban Communists, as your journalist John Gunther once reported, have never opposed Batista, for whom they have seemed to feel a closer kinship.[51]

Then Castro started asking the questions. He criticized U.S. policy for political and military support of the dictatorship. "Why is it assumed that outmoded dictators are the best guardians of our rights, and make our best allies? And what is the difference between dictatorship by a military caste, like Batista's, and the Communist or Fascist dictatorships you say you abhor?"

Castro offered a hypothetical example. "To any North American, it would be absurd, outrageous, if an army officer or police chief deposed or disposed of the governor of a state and then declared himself governor. Who would recognize him as such? Yet this happens all too frequently in Latin America. By furnishing arms to these usurpers of power—the men of the infamous 'international of sabers'—tyrants like Pérez Jimenez of Venezuela, exiled Rojas Pinella of Colombia, and Trujillo of the Dominican Republic—you kill the democratic spirit of Latin America."

Look's scoop ended with Castro's challenge to the U.S. government to stop sending arms to Batista. "Do you think your tanks, your planes, the guns you Americans ship Batista in good faith are used in hemisphere defense? He uses them to cow his defenseless people. How can he contribute to 'hemispheric defense'? He hasn't even been able to subdue us, even when we were only a dozen strong!

"I firmly believe that the nations of Latin America can achieve political stability under representative forms of government, just as other nations have. We need material progress, first, to raise low living standards; we need a climate of freedom in which we can develop democratic habits. This is never possible under tyranny. Efforts at self-government in many Latin nations are far from perfect, I realize. But we can cure ourselves of these ills—unless dictators step in and strangle this natural political evolution, and are given aid and recognition by other countries. I repeat, by arming Batista you are really making war against the Cuban people."[52]

By February 1958, when Andrew St. George's stories appeared in both *Look* and *Coronet*, the revolution was into its second year, attracting more American correspondents. In Chicago, the *Sun-Times* agreed to send a reporter, Ray Brennan, who was eager to catch up with the work done by Jules Dubois at their Chicago competitor, the *Tribune*. The reporter who volunteered for the assignment, Brennan specialized in covering Chicago mobsters and would also be looking for connections with the mob's investments in Havana's new hotels, nightclubs, and casinos. And in New York, the *Times*, having decided that Herbert Matthews should not write for the news department, settled on sending a veteran war reporter, Homer Bigart. Coincidentally, during the Greek Civil War a decade earlier, Bigart had won a prestigious journalism prize for interviewing the leader of the Greek rebels in his hideout—a daring exploit during which Bigart rode on horseback in the Greek mountains.

CHAPTER 8

IT IS NECESSARY TO HAVE FAITH

As the insurrection continued into a second year, U.S. news media began investing in more coverage of Fidel Castro. His so-called ragtag rebels had survived and even seemed to have gained strength in men, arms, and middle-class support. After the attacks by the student revolutionaries and the Miami exiles had been crushed, Castro's force appeared to be the one serious opposition to President-General Fulgencio Batista, even though it remained in the southeastern Sierra Maestra mountains.

The few American correspondents who had covered Castro's first year now had more competition. Two news agencies sent representatives—Harold Lidin for United Press and Ed Cannel for the Newspaper Enterprises Association. The *Chicago Sun-Times* sent Ray Brennan, who came straight from reporting on professional baseball's 1958 spring training in Florida. The *Sun-Times* editors had of course noticed all the Cuba dispatches by Jules Dubois at the rival *Chicago Tribune*, but until 1958 they considered Cuba beyond their editorial fairway. At last Brennan won the argument that he could produce something that Dubois had neglected—insider stories about Chicago mobsters ensconced in their flashy new Havana hotels, nightclubs, and casinos. Brennan's other agenda, however, was to follow Castro. The casino business also led a Las Vegas radio station, KRAM, to send Alan Jarlson to Havana. One big question was whether the insurrection was affecting the casinos that were drawing gamblers away from Las Vegas.

A new face also arrived in Havana for the *New York Times*. Editors in February assigned a fifty-year-old veteran war correspondent, the reliable straight-shooter Homer Bigart, who in 1954 had covered the civil war in Guatemala. In contrast to Herbert Matthews, Bigart had no personal involvement with Castro and was trusted to be unbiased. In fact, Bigart's current focus was on the superheated turmoil in the Middle East, and to him Cuba was a sideshow. While Matthews continued to write about Cuba, the *Times* regarded his contributions as suitable only for the opinion pages—as personal columns or editorials, or as essays for its *New York Times Magazine*.

As Matthews had, Bigart made connections with the 26th of July Movement. In Havana, he avoided the U.S. Embassy, went directly to Santiago, and then headed into the Sierra Maestra mountains. Ten years earlier he had done mountain trekking in Greece. During the Greek Civil War, Bigart made a perilous journey on horseback to the hideout of General Markos Vafiadis, leader of the Greek Communist guerrillas. For that feat, Bigart received the first George Polk Award, presented in remembrance of his friend, a CBS correspondent killed months earlier while attempting the same journey.[1]

Bigart recorded that he arrived in the "forested peaks of the Sierra Maestra" on February 10 and nine days later interviewed Castro "outside a squalid hut deep in the sierra" where Castro was resting after what he called "our biggest battle."[2] However, Bigart provided no information to prove how he managed to find Castro. After a full year, interviews with Castro had become believable and it seemed no longer essential to document, as Matthews and St. George had done, the intrigues, disguises, and ordeals involved with gaining the interviews.

Bigart's first story, about Castro's peace "plan" to end the rebellion, made the *Times*'s front page. Castro told Bigart that he had recently offered General Batista a "plan" for ending the "worsening civil war" and holding "general elections." The plan had been carried to Batista by a congressman whose main antiwar goal was to stop the rebels' raids on local cattle herds. But Bigart noted that the peace plan was unrealistic because Castro required three conditions—two of which, Bigart noted, "informed sources said President Batista could not conceivably accept.... Señor Castro demanded the withdrawal of all Government military forces" from the "most rebellious" Oriente Province. Castro also wanted the Cuban Army to leave all of its equipment. "Upon withdrawal of the Government forces, Señor Castro would agree to general elections under President Batista provided the elections were supervised throughout the island by the Organization of American States." If Batista did not withdraw the army, Castro told Bigart, fighting would continue "until we occupy the whole island."[3]

Bigart highlighted Castro's ongoing power struggle with the Miami exiles, now focused on who should succeed Batista. Castro preferred the former judge now in exile, Manuel Urrutia, as provisional president. Castro had liked Urrutia since May 1957 when the judge voted, alone in the minority, to acquit twenty-two captives from Castro's invasion force, arguing that armed resistance against the dictatorship was constitutional. But Castro seemed "much more conciliatory," Bigart reported. He no longer insisted on Urrutia "if public opinion wants another man." Exiles meeting in Washington the previous November had hurriedly formed a "unity" group, the Cuban Liberation Council, which called for a temporary military junta. Now, Castro told Bigart that he was "still deadset against" a military junta such as the one that backed Batista's coup. "I do not believe in military rule. And there is a strong tradition in Cuba against military juntas. All Latin Americans are tired of government by colonels and generals. We do not want professional soldiers oppressing the people."[4] On the power struggle, Bigart quoted Castro as uncompromising:

> The leadership of the struggle is and will continue to be in Cuba, in the hands of the revolutionary combatants. Those who wish now or in the future to be considered as revolutionary leaders should be in this country, confronting directly the responsibilities, risks and sacrifices that Cuba now demands.... The attitude of many compatriots could not be any more ignoble. But there is still time to rectify it and to help those who are fighting. ... Exiles should cooperate in the struggle, but it is absurd for them to try to tell us from abroad what peak we should take, what sugar cane field we should burn ... or at what moment or in what circumstance and form we should unloose the general strike.[5]

Other liberation groups worried that Castro's armed revolutionaries would threaten political activities after Batista departed. But Castro assured Bigart that his rebels would keep their weapons only "for a few months" after the provisional government came to power. "Our forces will help to maintain order for an interim period while the army is purged."[6]

Rather than ask Castro if he was a Communist, Bigart teased out his ideas. Bigart said Castro "showed some uneasiness when questioned about his economic and social platforms," saying only that a group of university professors was "working out his economic program." Then Bigart took the liberty of speculating about Castro's widening financial support and that perceived uneasiness. "The reason is obvious: he is a symbol of a middle-class reform movement rather than of economic and social revolution. His financial support has been derived mainly from wealthy and middle-income groups. But to gain the wide support of Cuban labor, which is essential if his general strike is to succeed, Señor Castro may have to promise reforms that could frighten other groups of his supporters," even middle-class supporters he was already attracting such as the economist Felipe Pazos, former president of the National Bank of Cuba.[7]

In a follow-up story published the next day, Bigart speculated about why Castro thought he could win. The reporter concluded that a military victory hardly seemed possible. He discounted Castro's "boast" that his small band of rebels could defeat an army supplied and trained by the U.S. military.

Castro's claim of success in fighting in the mountains did not impress a war correspondent as experienced as Bigart. "A rebel leader capable of throwing into battle only 400 riflemen boasts that within a few months he will oust the Batista dictatorship and occupy all Cuba," Bigart wrote. "Still unexplained, however, is the question of how Señor Castro can fight his way out of the Sierra Maestra in the southeast tip of Cuba. How could he defeat the Government forces equipped with tanks, armored cars and artillery? His only anti-tank weapons are a few bazookas." In fifteen days in the Sierra Maestra, Bigart saw "no rational solution. . . . To break out onto the plains, Señor Castro would have to rely on major Cuban military defections. But his program offers no attractions for power-hungry officers. On the contrary, the rebel leader has said he will tolerate no military junta. One harsh fact stands out: 400 men is the maximum combat force Senior Castro can safely commit at this moment against the government troops ringing the sierra. Señor Castro himself disclosed this figure in an interview last week as he rested after an action he described as 'our biggest battle.'"[8]

"To see our victory," Castro advised Bigart, "it is necessary to have faith."[9]

After some interviews in Havana, Bigart concluded that Castro's "boast" must be based on successful *economic* warfare. The rebels' urban cadre imagined a "general strike" that could shut down commerce, with far greater economic impact than setting fire to cane fields and raiding cattle ranches. Castro's plan for victory "provokes no scornful laughter in Havana," Bigart wrote. "Many Cubans believe it could be done with the help of a paralyzing general strike and the sabotage of utilities by the rebels' urban underground."[10]

As talk of an impending general strike circulated, more U.S. correspondents arrived in Cuba, among them three veterans: Matthews, St. George, and Taber. Matthews was there to see if a general strike was a serious threat. For St. George it was his third visit, this time as a freelance photographer for Henry Luce's *Time* and *Life* magazines. St. George would be taking abundant photographs so *Life* could catch up with what St. George had done for *Life*'s competitor, *Look*. St. George also agreed to guide *Time-Life*'s writer Sam Halper into the Sierra Maestra and introduce him to Castro.

CBS's Taber, also back for a third time, was probing how the revolutionary strategy had changed since the CBS telecast in May of "Cuba's Jungle Fighters." He noted that the rebels in Havana were "still looking for a short-cut to their objective" and now believed the way was through a general strike. Taber learned that originally "Fidel was opposed" to the strike for at least three reasons: "He did not believe that the underground was adequately prepared for a general uprising. . . . He had little faith in Havana, with its large foreign population, its Spanish merchant class, which formed the backbone of Cuban conservatism, its traditional disaffection from the struggles of the nation, its historical position as the exploiter of the wealth-producing provinces. . . . He was well aware of the firm grip in which Batista held organized labor, under the domination of Eusebio Mujal." Despite these obstacles, Taber noted, Castro "was nevertheless persuaded, against his better judgment." On March 12, 1958, Castro's Sierra Maestra manifesto called for "a revolutionary general strike."[11]

By contrast, Castro's talks with Bigart had emphasized that victory would come through the rebels' *military* prowess. When Castro told Bigart about their "biggest battle" around Pino de Agua, Bigart discounted it as no more than a series of skirmishes. In his story, Bigart ridiculed the battle that "will never make an addition to Sir Edward Creasy's *Fifteen Decisive Battles of the World*."[12] In that calculation, "Bigart failed to understand the dynamics of guerrilla war," wrote Matthews's biographer, "which was not surprising, given his experience with conventional war. Castro did not need to win one of the world's fifteen decisive battles. . . . Though he had been sent to Cuba to correct what the editors believed was Matthews' biased reporting, Bigart also apparently took sides, downplaying Castro's chances of winning the war."[13]

Despite his doubts about Castro's military potential, Bigart nonetheless recorded the rebels' tactic of ambushing the enemy in small "guerrilla" battles in the forests—a method that Taber later termed "the war of the flea."[14] The same method had been used on May 28, 1957, in the rebels' first surprise attack on the small military outpost at El Ubero, where they aimed to "capture weapons to arm more guerrillas," Taber wrote. "Other actions during the first year were on a similar scale, or smaller. . . . The scale of the action was miniature, yet propaganda victories came earlier and were international in their scope."[15]

Although Bigart had not witnessed Castro's so-called "biggest battle" at Pino de Agua, he dutifully recorded how Castro conducted his method of warfare. Che Guevara and Castro had led two columns. At dawn they started firing on the garrison, expecting the commander to send for reinforcements that could then be ambushed by a third column led by Raúl Castro. When they stormed the village at 9 a.m., most of the startled army garrison force fled to the woods, leaving behind weapons and four dead. When a group of sixteen army reinforcements rushed from a nearby garrison, the rebels killed ten, wounded three, and captured their lieutenant. However, a larger contingent of reinforcements avoided the ambush; forewarned, they approached warily, according to Castro, and "walked behind a screen of women and children."[16] Castro "was pleased with the over-all result," Bigart wrote, because Batista's army altogether lost fifteen killed and ten wounded. The rebels lost four killed and four wounded, but they captured the garrison's arsenal of weapons—many more than expected: five machine guns, 313 rifles, more than a thousand cartridges.[17]

By the time Bigart's stories were published, he had already flown to a new assignment in the Middle East, switching gears to write about a meeting of Arab leaders in Egypt. Leaving Cuba when he did, he missed at least two rebel achievements, the launch of "Rebel Radio" and a sensational kidnapping that infuriated President-General Batista. On February 24, the rebels launched their shortwave radio station, with an announcement to Cubans: "Aquí Radio Rebelde! Transmitiendo desde la Sierra Maestra en Territorio Libre de Cuba!" (Rebel Radio Here! Transmitting from the Sierra Maestra in Free Territory of Cuba!) There followed a statement: "Tonight, and every night at this time, we will bring you the true story of Cuba and about the people's revolution." Then, noted the *Sun-Times*'s Ray Brennan, Fidel Castro in a "mild, softly persuasive" voice thanked followers, assured families of rebels that their loved ones were "doing as well as could be expected under primitive conditions," and "assured his listeners that the revolution would be won." Addressing Batista, Castro said the "working people would be called upon to go on a general strike" that would "cripple the dictatorship beyond any reconstruction." Very soon, the *Tribune*'s Jules Dubois learned that Radio Rebelde "had the highest rating of any of Cuba's stations" and President-General Batista was "jamming its broadcasts, especially in Havana."[18]

Two days later, on February 26, the rebels demonstrated their capacity for disturbing the peace and grabbing headlines. They kidnapped a celebrity, an act which Dubois claimed "was one of their greatest psychological blows."

The victim was the world-champion Argentine racing driver Juan Manuel Fangio, who had been invited to race in Havana's Gran Premio II. Dubois wrote that Fangio was "politely snatched from the lobby of the Lincoln Hotel in downtown Havana."[19]

Brennan dug deeper to get an insider's story. In the hotel lobby Fangio was kidnapped moments after he left a group of admirers and headed alone to the cigar counter. A rebel named Oscar Lucero stopped him, showed him a revolver, and said quietly, "Do not worry, señor. You will not be harmed if you do as I say. I and my friends are from the 26th of July Movement. We are kidnapping you but only for propaganda purposes. You will be released after the race."[20]

Radio and television stations soon broadcast appeals to "return Fangio safely." Brennan noted that some reports speculated that Fangio "was being tortured, held for ransom, probably murdered." The kidnapping embarrassed President-General Batista, who was promoting the race, as well as his brother-in-law, General Roberto Fernandez Miranda, who had invited Fangio to Cuba. "The Malecón race without Fangio," Brennan wrote, "would be like a baseball world series without a star in the line-up." Fangio meanwhile listened to the race on radio, and afterward the rebels delivered him unharmed to the Argentine ambassador "with a letter of regret signed by Faustino Pérez," the Movement's chief in Havana. "To be kidnapped by those people," Fangio said, "was a fine, restful vacation." For two days the racing star had been pampered; he was given silk pajamas, fed well, including breakfast in bed, and indoctrinated about the revolution. "Your kidnapping may save other good Cubans from being tortured, as thousands of us have been," he was told by Ramón García, who showed the whip welts across his back. Castro had urged Faustino Pérez to do something spectacular and Pérez had come up with the idea while reading about Fangio in the newspaper. The kidnapper, Oscar Lucero, who already was Batista's most-wanted man, was soon after found dead, murdered after being tortured.[21]

The publicity accorded the kidnapping in Cuba and in U.S. media lent credibility to the rebels' threat of a general strike. While some thought the rebels were "fools, idiots and dolts to do such a thing," Brennan noted, "the Fangio abduction gave momentum to the revolution. Fidel sent his congratulations to Perez, Lucero, and others." Taking Fangio out of the race increased the worries of American mobsters, who already noted seriously diminished cash flow attributed directly to declining tourism.[22]

Brennan had taken a special interest in mobsters from Chicago and elsewhere who had invested big in Cuba. Their migration had begun in 1933, coinciding with Batista's rise to power in the military and in politics. That year, Batista made a multi-million-dollar deal with the American mob for a gambling monopoly.[23] By the 1950s Havana had become a lucrative and comfortable haven for a diverse group called the Havana Mob. By 1956, wrote a historian of the mob, "it was an exciting time for anyone associated with the Havana Mob. Over the next year three major hotel-casinos were scheduled to open. The city was seemingly alive with opportunities and activity."[24]

But early in 1958, the rebels' impact on tourism began to drive down the hotel and casino business. In March, a story circulated that "the Mafia had placed a $5 million price on Castro's head," according to Washington columnist Drew Pearson, who heard that Castro "has caused so much turmoil in the islands that the gambling business is practically dead and they want the revolution stopped. No tourists are gambling." On March 28, Pearson's friend Ted Scott of the *Havana Post* "went over to Miami and telephoned me [Pearson] collect. He says that all hell is going to break in Havana. Batista is not going to budge and is a tough fighter.... Batista has about 4,000 men tied up guarding the sugar crop. But it [the harvest] will be over in about two weeks and then he will have more troops at his disposal. Local investors are getting so jittery that they are trying to close up the Seville Biltmore Hotel.... Some of the people around him [Batista] are deserting." Pearson noted one very prominent deserter: "apparently my old friend Ed Chester." Edmund Chester, the former CBS executive who in December 1956 wrote Batista's press statement accusing Herbert Matthews of fabricating the interview with Castro, had tried to promote Batista as a benevolent leader, including arranging in 1954 for Batista's cordial interview with Pearson.[25]

Events in March drew Bigart back to the Cuban insurrection, but this time he went to Miami. There he found the Cuban exile community "bitterly disunited," although most exile groups in Miami were increasingly impressed with Castro. They "seem ready to obey an impending call for an island-wide general strike led by the 26th of July Movement." Many of Miami's exiles unhappily conceded that real revolutionary power resided with the combatants in Cuba, as Castro insisted. Yet, a key holdout was former president Carlos Prío Socarrás, who insisted on having a voice in any final solution. He told Bigart that his followers "would refuse to participate in any [general] strike ... unless they were given representation on a central strike committee. He implied that the strike would meet tragic failure unless prior agreement on strategy had been reached between himself and Señor Castro."[26]

All this seemed to doom Batista. Bigart saw "mounting evidence that the Cuban dictatorship of President Batista is on its last legs," even though the disunity among Batista's "foes" was significant. "Señor Castro seems to be convinced that he can win without Dr. Prio Socarras. Interviewed two weeks ago . . . he [Castro] told this correspondent: 'Prio represents the past; we are the future.'" However, Bigart recalled that a prominent Castro supporter had advised against alienating Prío Socarrás. Felipe Pazos "warned that Señor Castro might need all available help to conduct a successful strike."[27]

In mid-March, Herbert Matthews returned to Havana to check on the mood of the city amid the talk of a general strike. Matthews found no support from organized labor. The powerful labor leader Eusebio Mujal told him that the Cuban Workers Federation would remain loyal to Batista and oppose such a strike. "Mujal's unwillingness to support the strike probably doomed it to failure," wrote Matthews's biographer, "but Matthews did not report the labor leader's comments. Instead, he said the strike would cause chaos."[28]

At this time in Washington, the 26th of July Movement secured a major concession from Congress and the State Department. Castro's lobbyists and supporters had been pressuring Congress to end U.S. arms shipments to the dictatorship, a position also advocated in the *New York Times* by Matthews.[29] In response, Congress passed an embargo against arming the Batista regime. Representative Charles O. Porter, Democrat of Oregon, said that arming Cuba had been "identifying us with the vicious police state ruled by Batista." In response, the State Department—acting against advice from its ambassador to Cuba, Earl Smith—suspended all further arms shipments. That included even the 1,950 Garand rifles waiting for shipment on a New York dock and a paid order for twenty armored vehicles. The State Department diplomatic statement noted that "it would be entirely contrary to our policy to intervene in [Cuban] affairs and we do not intend to become involved." The *New York Times* noted that U.S. policy was to "sell arms to 'friendly' Latin-American countries that are signatories of the Rio de Janeiro treaty of reciprocal assistance provided that the arms are not used for aggressive purposes."[30]

In Cuba, the embargo was unwelcome news to political centrists and moderates who opposed Castro far more than Batista and sought a middle ground. Their numbers and influence had been shrinking, but they still hoped for a free and fair presidential election to choose Batista's successor. Presidential hopeful Carlos Marquéz Sterling worried that the arms embargo aided Castro in that it limited the range of political possibilities. As his son Manuel Marquéz Sterling later wrote, the centrists blamed two "influential and openly pro-Castro legislators"—Representative Adam Clayton Powell of New York and the Oregon senator Wayne Morse, both Democrats. "Rather than support a constitutional and legal solution . . . Washington behind its ambassador's back had strangely chosen to leap into the dark, hand in hand, with Castro and his movement."[31] Carlos Marquéz Sterling agreed with Ambassador Earl Smith's opinion that "Castro would be ten times worse than Batista."[32]

I n the first week of April 1958, the date for a general strike was still uncertain, but more American journalists were arriving in Cuba, taking Castro's threat seriously. Cubans had used the general strike once before to get rid of a dictator, President Gerardo "the butcher" Machado. That strike in 1933 had paralyzed Havana and other cities for days as railway workers struck, food was scarce, and deliveries of ice and milk stopped. Havana bars, cafés, shops, banks, and newspapers shut down. Urged to resign by President Franklin Roosevelt's new U.S. ambassador to Cuba, Sumner Welles, Machado fled, cushioned by money hidden abroad. In the chaos, his immediate successors were opposed by the army, in whose ranks Fulgencio Batista rose in short order from corporal to colonel and eventually general. Within months, Batista established military control over the island and by January 1934 achieved a counter-revolution, eventually becoming the "real center of power in Cuba" for the generation of Fidel Castro, born in 1927.[33]

Jules Dubois, moving fluently between the realms of Castro and Batista, kept trying to persuade the Batista regime to restore press freedom. As chairman of the IAPA Freedom of the Press Committee, Dubois threatened to publish the names of all Cuban editors and journalists who received hush money from the regime.[34] Through rewards, threats, and punishments, the regime aimed to make Castro's name "disappear." Censorship of even oblique suggestions of Castro seemed ridiculous to the visiting British novelist Norman Lewis, amused that "a newspaper advertisement for a watch was banned not long ago because the celebrity shown wearing it was a bearded explorer, and every Cuban knows that Castro has a beard."[35]

Guarding against the potential strike, President-General Batista invoked emergency powers. "He had the congress vote him powers which enabled him to act as total dictator of Cuba," Dubois wrote, "under what he considered a phase of legality." An amendment gave him authority to dismiss "unreliable" judges. He threatened potential strikers with a "decree-law which authorized the firing of any worker who absented himself" together with "the loss of all benefits, privileges and severance pay."[36] Despite censorship, Dubois reported the regime's secret crackdown of suspected insurgents in the military. He reported that on April 7 the regime conducted a closed trial of eight former army and navy officers. One of them had helped Batista's coup in 1952.[37]

Next, the Cuban Army moved against reporters who traveled to Santiago, where they rightly expected the strike to arouse greater public response. Acting under another emergency order, soldiers began arresting journalists, forcing some to fly back to Havana and jailing others. On April 7, in one swoop at Santiago's Hotel Casa Grande, soldiers apprehended six U.S. newsmen. Arrested and told to leave the city were Harold Lidin of United Press, the *Times*'s Homer Bigart (back in Cuba for the second time), and CBS's Robert Taber. The other three, taken to the army's notorious Moncada fortress, were the Las Vegas radio reporter Alan Jarlson, Ed Cannel of the Newspaper Enterprises Association, and the *Chicago Sun-Times*'s Ray Brennan. In a story for the *Times*, Bigart reported that Brennan, Taber, and Cannel were held "presumably on suspicion that they were attempting to join Señor Castro's guerrilla forces." Moncada was the ominous place where soldiers in 1953 had tortured and killed Castro's rebels, and where months earlier Andrew St. George feared he would be lashed with the whip he saw in an officer's hand. Through fortunate intervention, Brennan, Jarlson, and Cannel were released the next day, April 8, and ordered back to Havana.[38]

Brennan had been incarcerated in the Moncada fortress, guarded by soldiers with submachine guns, for twenty-one hours, and he knew it could have been much longer. Fortunately, St. George contacted the consulate, and the U.S. consul in Santiago, Park Wollam, intervened. "Otherwise," Brennan feared, "we might have vanished for days or weeks."[39] Brennan managed to find a telephone to send the *Sun-Times* his story about "that night of confinement and of censorship troubles the following day." He began by giving a macabre glimpse of his cell and the menacing guards. "We sat in a window-barred room while machine gunners, festooned with hand grenades like pineapples on trees, stood guard. A sullen sergeant provided comedy of a kind by glowering at us, making throat-cutting gestures and saying: 'Government does that to you.' It didn't seem funny at the time."[40]

At that point in the dictation, censors cut Brennan's phone connection. A Cuban telephone operator interrupted to say, "Due to superior orders the connection cannot be established again." Thirty minutes later, however, Brennan was reconnected and resumed dictating, but now more diplomatically, as his editor later noted to readers, "in a tongue-in-cheek manner, telling as best he could—without again running into censor trouble—about his night in jail." Now Brennan referred to prisoners as "guests," jailors as "hosts," the jail as "clean" and the food as "wonderful":

> When one of the guests wanted to rest briefly, there was an army cot.
> I can't describe to you how clean its mattress was. There was a washroom, too, a lovely washroom. Something like the ones in the Elevated Line stations in Chicago—delightfully clean.
> They served a wonderful breakfast. The bread was a delicious gray color. And the coffee was equally delightful.

In Brennan's doublespeak, the city of Santiago was "a wonderful place" where authorities "take care of the citizens very well. . . . They protect them every hour. There are machine guns on the roofs to make sure no harm comes to them. It's a very fine, well-run democratic community. . . . After we arrived in Santiago by plane, we were met by our hosts in the lobby of our hotel, the Casa Granda. Our hosts took care of us from that point on."

When the *Sun-Times* published this account, so there would be no misunderstanding on the streets of Chicago, his editor translated "tongue-in-cheek" into plain language: "With the newsmen in the jail were political prisoners of the government. The jail was filthy. There was one cot, and it was filthy. Moldy bread and bad coffee were served for breakfast. Brennan and his two companions . . . were harassed by Cuban police from the moment they arrived in Santiago." The "protection" extended the citizens by the government meant that a state of virtual martial law prevailed in heavily defended Santiago.[41]

In Havana the Batista regime "admonished" the American correspondents, as Dubois put it. Cuban prime minister Gonzalo Güell stated that the army arrested them because the government "feels responsible for the safety of Americans and does not want any American newspaperman to wind up on the end of a bullet."[42] Reporters were told they had wandered into "a military zone during a state of emergency without proper authorization." In Santiago, the regime told U.S. consul Park Wollam that a new military order barred newsmen from the "zone of operations"—now including all of Oriente Province. Ray Brennan noted that the order was issued only after "a number of reporters had slipped into the nearby mountains to interview Rebel followers of Fidel Castro and to watch set-tos between his guerrillas and army regulars."[43]

Two of those who had "slipped into" the Sierra were Sam Halper, representing *Time* and *Life*, and his guide and photographer, Andrew St. George. Soon after they came down from the mountain, news leaked about their expedition. St. George went into hiding in Santiago. Halper, alone in Havana, waited for his flight to New York, worried that he might be caught in possession of hundreds of photographs of the rebels. Censorship had been tightened. Foreign journalists risked detainment and jail, and their Cuban accomplices always feared torture. In the middle of the night, Halper thought he heard an intruder at the door to his hotel room, so he telephoned Jay Mallin, *Time*'s resident correspondent. Mallin had a reputation for helping other reporters as well as reporting atrocities; he earned praise from Dubois: "Religiously, almost every week Mallin had documented for *Time* the atrocities committed by Batista's police, often flying to Miami to file his copy from there."[44] Modestly, Mallin said he merely "provided visiting correspondents out to make names for themselves with contacts and info. Sam Halper was one of those." Mallin recalled of Halper, "As for his fears, coming down out of the mountains he phoned the U.S. consul in Santiago to please come and get him in Manzanillo. Bob Wiecha [assistant consul] did. Later, back at the Hotel Nacional [in Havana], he phoned me, terrified, at 3 in the morning and asked me to rush down to the hotel because he thought someone was trying to get into his room." Mallin knew he could be deported if he got tangled in Halper's adventure. "I refused, told him to call the desk."[45] Without incident, Halper got his flight to New York.

While reporters waited days for clues about the impending strike, Dubois was favored with confidential information from Castro's Movement leader in Havana. "We promised we would keep you informed," Faustino Pérez told him. Dubois had given Castro and his movement continuous attention since early 1957, while maintaining access with President-General Batista and with Carlos Prío Socarrás in Miami. On April 6, Easter Sunday, a Movement guide led Dubois to a doctor's office only a block and a half from Hotel Nacional. There he met with the head of the 26th of July strike committee in Havana, Faustino Pérez, and members of the "rebel underground high command." They showed him Castro's manifesto calling for the "revolutionary general strike." They told Dubois that Castro's manifesto called on all Cubans to rise in "total war" against Batista. Already the rebels had made preliminary attacks in the east: "Trains were derailed and burned and passengers had to complete their journeys on foot. Freight cars carrying sugar cane were derailed and burned."[46]

"How about your communications?" Dubois asked. "Are they all right this time? You had none for the strike on August 5." Dubois had written in August 1957 about the police shooting of the Movement's daring leader in Santiago, Frank País, and how that killing sparked spontaneous—but uncoordinated—uprisings in Santiago and other cities in the east, all of which were suppressed.[47]

"Our communications are all set," Dubois was told. "We will be in contact with all points and other cities. We can now tell you that the strike call will be issued soon, possibly within the next few days."[48]

Dubois bypassed Cuba's censors and got his scoop to the *Chicago Tribune*. "Castro's rebel movement issued a manifesto today . . . signed by Faustino Pérez, who is directing the movement from a hideout. . . . Pérez, who says he will give the order for the long-promised general strike, issued the manifesto which said that only Batista's resignation could avoid the strike."[49]

Dubois's story mentioned three rebel claims. First, the Movement declared the strike would have wide support. Castro's "forces of liberation" included "many capable business and professional men who are willing to serve in the provisional government." Second, Faustino Pérez "promised that Castro will not be in the provisional government." Third, the Movement spurned the support offered by Cuban Communists. Dubois wrote that Cuba's Communist leaders had requested a meeting with Castro's Movement and that "the rebels are reported to have refused an appeal to allow the Communists to sign the strike proclamation."[50]

Leaders of the Cuban Communist Party allegedly "tried to infiltrate into the general strike," Dubois reported. Castro, seeking to "counter the Communist maneuver" and deny opponents' allegations of Communist connections with the general strike, had written two paragraphs that Dubois quoted:

> One of the excuses put forth by totalitarian tyrannies when destroying elementary human rights is that their opponents are Communists. This form of deceit was used by Hitler and other European totalitarian regimes, and is still being used by hated dictators in this hemisphere in their efforts to win the support of public opinion in the United States. Deceit, plunder and terror have been the basic elements of tyrannical regimes everywhere.
>
> The present revolutionary movement to remove totalitarian tyranny and restore elementary human rights to the Cuban people is far from be-

ing Communist. All classes of our population including professional, religious and business organizations issued their courageous joint statement, requesting the resignation of the dictator.[51]

The threat of a looming shutdown worried practically everyone. What would the rebels do? What would the army do? Some journalists agreed with what Ted Scott at the *Havana Post* had told Drew Pearson, that "all hell is going to break in Havana." Particularly worried were Meyer Lansky and other U.S. mobsters with huge investments in the new casinos. The decline in tourists was a run of bad luck. The mob was said to be betting against Castro. "Ted [Scott] didn't know about the report I had heard that the Mafia had placed a $5 million price on Castro's head," Pearson noted. The turmoil was also disturbing the Catholic Church. Pearson learned that the governing papal nuncio had come from Rome and "met with the bishops in Havana last night (March 27, 1958), but could not decide what to do."[52]

Ray Brennan had gotten assigned to Cuba by arguing that the *Sun-Times* needed to start competing there with rival *Chicago Tribune*'s Dubois, who had scored repeated scoops about Castro's revolution. But Brennan knew there was an untold, sinister story involving the Havana Mob's investments in the new casinos and their connections to flush bank accounts of the mob's major enabler, President-General Batista.[53]

Brennan was a risk taker who in Chicago had been in precarious situations with mobsters. In Chicago journalism, he was among the breed of reporters remembered as being "hard-bitten, big-hearted, passionate writers who brought the stories of people to life." By his own choice, he was the *Sun-Times*'s organized crime reporter who probed the secrets in Chicago's underworld mobs and police force. Over time, Brennan gained a national reputation for writing about greed and treachery involving men with mob monikers. There was Daniel "Tubbo" Gilbert, an allegedly corrupt police captain; John "Jake the Barber" Factor; and Roger "the Terrible" Touhy—often called "the richest cop in the world." *Time* magazine's "Press" section recognized Brennan as "fast-thinking, fast-moving," as well as "hard-digging, tough and growling." He was earning a place in the hallowed Chicago Newspaper Hall of Fame.[54]

Brennan was fascinated with the mob's new frontier in Havana. With a combination of protection and payoffs to President-General Batista, the underworld bosses had been growing this gambling and gangster haven safe from the prying eyes of the U.S. federal and state prosecutors. Fresh in mob minds was the nightmarish hounding from the U.S. Senate's Special Judiciary Committee to Investigate Crime in Interstate Commerce. A few years earlier the committee had required testimony from the very mobster who now was the undisputed top man in the Havana Mob, its biggest dreamer and investor, Meyer Lansky. Lansky's "entire existence was based on creating the illusion that life was one big party, with champagne, music, and exquisite women all around. It was a vision shared by his most powerful partner—President Batista."[55]

Brennan had his own distinctive opinions of the leading characters in his Havana stories. President-General Batista seemed the major personality, dominating with his avarice and his army. He was the self-assured dictator with the Cheshire-cat smile, who "once promoted himself from army sergeant to colonel in one jump" and was "the most adept thief in the Western Hemisphere, but everybody present knew that." By contrast, Fidel Castro was "the swashbuckling leader, the mystical messiah, the twenty-four-hour-a-day zealot, the man who preached that life was a zero without democracy." Then, there were the American mobsters who fed Batista bribes for protection and cooperation and moved around Havana with the authority of government officials. They were busily building this new base of operations safely away from U.S. probity. Proud of their new hotels, nightclubs, and casinos—notably the Habana Riviera, the Capri, the Nacional, and the new Habana Hilton—Lansky and company were realizing a grand scheme to make Havana the Monte Carlo of the Caribbean. The action in Havana expanded Brennan's cast of shady characters. Now Havana had mob representatives from Buffalo, Kansas City, Pittsburgh, New Orleans, and five families in New York, notably Santo Trafficante Sr., Sam Tucker, Morris Kleinman, Moe Dalitz, and, representing Chicago interests, "Jimmy Blue Eyes" Alo. "Havana," Brennan asserted, "had more gangsters per square foot in government than the Chicago suburb of Cicero was infested with under the late Al Capone."[56]

At 11 a.m. on April 9, the 26th of July Movement leaders in Havana suddenly issued the order to launch the general strike. "According to the plan," Dubois wrote, "half of Havana was to go up in smoke, electric power lines and gas lines were to be damaged and there was to be a series of explosions and fires that would terrorize the populace, forcing everyone to remain away from work and stay indoors." Brennan thought the strike "seemed—deceptively at that time—to be fairly effective. Banks were closed, and so were a few stores. . . . Armed rebels had grabbed control of two radio stations. They had shouted over the air for all working people to walk off their jobs. . . . The most successful sabotage had been on the Prado, only a short distance from Sevilla Biltmore. Half a dozen rebel young men, riding in an ancient car, had stopped long enough to lift a manhole cover in the street and drop a bomb into the opening. A bright orange flame from smashed gas mains roared forty feet or more into the air. Gas, electricity, and water had been cut off by the explosion over an area of about thirty square blocks."

It seemed that the police and army were far more ready to act than the rebels. Police security "was so tight that word was not transmitted properly to cell leaders," Dubois learned. "Some cell leaders were not even notified, and heads of certain unions who were to issue orders for walkouts at eleven o'clock were not even given the order to strike until fifteen minutes before." Many, he said, were "confused" or "suspicious" that police, not Castro's Movement, had made a trick announcement. Dubois reported sporadic gun battles in Havana streets and the one gas main explosion downtown on the Prado. Meanwhile, President-General Batista was "lunching comfortably in his (other) residence at Camp Columbia, the only chief executive of Latin America who maintained a home in his principal military fortress."[57]

In the *Prensa Libre* newspaper office, Dubois heard "terrifying reports" over the police radio relating shoot-to-kill orders at 2 p.m. from Lieutenant Francisco Becquer, speaking for General Pilar Garcia, the new chief of the Havana police.

"No prisoners are to be reported. Only deaths."

"We have arrested a suspicious character," an officer advised. "He is unarmed. Shall we take him prisoner or kill him? Wounded or dead?"

"We don't want wounded or prisoners," came the answer.

"We have a man who says he is a lawyer," another officer stated. "He has a gun in the glove compartment of his car and a permit to carry it."

"Kill him!"

"But he says he's a friend of Santiago Rey!"

"We don't want double-talk. Kill him."[58]

The strike in Havana had "failed abysmally," Brennan concluded. "By 2 p.m., at the end of Havana's two-hour, hot-weather siesta, stores were open again and taxicabs were rolling. Bars were getting deliveries of big cakes of ice in order to continue business." Tourists trying to let families know they were unharmed found "it was all but impossible to make a call to the United States." In the confusion, Brennan wrote, "a few lucky reporters managed to get through to their offices and dictate stories with little annoyance of censorship." The strike had failed, he concluded, plainly because "many Havana civilians didn't have the courage, the toughness to go up against the power of Batista's gunmen." One taxi driver told him, "I was like thousands of others. I have a wife and kids.... I really planned to go through with the strike. I was going to park my cab sidewise across the street to help tie up traffic, set the brakes, grab the ignition keys, lock the doors, and run.... I kept looking at the other taxi drivers parked near me.... Each of us waited for the other to do something. Nobody did anything, and pretty soon it was too late."[59]

Although Havana was the main target, the rebels inspired action in areas where they caught police and army off guard. "The strikes were total in most interior cities," Dubois wrote, especially in Santiago. In Camagüey Province, rebels blocked traffic on the central highway. And in Sagua la Grande, 150 youths took over the city and "held it for several hours and then fled into the sugar cane fields, only to be bombed and strafed by aircraft and left for dead."[60]

Dubois blamed the failure on a "lack of unity among the insurrectional forces," especially the rebels' refusal "to accept the co-operation of Prío Socarrás's Organization Autentico." Dubois wrote that the failure in turn empowered Batista, who was "turning the tables on Fidel Castro in Havana. He had declared his own total war against the rebels." After April 9, Brennan wrote, many journalists' stories were "gloomy as to the Fidelistas' prospects. But the reporters reported as best they could from the meager and frequently untruthful ... sources. They didn't report the real facts—that much is certain."[61]

Meanwhile, Brennan's rival, Dubois, was looking at the bigger picture, paying close attention to other facets of the conflict. Traveling frequently between his home in Miami and Havana and Santiago de Cuba, Dubois still had access to Prío Socarras's exile group, the regime, and the 26th of July Movement. Better than any other U.S. reporter, he understood that Castro's strategy was beginning to drive middle-class Cubans to support him as the only viable alternative to the increasingly brutal dictator determined to hold on to power.

A ndrew St. George had become the most elusive foreign correspondent and now he was getting paid well, as he had hoped. In March, he had been very pleased to have the assignment as photographer and guide for Sam Halper, the *Time-Life* Latin American editor. Halper normally covered the region from his desk in the New York office, but pressure had been building for him to go to the Sierra Maestra. Until then *Life* and *Time* had depended on reports from their reliable resident correspondent in Havana, Jay Mallin, and on the few photographs of Castro offered them in 1957 by CBS's Robert Taber. But *Life*'s editors took a keener interest in Castro after *Look*'s exclusive photo essay in February in which St. George documented the rebels' strength and persistence into a second year. Amid talk about a general strike, the editors decided they needed a photo essay for April. They turned to Halper, and Halper turned to St. George.

St. George, with his proven access to Castro, had become a primary go-to person for U.S. correspondents, a relationship he enjoyed. So far, no journalist matched what he had delivered: a comprehensive picture of the rebels' life in the mountains, and Castro's own words describing his military and political aims. On meeting Halper, St. George realized the greatest challenge of this mission. He would be leading a desk-bound New York writer on an arduous journey by ponyback up and down "a precipitous trail in Cuba's eastern Sierra Maestra."[62]

Halper, however, relished the opportunity. He hoped this story would lead to his getting a foreign posting as *Time*'s correspondent in Latin America. So long as he remained at a desk in New York, he was at the bottom of a high editorial totem pole. "Every story in *Time* went through some seven hands," as Havana correspondent Mallin knew, including fact checkers, senior editors, department editors, and "at the top was the powerful managing editor. You can see why ambitious Halper wanted to get a foreign post."[63]

St. George was delighted to do for Henry Luce's wealthy organization what he had done for *Look* and *Coronet*. With his experience and aptitude for revolution, he had invested heavily in Castro and it had paid off. The impact of the stories and photographs in both *Time* and *Life* could be greater than that of the work he published in *Look* and *Coronet*. Founded in 1923, *Time* had become the nation's leading weekly news magazine. And *Life* now commanded a fifth of all revenues in magazine advertising, although *Look* was close behind in peak circulation.[64]

Even more important than circulation were the political implications. To the Batista regime the attention given to Fidel Castro by Henry Luce's politically conservative organization indicated a turning point in U.S. media coverage. Luce's editors evidently concluded that the 26th of July Movement now seriously challenged the dictatorship. Despite President-General Batista's branding Castro as a Communist, the rebel *comandante* appeared to have some legitimacy with one of America's most public anti-Communists.

Because of Luce's well-known control of editorial content, especially when communism was involved, one could assume that his editors acted in his interests. During World War II, when reports from China indicated that the Chinese Communists were gaining legitimacy, Luce responded by supporting the anti-Communist Nationalist general Chiang Kai-Shek, twice putting his picture on the cover of *Time*. As one historian of American foreign correspondents noted, "So much control did Luce exert over the contents of his magazines that his wartime correspondent in China, Theodore White, posted a sign on his office door in Chungking: 'Any similarity between this correspondent's dispatches and what appears in *Time* is purely coincidental.'"[65]

One week after the general strike, with Cuba freshly in the news, *Time* and *Life* scored hits with St. George's photo essay from the rebels' camps and Halper's interview with Castro. The interview in *Time* and the photographic display in *Life* were presented as stunning accomplishments. "These pictures provide the best look yet at Cuban rebel Fidel Castro in his hideout in the Sierra Maestra country of eastern Cuba." The interview—where Castro was described as talking "at length"—was presented more fully in *Time* and was abbreviated in *Life*'s picture magazine format to only 366 words accompanying six photographs of Castro.[66]

Writing in the first person in *Time*, Halper basked in the limelight of his achievement, as underscored in an editor's note: "By ponyback and down a precipitous trail . . . Sam Halper last week brought out a dispatch on Rebel Commander Fidel Castro's personality, plans and politics." One evening Halper had witnessed "an extraordinary scene: an old woman tending grandchildren, rebel troops milling around, guitarists strumming, and under a dim kerosene lamp, rocking in a chair, surrounded by kids seated on upturned 5-gal. cans, the bearded Rebel Castro. In the next days and nights, always on the move, I talked at length to Fidel Castro and got a thorough look at his ragtag, fanatic force." Halper did not give a count of Castro's army, but he stated that only 10 percent had modern weapons, captured from the Cuban Army, and the rest had light rifles, shotguns, and revolvers. He noticed four women in camp and said they helped run messages, kept records, guarded the camp, and prepared meals—usually rice or boiled starchy roots, dried codfish or bananas, and sometimes boa constrictor or raccoon. Like Homer Bigart, Halper was unimpressed with Castro's rebels: "Nothing about the appearance of Fidel's force would lead me to think it could fight."[67]

One of Halper's tasks was to confirm what Castro told St. George in the stories published in *Look* and *Coronet*. Castro repeated everything, with new emphasis on the elevated importance of rebels since St. George visited in the fall. Now, Castro stressed that his revolution was the only legitimate force against the dictatorship, thus dismissing any legitimacy for Batista's proposed national election. "We have assumed the responsibility of throwing out Batista's dictatorship," he said, "and re-establishing the constitutional rights and freedoms of the people. Our first fight is for political rights—and after that for social rights."[68] Halper noted that at the University of Havana Castro had "hotheadedly espoused a series of student-radical notions" including "nationalization of Cuba's U.S.-owned power and telephone companies."

"I am still the same revolutionary," Castro declared, "but I have had time to study the political and economic factors. I understand that some ideas I used to have would not be good for Cuba. I do not believe in nationalization."

Halper added that Castro "now advocates amplified social security, along with speeded up industrialization, to fight Cuba's chronic joblessness."

What of Batista's claim that Castro was pro-Soviet and pro-Communist? Evidently Halper did not put that question directly to Castro, perhaps trusting that he would get a more accurate response from Castro's "friends." He stated that "friends of Castro point to the character of his army. "Almost to a man, they are Roman Catholics, who wear religious medals on their caps and on strings around their necks," Halper wrote. "For the sake of getting on with the war, Castro says, he avoids fruitless political discussions with his one outwardly pro-Red captain." Halper did not name the captain.[69]

How was it possible that this "disorganized, barebones partisan army... has not been subdued by Batista's 29,000 men?"

Castro reasoned that the government's "soldiers are not convinced of the justice of their work.... If they had been fighting for an ideal, they could have beaten us 30 times. But no man is supposed to die for $35 a month."[70]

What of Castro's ambitions after victory? "If he wins, Castro says, he proposes freer labor unions, a crackdown on corruption, and punishment for government 'criminals'—including bringing Batista to book." Halper concluded that such plans "imply a great deal of control over Cuba's future by Fidel Castro." Yet, Halper wrote, Castro "denies all presidential (or dictatorial) ambitions."

"I can do more for my country giving an example of disinterestedness," Castro stated. "After we win, I am going to live in the Sierra Maestra, building roads and hospitals which we have promised." Castro "insisted that the provisional president should be Judge Manuel Urrutia. 'Our movement has the right to appoint the Provisional President.'"

Halper's editors at *Life* doubted that Castro would give up power. "This was at variance with the impression an earlier Castro pronouncement had made on some of his Cuban backers, who had begun to fear him as another dictator." Given Castro's growing strength, it seemed that he wanted to "step into Batista's shoes."[71]

The interview had been conducted before the threatened general strike, so Halper asked Castro to speculate on the consequences of success—or failure. "Batista could be out within 20 days. But if Batista crushes the strike, the revolution will not be lost. Then we will see what happens in six months. If Batista loses, he loses for good; if I lose, I will just start again."[72]

CHAPTER 9

HOW CAN WE PROVE
WE ARE NOT SOMETHING?

By Homer Bigart's calculations, the failure of the general strike signified the defeat of Castro's only viable strategy, economic warfare. In the Sierra Maestra, Castro had told him, "To see our victory, you must have faith." Now Bigart wrote that "apparently there was more faith than realism." Based on his unnamed "informed sources," the journalist concluded that "the days of Fidel Castro are numbered."

Others were not willing to write the revolution's obituary, although they recognized the sudden change in momentum. "For a week or so after April 9, Batista seemed to be genuinely confident that the revolution was dead," Ray Brennan wrote. "He boasted that his government had won a great moral and military victory.... He predicted to friends that Raúl and Fidel Castro... would flee to the United States or Mexico."[1]

Jules Dubois agreed that these were dark days for Castro's 26th of July Movement and for his allies in Havana with the Civic Resistance Movement (CRM). "The terror of Batista's police struck everywhere," Dubois wrote. He described the torture of a CRM member, a University of Havana medical student, Omar Fernandez. He was "beaten into unconsciousness in the police station and was then taken, almost dead, to the police hospital." In the hospital room, the chief of police and an army colonel, trying to make Fernandez reveal the names of other student leaders in hiding, "yanked off the oxygen mask which the doctor had placed over his face to keep him alive. The doctor arrived just in time to restore it over... [their] threats."[2] Five days after the strike, Dubois was led to an interview with Castro's strike leader, Faustino Pérez, "the most hunted man in Havana.... Here was a rebel movement that had just suffered its worst military and psychological defeat since the civil war began and Pérez, who was thoroughly saturated with the thinking and confidence of Fidel Castro in the face of adversity, was voicing certainty that the battle was going to be won."[3]

The Movement leaders were soon communicating Castro's confident outlook. Faustino Pérez issued a statement that was also read over the rebels' shortwave Radio Rebelde: "The events of Wednesday in Havana once more pointed up the appetite for blood of the dictatorship, its disdain of the truth, and its mockery of public opinion. . . . The dictatorship is disintegrating. It depends entirely on a gang of assassins who carry out the jungle law—not attending to the wounded, refusing to take prisoners, only showing corpses. Innumerable people have been tortured and even young people have been taken from the jails and killed after having been terribly tortured. . . . Our armies in the provinces have been reinforced with the loyal elements of the armed forces of the nation. . . . Others in the cities have joined the underground movement . . . The fight continues firmer and fiercer than ever."[4]

Castro announced that those who died during and after the strike were to be honored as martyrs. "The debacle of April 9 was turned into a triumph of propaganda by the Fidelistas," Brennan wrote. "Fidel had turned ignominious defeat to his advantage many times—starting with Fort Moncada on July 26, 1953—and now he was doing it again."[5]

That the "fight" was continuing could be seen and heard. Some actions were evident when citizens in Havana or Santiago heard a bomb blast. Others were carefully concealed. On April 1, before the general strike, Fidel Castro sent his brother Raúl with eighty men to open a "Frank País second front" in honor of Santiago's courageous 26th of July organizer who had been killed by police in 1957. The second front would operate in northeastern Oriente Province in the mountain ranges of the Sierra del Cristal and Sierra de Puriales. Its mission was to harass transportation along the Central Highway and disrupt communications. To distract the army from detecting the men on that "long and arduous march," the Movement's militia in Santiago attacked the army garrison there.[6]

President-General Batista was now planning to go on the attack. Because Batista "read and listened to the Rebel propaganda," Brennan surmised, "he became convinced that he was holding the short end of the stick in the war. He resolved to mount a full-scale invasion" that would end the revolt for all time, so he could "go back to running the country that he had stolen for his own." In the mountains, Brennan stated, "Fidel sat back and waited patiently, like a man who had built a series of the world's best mousetraps."[7] Brennan was among the coterie of American correspondents—especially Jules Dubois, Robert Taber, and Andrew St. George—eager to see the fighting up close.

In May the army began a massive troop movement. Against Castro's few hundred experienced fighters in the southeastern mountains, Batista committed twelve thousand men from his total army of twenty-nine thousand "to a spare-nothing effort to put an end to Fidel Castro and his bearded, payless bravados," wrote Brennan, who witnessed the showdown. "By train, airplane, truck, and bus, the Batista Army poured into Oriente Province." They came with U.S. Sherman tanks out of Fort Moncada, automatic weapons, mortars, bazookas.

The Cuban Air Force attacked the swath of mountain forests. In 1957, before the first bombing raids, the regime had dropped leaflets warning settlers to vacate their huts. This time the regime assumed that the mountain people were supporting Castro. The planes fired rockets supplied by the United States and napalm bombs provided by the Dominican Republic's dictator, Rafael Trujillo.[8] "Clusters of bombs came slicing down on the miserable shacks of the dirt-poor *guajiros*. The strategy was to annihilate the farmers or to terrorize them out of giving information to the Rebels on army troop movements. The psychology failed, utterly. Fires from the napalm bombs burned all night long in the mountains, and still the peasants remained loyal to Fidel."[9]

The bombing was not effective against the rebels, Taber discovered. "For the most part, the aircraft did little damage... because of the steepness and height of the mountains which kept the army planes from flying too low, and the thickness of the jungle growth which provided protection and absorbed the force and shrapnel of the bomb explosions."[10] Brennan found that the tons of bombs killed one rebel soldier, but "the death toll ran into the hundreds for helpless civilians."[11]

And the army was unprepared and too often surprised. After April 9, President-General Batista wanted a quick victory. The commanders had been hastily ordered to attack without adequate troop training or reconnaissance. "Before the ground troops reached the combat area," Brennan wrote, "the invaders of *Cuba Libre* learned that they were up against a dangerous, ingenious foe." The rebels had blown up railroad and highway bridges. "Snipers peppered at them from the hills. Molotov cocktails, some them thrown by *guajiros*, smashed against their vehicles." Higher up, soldiers and their vehicles struggled in the rugged and damp wilderness that had been described by Matthews, Taber, and St. George in their climbs to find Castro. They had discovered a wild world of sheer cliffs, deep gorges, rushing streams, thick forest, and jagged rocks, home to various snakes and nasty insects. "The army soldiers were physically flabby, poorly trained," Brennan noted. "Most of them never had even been on maneuvers in mountain country. Two hours of marching left them exhausted, and when they sat down to rest Rebels fired on them." Quite the opposite, Castro's men had become experienced with fighting from the high ground, from behind trees, or from earth-covered camouflaged bunkers. The army simply did not yet understand that "the Rebel tactics were to bleed, starve, harass, exhaust, and terrorize the enemy."[12]

The army had lied to its troops. "They had been told by their officers that their opponents would have no weapons more dangerous than shotguns and squirrel rifles," Brennan learned from captives. "Many of the soldiers were demoralized, therefore, when they came up against automatic weapons and mortar fire. Furthermore, the marksmanship of the freedom fighters was ter-rifyingly accurate. Desertions from the Batista ranks began."[13]

As troops moved upward, they ran into more obstacles unanticipated by army general Francisco Tabernilla and his commanders. They made "a griev-ous mistake," Brennan noted, by bringing bazookas, "for which there were no targets in the Sierra. The Fidelistas captured the rocket-firing weapons and used them to cripple or destroy army tanks." In areas where Sherman tanks could advance, Castro's men had dug traps. Some tanks "toppled nose-first into pits dug in the road. The Rebels thoughtfully had saturated the ground around the traps with gasoline." Incendiary bullets ignited the gasoline. "Out of the tank would tumble the crew members, fearful of being roasted to death."[14]

During May and June, the rebels fought a hit-and-run war, stocking their arsenal with seized weapons. "They concentrated on capturing guns and am-munition. Every time the revolutionaries caught an armed Batista soldier, Fidel had the weapons to put another combat man into the field."[15]

Meanwhile, Raúl Castro's second-front fighters "went boldly into Guan-tánamo City, Santiago, and Bayamo to bomb and shoot." That tactic forced the army "to leave hundreds of soldiers in the cities to help the police keep order."[16]

B y summer, Castro shifted from defense to offense. In July, during the thick of the fighting, the *New York Times* had no reporter in the Sierra. Nonetheless, Homer Bigart was able to produce a lengthy story for the July 10 paper. He based the story completely on information from an adven-turesome twenty-eight-year-old television executive just returned to New York from the Sierra Maestra. Morton "Mort" Silverstein had some credibil-ity as the producer for ABC's increasingly popular network celebrity show, "The Mike Wallace Interview." Also, a week earlier, when Silverstein was still in rebel territory he had sent the *Times* another timely story, transmitted by radio. The *Times* published his story on July 3 after Silverstein's wife, back in New York, vouched for its authenticity. She explained that they had been vacationing in Cuba when Mort "decided to go visit the rebel forces" and she flew home.[17]

Within days, Mort Silverstein was in the *Times* newsroom. He handed Bigart a "crude" battle map that Castro had drawn and authenticated with an autograph to Silverstein. With the map as an aid, Bigart composed a nineteen-paragraph story, reconstructing a battle that Bigart estimated was "the most crucial of the twenty-month campaign" since Castro's invasion in December 1956.

This was clearly a scoop. Amid the sporadic and spontaneous guerrilla warfare, no one had yet reported this close encounter. "Cuban government forces," Bigart wrote, "penetrated within a half day's march of Fidel Castro's base in the Sierra Maestra last week, but were halted with heavy casualties, according to Morton Silverstein, a New York television producer. Mr. Silverstein returned Tuesday from the Castro camp in eastern Cuba. The fight started June 28 when the rebels started a counter-offensive against two Cuban Army battalions that had reached the village of Las Vegas and Santo Domingo and were within about seven miles of the rebel base."[18]

Relying on Castro's drawn lines on the map, Bigart described how the rebels enveloped the army's left flank: "As usual," he wrote, touting his knowledge of Castro's "usual" tactics, "the rebels marched along the forested crests of the steep ridges." Bigart emphasized a quote that Silverstein got from Castro, who said his troops "had 'routed' what he identified as the Twenty-second Battalion of President Fulgencio Batista's army. The battalion abandoned large quantities of arms including mortars, light machine-guns and automatic rifles."[19]

The rebels found even more treasure. According to Silverstein, Fidel was "elated over the capture of Army papers" found on the body of a Cuban Army captain, one of thirty-six soldiers killed. The papers showed a "table of organization of the Government column" and "the strength of each Army unit in the area," as well as "the Army Commands code numbers for the zones into which it divided the Sierra for operations."

Silverstein also related what he learned from talking with some of the twenty-eight army prisoners. Bigart wrote that some "joined the army because they had no work. They said that they had been assured by army officials that, although they would be stationed in Oriente Province, they would

not have to go into the mountains." Castro was quoted as saying the government troops were mostly ill-trained teenagers.[20] The hand-drawn battle map,
inscribed to "Morton" and signed "Fidel Castro on Julio 4, 58" was published
as an artifact to substantiate Silverstein's information. An elaborate caption
explained the drawn battle lines: "The horizontal parallel lines in the center
represent a road, and the wavy verticals and diagonals indicate the ridges.
In the road are three black dots, and above the center dot is a fourth—they
show the position of the Government battalions. The single dot shows that
the Government troops got within seven miles of Castro's base, the scrawled
area in the upper center. The chevron-like symbols depict rebel units and
the directions in which they moved along ridges as they sought to isolate the
government forces."[21]

One week earlier, while Silverstein was still in the Sierra Maestra, he had
sent the *Times* an exclusive report on another kidnapping by the rebels—this
time of U.S. servicemen. On June 28, Raúl Castro's men in the Frank País second front ambushed a bus and took as hostages forty-eight U.S. sailors and
marines returning from leave to the Guantánamo Bay Naval Base. Jules Dubois hurried to the naval base, as did some twenty other U.S. correspondents.

In Fidel's camp, Silverstein heard the news on Havana radio and relayed
Fidel's statement about it to the *Times* via a shortwave radio broadcast that
was picked up in Florida by a fifteen-year-old ham-radio operator in Panama
City, Bart Fay, who relayed it to Silverstein's wife, who alerted the *Times*.

On July 3, the *Times* printed Fidel's order to Raúl to release the hostages
immediately and Fidel's claim that the U.S. military recently had shipped
rockets to Batista in violation of the March 12 U.S. arms embargo. According
to Silverstein, Castro stated that he "will give an immediate order that these
Americans be granted their liberty, if it is true that they are in the hands of
rebel troops." Fidel said he did not know what was happening in Raúl's second front, but thought Raúl might be acting to protest a violation of the arms
embargo. "If the news of the arrest is true... it is possible that it has been due
to the reaction to the recent gift of 300 rockets from the American naval base
at Guantánamo, given to Batista's airplanes with which the civilian population of this territory, occupied by our rebels, has been bombed in the last few
weeks."[22] Castro's accusation was accurate. As Dubois learned, proof of the
shipment of rockets was sent to Cuba by a 26th of July "secret agent" in Batista's embassy in Washington. "Photostats of the requisition had been flown
into the Sierra Maestra to Castro from Washington via Florida and were distributed to the rebel underground everywhere."[23]

The hostage situation was an awkward distraction for President Eisenhower's State Department and the U.S. Embassy in Havana. A State Department spokesman, Lincoln White, issued the official explanation. Technically, it was true that three hundred rocket warheads had been shipped on May 19, two months after the embargo. However, those warheads were not a *new* order, only an *exchange* "for a similar number of warheads" delivered *before* the embargo that were faulty because they had "inert" nonexplosive warheads. The recent shipment of explosive warheads was thus "merely a rectification of a mistake." The rebels rejected the explanation, stating that "mistake or no mistake, their people would be just as dead or maimed by those rockets with their newly acquired live heads," Dubois wrote. "Neither Fidel Castro nor many other Cubans, except Batista and his minority of supporters, could reconcile the March embargo on arms shipments with the replacement of the inert rocket heads."[24]

Meanwhile, the 26th of July Movement scored headlines in the U.S. press for days. Although Castro had radioed Raúl to release all hostages, Raúl stalled, awaiting, he explained, Fidel's *written* order. He then released only a few at a time, meanwhile negotiating with the very busy U.S. consul from Santiago, Park Wollam. "Most Americans considered the kidnappings abominable," Dubois wrote. "But for the Cubans they were a means of forcing the United States, at long last, to give some recognition to the existence of a civil war: consuls had to parley with Raúl Castro and his officers."[25]

For his exclusive stories, Dubois left the pack of journalists in Guantánamo and traveled by jeep into the mountains to interview Raúl Castro. In the rugged terrain, the jeep crashed and Dubois was injured. Nonetheless, after thirteen hours he arrived in Raúl's camp and got the interview. While Dubois was recuperating in a rebel base hospital, Raúl visited him, accompanied by his constant female companion and translator, "Deborah." She was actually Vilma Espin, daughter of the attorney for the Bacardi Company in Santiago, and she was also hunted by the police.[26]

Dubois had a long list of questions. Why had Raúl ignored Fidel's order to release the servicemen immediately? "I told Fidel not to send me any serious orders by radio, but to transmit them in writing," Raúl said. Across the terrain and during the fighting, it had taken twenty-five days for the courier to reach Raúl.

Dubois raised the Communist question. "I asked Raúl about his trip to Vienna to attend a Communist Youth Congress and his subsequent journey behind the Iron Curtain when he was a student at the University of Havana."

"The Communists," Raúl said, "approached me for a contribution so they could send a delegate to the World Youth Congress at Vienna in 1953. I wanted to travel and thought this an excellent opportunity. I offered to pay my entire fare if they would let me go and they agreed. So I went. At the Congress I had an argument with a Rumanian delegate on the floor, which led the head of that delegation to invite me to visit his country. I also visited Budapest, Hungary, on that tour. I would travel to China if I had the chance because I enjoy it and I want to see the world, but that doesn't mean I am a Communist." That night, Dubois wrote, "Raúl slept in the bed opposite me in the hospital." The next day, Dubois submitted a longer list of questions. Raúl soon "answered in longhand; he had both questions and answers typed for delivery to me."[27]

Why did Raúl's men kidnap the servicemen? Raúl answered that he wanted to attract U.S. and world attention "to the crime that was being committed against our people with the arms" that the United States supplied for defense of the hemisphere, not for killing Batista's own people. Also, he needed the servicemen as human shields "to deter the criminal bombardments—with incendiary bombs, rockets and even napalm bombs—which in those moments were being carried out against our forces above all against the defenseless towns of the *campesinos* without taking into account at all the fact that they were not military objectives."

Dubois had asked another Communist question. "Certain elements, including President Batista, say you are a Communist. Why does this accusation prevail?"

Instead of denying the accusation, Raúl repeated previous attacks on Batista's credibility. "That Batista accuses me of being a Communist is not strange, for it is just the way every Latin-American dictator tries to label his political adversaries. If I were a Communist, I would belong to that party and not to the 26th of July. Therefore, I don't care about Batista's opinion of me. What does surprise me is the attention that is given to this matter when everyone knows he doesn't do anything but repeat stupid accusations like a parrot. I feel that every time he says that, he is pulling the leg of his interviewers with the same childish tale."

Dubois then prodded him with a third Communist question: "Do you consider communism as nefarious and as dangerous as the so-called dictatorships of the extreme right?" Raúl replied, "I consider nefarious every government imposed by force be it of the right or the left."

Q. What is your political philosophy?

A. I don't like to consider these questions from a personal point of view because I consider myself only another soldier of our cause. But mine, like those of all the members of the 26th of July, are the doctrines of Martí. We consider ourselves followers of his unfinished work. If we cannot conclude it we will nevertheless have fulfilled our historic role, sustaining until the end the standard of his ideological principles.

Q. What do you forecast for the future of Cuba?

A. With a people like ours, who in these tragic and terrible moments have given such a great example of civic virtue, bravery and the spirit of sacrifice, it is easy to forecast a future of real hope for the conquest of their lost freedoms, the conquest of their full sovereignty and a flourishing economy which would bring everything together. Finally, referring to our relations with the United States of North America, we sincerely believe that in "our America"—as Martí called it—it would be more convenient for them to have friends of the heart in an equality of conditions than false friends obligated by circumstances.[28]

On July 17, Raúl released the last sailors and marines. One day later, Dubois, still hurting from the jeep wreck and hardly able to walk, was airlifted from the rebel base aboard a navy helicopter. "Because of my accident and the rebel doctor's refusal to let me attempt returning to the naval base by road, [Raúl] Castro requested [Consul Park] Wollam and Admiral [Robert B.] Ellis to evacuate me by helicopter."[29]

As Dubois was flown out of the mountains, a U.S. news executive from Philadelphia was making his way up to Raúl Castro's camp. Charles Shaw, at forty-seven, was an award-winning radio and television news director at the CBS affiliate in Philadelphia, WCAU. Twice, his news department had been honored for "distinguished achievement" by the Radio-Television News Directors Association. And he had been personally honored by the Society of Professional Journalists and by the Freedoms Foundation. Now he had a serious compulsion to take a break from his desk job, especially since the hostage-taking incident had become an ongoing story. He wanted to see the revolution firsthand.[30]

Shaw had plenty of wartime experience. In his twenties, he was working in radio in San Antonio when Edward R. Murrow came for a visit and hired him for his new CBS radio team. Murrow was developing network radio's first serious newsgathering staff, breaking with the practice of having announcers who read the news from newspapers and news agencies. During World War II, Shaw rose in prominence by going to Europe as a reporter for Murrow's famous team of correspondents that broadcast from European capitals during Adolf Hitler's rise and the world war. Shaw was a junior member of "Murrow's Boys," a group that included Richard C. Hottelet, Larry LeSueur, Eric Sevareid, and William Shirer. They reported at various stages from capitals in Germany, Italy, France, Norway, Sweden, and Greece, while Murrow broadcast from London.

The lure of the fighting in Cuba awakened something of that past in Charles Shaw. In July of 1958, before slipping away to Cuba, Shaw broadcast his opinion that the revolution could restore Cuba's democracy. As news director of the Philadelphia station, he bypassed peer review in airing his editorial: "It would now seem that the hopes for democracy in Cuba rest with the rebels in the Sierra Maestra of eastern Cuba led by the 31-year-old lawyer-patriot, Fidel Castro."[31]

In the same broadcast, he cautioned Castro against further political missteps that could cost him U.S. support. The kidnapping of the sailors and marines offended many who, Shaw said, "had been in sympathy with the rebellion against the police state regime. . . . Those of us who wish Castro well must advise him and his friends not to repeat such acts, no matter how provoked they may be at United States government aid to Batista, no matter how such deeds may call attention to their revolution and help spread the story of their fight." After all, the "Castro movement" was preferable to "tyranny as represented by Batista."[32]

When Shaw left for Cuba, his substitute anchor, George Lord, gave out a cover story, telling his audience that Shaw was "away on vacation." When Shaw returned, after a week and a half, he broadcast a series of reports on radio from July 2 through July 31. He apologized to listeners for "misleading you. . . . Had I reported my plans in advance, I would have been unable to cover this story, because the Cuban government would not have let me go where I went, or, worse yet, they might have let me make my rounds so that I could lead them to members of Castro's underground. And the record is clear as to what would have happened to anybody thus exposed."[33]

In Cuba, Shaw was determined to find the truth, including the answer to the lingering Communist question. He decided to question "every important rebel leader I met in Cuba." The 26th of July Movement arranged contacts first in Havana with religious leaders. His conversation with "the wife of a Protestant churchman" gave him "evidence of considerable Castro support among the 250 thousand Protestants of Cuba." Next he was conducted to the Catholic cathedral, where an "eminent cleric" responded to the Communist question with his own question: "My friend, do you think that I, in my position, would support a movement about which there was the slightest suspicion of communism?"[34]

While in Havana, Shaw mingled with American journalists, none of whom he identified. But he wrote that several told him they distrusted Castro. Some even lectured this newcomer headed to the mountains. "Don't believe any of this guff these rebels hand you, if you happen to get to them." They told him to beware of the brothers: "Fidel Castro and his brother, Raoul [sic], are a couple of bums. They've been agitators all their lives.... Raoul [if not Fidel] probably is a Communist." They "don't have any real support" and "they don't have a chance." On the other hand, "Batista's no good ... everybody knows that, but a couple of bums like the Castro Brothers aren't going to oust him. If he is ousted, it will be by somebody like him because.... You have to know these people; these Latins are all alike ... they're used to corruption ... they have the morals of alley cats."[35]

Shaw disregarded the journalists' comments as uninformed. They "don't have much more appreciation of the political and military situation than the average tourist," he wrote. "On one hand, they were censored in the city and, on the other hand, they did not go to the war zone." Furthermore, they were "operating under a censorship tighter than any under which I worked in an actual Theatre of Operations during war-time.... They are permitted to transmit much less information than I was permitted to transmit from London before D-Day and the front lines of Western Europe after that."[36]

Their pretense to knowledge without going to the Sierra Maestra offended him. "Much to my anguished disappointment there are some old-time American newspaper correspondents—the kind whose breed is fast dying out, thank Heaven ... the kind who think you can cover a country from its luxury hotels and its government offices.... Reporters like these, having given up the habit of covering stories for themselves, because, perhaps, its [sic] too uncomfortable, maybe even a little risky in Oriente, will lecture a visiting reporter most patronizingly."[37]

Shaw suspected that American correspondents living in Havana regularly self-censored their stories to avoid being deported. He seemed unaware that some Americans were dodging the Cuban censors. Jay Mallin regularly smuggled stories to *Time*'s Sam Halper in New York. And Ted Scott of the *Havana Post* bypassed the censors by flying to Miami to divulge insider information to columnist Drew Pearson and others.[38]

To Shaw, the silence of the press was a moral failing, the more so because of the brutality of the Batista dictatorship. Instead of reporting on the hot war and bloodshed close by in Cuba, the U.S. media focused on the Cold War being waged in the distant Middle East—"six times farther from Philadelphia than Cuba," although "it is safe to say that more lives have been lost in Cuba during the past year than in Iraq, Lebanon, and Cyprus combined."[39]

One of Shaw's main contributions was his Cuban travelogue. While almost all reporters flew to Santiago, he took the bus. Amid the heightened tensions, his 26th of July fixers advised he could avoid arrest by riding overland for more than five hundred miles from Havana to Santiago. On board, among fifty passengers, he was the only American, the only one who spoke English. In the manner of a travel writer, he explained that the thirteen-hour trip was in "a most comfortable carriage of the same type as our Greyhound busses, air-conditioned and with soft reclining seats." The bus followed the Central Highway, and Shaw noted the towns listed on a road map issued by a gasoline company. As they got closer and closer to Oriente Province, army patrols stopped the bus four times and searched passengers' luggage and wallets. This was the declared Zone of Hostilities, where, he noted, "suspected rebel sympathizers disappear, and their brutalized bodies are found days later. National Police and soldiers have the authority to shoot on sight. Criminal assaults on women are blamed on hoodlums." At one point, the police saw him filming and demanded the film, but they returned it when he gave a donation to "what I euphemistically called the Police Pension Fund."[40] At Holguin, the bus turned south off the Central Highway, giving Shaw his first glimpse of the silhouette of the Sierra Maestra and, miles later, a closer view when "some of the peaks were bare rocks, others were verdant." The mountains roused his imagination. "Somewhere in that vastness, I thought, was Fidel Castro, disciple of the poet-philosopher José Martí, apostle of the 1895 revolution, who was killed in a skirmish in Oriente just as his revolution was on the verge of success. Castro might be reading from Martí...more likely he was deploying his rebel troops against a government offensive."[41]

Arriving in Santiago, Shaw directed the taxi driver to a private home where he asked for Yolanda, who soon arrived. "You have the letter?" Yolanda asked. Shaw retrieved the letter from "its hiding place."

After lunch, a Movement fixer arrived with news that required a change of plan. Fidel was in the midst of a battle and a meeting was now unlikely. Shaw planned to stay only three days with the rebels, but during ongoing fighting it would take several days to get to Fidel. Instead, he accepted an alternative plan to go the next day to meet Raúl, whose second front was nearer Santiago. "Since I was beginning to conclude," Shaw wrote, "that the revolution story was as much a story of the underground—the cross-section of Cuban decency which worked for freedom in the cities and towns—as it was a story of men in the mountains, we agreed that I would visit Raoul and his men, while an explorer who had to make the trip anyway, went to Fidel's headquarters; and if time permitted, I would go back with him."[42]

That evening, Shaw checked into Santiago's Casa Grande Hotel, where, before the general strike in April, the army had rounded up six U.S. correspondents, including Bigart, Taber, and Brennan. Playing the vacationer with a group of men on the balcony veranda, Shaw started asking touristy questions about Teddy Roosevelt's historic San Juan Hill nearby and "other landmarks of the Spanish-American War." A man who spoke English changed the subject to the current revolution. "You see that bank building across the Square. Just last Saturday...two boys threw a grenade into an Army car. The grenade was a dud. The soldiers jumped out and killed those boys right there. They were only 14 or 15 years old. An American businessman ran over there, and, crying, he cursed those soldiers as murderers and butchers. It's a good thing those soldiers didn't understand English." Another English speaker added, "Almost every day, something like that. Look around...do you see any young men? No...they're all in the hills, or their parents keep them home. Just to be young in this province is suspect." Another referred to the revolution as "the trouble": "Observe the Square: it is almost empty. Before the trouble it would be filled at this time of night, especially in July, for this is the month of the Carnival. But no Carnival these days. Almost every family is in mourning. Maybe six thousand young men have been murdered...murdered, not just killed in battle." A fourth man spoke, "But the more Batista kills, the more friends Castro has. It's like—how you say?—he sows the teeth of dragons." As they spoke, Shaw saw two army patrol cars screech by the Casa Grande, and a fifth man in the group predicted, "More boys will die tonight."[43]

The next day, Shaw continued his pretense as a tourist going sightseeing and picnicking, accompanied by two women and a man who drove him off in a jeep. Thus began his hero's journey into the mountains, a trek he shared with his listeners from the beginning—with the change of clothes "from my suit and shirt with necktie into a pair of light slacks, pull-over sports shirt and heavy-soled shoes." He was amused to be posing as "Mr. Charlie," the younger woman's husband. "Here was I with a girl young enough to be my daughter, a girl who spoke no English, who, in case we were stopped by Batista's soldiers, was supposed to be my wife." In two and a half hours, the jeep traveled first on the highway, then on cuts through sugar plantations and dirt roads that went from smooth to rutty, to lanes through "jungle-like growth," into rebel territory. "We saw the branches of a bush quiver and a uniformed young man step into the middle of the road. He was the first rebel soldier I was to see, and Hollywood could not have a better job of casting. A field cap sat jauntily on long, wavy coal-black hair, which lapped over the collar of his blue-green uniform. His bronze face seemed to be sculptured . . . a good-sized nose, a strong jutting chin and large black eyes. He carried a Winchester rifle, a bandolier of shells. Two hand grenades hung from his belt. On his left arm, a brassard with the figure '26' and the words 'de Julio,' '26th of July' the name of the revolutionary movement. His pants were tucked into paratrooper boots."[44]

The jeep continued for several hours as rebels "waved and smiled as we passed by." Then they climbed on paths with ruts as deep as three feet. Late in the day they arrived at Raúl Castro's command post—"a veritable village of rebel soldiers and civilians" surrounding a wooden structure. Inside, young women were cooking and making and altering uniforms. He learned that women had trekked there from villages or Santiago and Guantánamo, and they trekked back home each night. Shaw regarded this revelation as indicative of a high degree of dedication, patriotism, and faith. He noticed a fourteen-year-old boy who appeared dismayed that he could not grow the beard that was "a sort of act of faith" among the rebels. There was "a shrine to the Virgin . . . and a bust of José Martí. . . . I noticed that most of the men wore necklace medals of Nuestra Senora de la Caridad del Cobre, Cuba's patron."[45]

At last he met Raúl. His boyish face and mere "wisps of beard" gave Shaw an impression of "gentleness and softness," stunningly different from his reputation as the tough, daring, and fearless commander who had kidnapped the Americans. Shaw soon got down to business with his prepared questions, addressing them through a translator, Raúl's companion, the same woman who days earlier translated for Dubois—"Deborah," the code name for Vilma Espin.[46]

"Why a revolution? Elections are scheduled for November 3. Why not settle this with ballots rather than bullets?"

Raúl Castro smiled and answered first in English, "The elections are a fake." And then continued in Spanish, as Deborah translated. "Batista doesn't dare hold honest elections. If he did, and the people's choices would be elected, the crimes of his administration would be exposed and just about everybody in the government would be put on trial. All the government officials are in this together, and they have to stay together for mere self-preservation. If the elections are held, they will be rigged. But they'll probably be postponed."

Shaw changed the topic to the fighting. "How are you doing up here? Are you gaining or losing or standing still?"

"We are gaining day by day, and if you want proof, consider this: Fidel went into the Sierra Maestra in December of 1956, just 19 months ago, with 12 men. Today, he has thousands. Don't take my word for it. You saw for yourself some of the army activity in Oriente Province along the road to Santiago. Batista has committed one-third of his army to fighting Fidel. Fidel must have made a lot of gains."

"All right," Shaw said, then dealt the Red card: "Now prove to me that this isn't a Communist movement."

Raúl Castro shrugged his shoulders and smiled, and he and Deborah spoke in turn. Shaw recorded what they said "in essence."

The answer was enigmatic, more evasive even than Raúl's response to Dubois. "How can we prove we are *not* something? Ask us to prove that we *are* something that we say we are, and we shall prove it. But prove we are *not* Communists? Well, look at our weapons. Go where you will and look at all of them. What will you see? American weapons, which we have taken from the Cuban Army. Those are our only weapons, plus ones we make. You won't see any Russian weapons. . . . But really, why should the Russians want to help us? What do the Communists have in common with us? We are out to bring stability and decency to Cuba, to end corruption, to restore Cuba's strength. Batista serves communism much better than we do. He is bankrupting the country; he is undermining the moral foundations of our society. He is creating conditions ideal for communism. There is no substantial Communist movement in Cuba; but if we should fail, the people might turn to any group that would promise them relief from Batista even if they should jump from the frying pan into the fire."

To dispense with the Communist worries, Raúl cited support from the church leaders. "And perhaps most important of all, we have the vast majority of the church leaders behind us—Catholics and Protestants alike. They are not fools. They would not support Communists in preference to anybody, even Batista."

Shaw suspected Deborah was editing Raúl's comments. He was impressed that she was "startlingly beautiful—a young Dolores del Río—tall, slim with straight jet black hair" in a ponytail. Shaw turned to her. "What about you? May I write anything about you? Frankly, I had never heard about you until today ... and I find you're quite a woman ... educated in the United States ... high up the Movement. I would like to write about you. What may I say?"

"Well, I believe it is known that I am here and that I am called Deborah. That is not my right name. I shall tell you my right name, but I ask you not to use it for a while." Anonymously, she answered a number of questions, which Shaw presented as one response.

"I am a member of the Council of Twelve. I am 28 years old. I studied Chemical Engineering at the University of Havana and at Massachusetts Institute of Technology ... for one year. I wanted to be a chemical engineer, but I knew that one could do nothing worthwhile until Cuba was freed. I joined the 26th of July Movement to do organization work. I worked in the cities until a few months ago, and then I came up to the mountains. I shall remain here until we have won."

At that point in the interview, which became part of the broadcast script, Shaw shared his own passion for freedom. "I am not particularly interested in Cuba, but I am interested in freedom ... for a very selfish reason. Today I am free. But I shall have greater assurance of retaining my freedom, and of my son's living the life of a free man, as freedom is extended."

To drive home the point, he quoted an English poet. "Just as John Donne said that 'any man's death diminishes me,' so do I feel that any man's loss of freedom diminishes my freedom. If what you have told me is true, and only time will determine that because I don't know any of you well enough to judge for myself, you are doing a great thing. As far as I am concerned, you are not fighting for Cuban freedom ... you are fighting for *freedom*." When he finished, Deborah looked at him "with her big black eyes." She "glanced toward the ceiling of that ramshackle old barn" and said only: "Freedom! That's a big word."

Shaw had completed his mission. He had not interviewed Fidel, but he had done "all that I should have done." He made his way back to Havana, and as he took off toward Miami, looking down upon the coastline of Cuba, he drew the conclusions he would tell his Philadelphia audience. "I hope that Fidel Castro and his brother are everything their followers think they are; although it would be impossible for any man to be the kind of man Fidel's followers think he is. But Fidel Castro is not nearly so important as the people who follow him." Castro's supporters had won his own support. "They, to me, are Cuba as I would like to think of Cuba.... There are decent people everywhere, the great consolation I shall have when I become discouraged." He wondered if they would remember him. "I don't suppose I shall ever see them again. If their Movement succeeds, and I should cover the inauguration of their President, I'm sure that none of them will be in the Presidential Palace. None of them expects to be. They are the nameless heroes and heroines without whom no fight for freedom can be won. Those who have survived will listen to the ceremonies by radio, and perhaps they will remember me for one thing . . . for passing on to them what Deborah said to me that afternoon in the Sierra del Cristal: 'Freedom! It's a big word.'"[47]

Back in Philadelphia, Shaw continued throughout the fall to report on developments he heard by monitoring the rebels' shortwave radio broadcasts from the Sierra Maestra relayed through Venezuela "and picked up by tuning to Caracas."[48] On August 20, Shaw reported Castro's announcement of a "tremendous" victory. "Out of short-wave radio receivers last night and early this morning crackled news that no censorship could stop . . . news broadcast from the Sierra Maestra by Fidel Castro, commander-in-chief of the Cuban Freedom Fighters, that his forces had just scored a tremendous victory over the troops of President Batista's government in Oriente Province."[49] He vouched for the report's credibility, largely because of Castro's detailed accounting of weapons and captives: "The chief of the Freedom Fighters, organized into the 26th of July Movement, reported that 14 government battalions had been defeated, one being annihilated; that hundreds of government soldiers had been killed and wounded; hundreds more had been captured—442 of the wounded captives were turned over to the International and Cuban Red Cross."[50]

Shaw found the rebels more credible than the government, especially when an economic target was attacked. "When the rebels tell you they were the ones who set the three-million-dollar fire which just about destroyed the administration building at Havana Airport last night and shut down the airport for three hours, and the government blames the fire on an accident, you wonder whether it's only a coincidence that the government reports a few hours later that a political prisoner being held in an Havana jail was shot to death while he and others were trying to escape. The rebels say the political prisoners are held as hostages and that the man shot to death last night was executed for the Havana Airport fire, not while trying to escape."[51]

Shaw was among the journalists who learned that decisions about Cuba's future had been made on July 20 while he was in the Sierra Maestra. A deal had been reached in Caracas among the various anti-Batista factions. The so-called unity Pact of Caracas meant to Shaw that "all of the revolutionaries have accepted the political leadership of the Castro-led forces."[52]

Shaw misunderstood the unity pact's significance as a rebel victory. Dubois, however, knew that Fidel Castro, while fighting the army in the Sierra Maestra in July, dictated the final document and sent it secretly over rebel radio to Caracas. The significance was that the followers of former president Carlos Prío Socarrás and other exile groups now officially conceded the leadership to Castro's armed movement. All signatories to the unity pact pledged to join with Castro in the final phase of the revolution, accepting his proposal for a provisional president, and his choice for president, Judge Manuel Urrutia.[53] To the relief of the exiles meeting in Caracas, Fidel made no claim to the presidency or any high office. Nonetheless, they suspected he still desired power despite his constant statements to the contrary. Naïvely, Shaw reiterated that "Castro himself is too young to be president under the Cuban constitution, and he has sworn to uphold that constitution."[54]

At home, after Shaw delivered his broadcasts, he submitted the series to compete for the high broadcasting honor of a Peabody Award, considered by many equivalent to the Pulitzer Prize. CBS radio had done well in the Peabody competition in years past. Shaw's mentor and former boss at CBS, Edward R. Murrow, had won three Peabodys, in 1950 for *Hear It Now*, in 1951 for converting *Hear It Now* to television as *See It Now,* and in 1953 a "personal award" for overall contributions to broadcasting. Shaw had high hopes.[55]

Meanwhile, he continued to follow the rebels by radio. In September, he was among the first to realize that the hijacking of a train bound for Santiago appeared to be part of the "current drive westward from Oriente province." The rebels were on the move toward Havana.[56]

CHAPTER 10

LIBERATOR OR DICTATOR?

T
he tempo of bulletins out of Cuba in the summer of 1958 moved the country higher on the daily news agenda. At the same time, it troubled editors and broadcasters that they relied heavily on official and other sources they did not entirely trust. The "reputable" sources in the State Department in Washington and the U.S. Embassy and Presidential Palace in Havana were at great odds with what was being reported on Radio Rebelde. At the *Washington Post and Times-Herald,* an ambitious young editorial writer, Karl E. Meyer, thought that his newspaper—situated in the nation's capital—should act more aggressively. He was motivated to go and get the real story.

But Meyer knew nobody would ask *him* to go and get it. As a new hire at the *Post,* he lacked seniority. Also, he was assigned to the editorial department, not the news desk. He was in his mid-twenties but was relatively inexperienced by the standards of the *Washington Post and Times-Herald.* If the *Post* sent someone, most certainly it would be a senior news reporter or investigative writer.

Yet, he was competitive and eager to do something significant, as had two generations of his family before him. Meyer's father, Ernest "Ernie" L. Meyer, had been an editorial columnist for the *Capital Times* in Madison, Wisconsin, and then left the Midwest for a bigger stage at the *New York Post.* Karl Meyer's grandfather, Georg Meyer, had edited a leading German-language newspaper in Milwaukee, *Die Germania,* back when the city had five German newspapers and only two in English.[1]

With a virtual pedigree in journalism, Karl Meyer had scored triple press credits at the University of Wisconsin–Madison. He was editor of the student newspaper, the *Daily Cardinal;* editor of the university's literary magazine, the *Athenaean;* and campus correspondent for the *Milwaukee Journal.* Then he prepared intellectually for writing about foreign relations, arriving at the *Post* with a PhD in international affairs from Princeton, one reason why he was assigned to write for the editorial opinion pages. "When I became an editorial writer in my mid-twenties," Meyer recalled, "the editor Bob Esterbrook said I had two jobs—first pick out the letters to the editor, and second, you have to write about Latin America."[2]

Meyer had settled into the constant and time-consuming clerical task sorting through the continuous flow of letters to the editor and picking those he considered worthy of being published—mainly those with cogent arguments that were both timely and necessarily brief. Then he turned to the more interesting task of writing about Latin America. As he found it difficult to write something meaningful about Cuba from his desk in Washington, Meyer grew more determined to go there.

The revolution was generating a good deal of excitement. In reading the *New York Times*, Meyer followed and respected Herbert Matthews, both for his scoop and for his editorials. "I got to know Herb Matthews, was very much influenced by Herb," he recalled. "He was absolutely sure" there was no truth in "all this talk about Fidel being a Communist."[3] Matthews accepted Castro's argument that all Latin American dictators routinely call their opponents Communists.

Nonetheless, Meyer was enticed by questions that remained unanswered by Matthews and others who interviewed Castro. What did Americans really know about El Comandante, the "Maximum Leader"? If Castro prevailed—as seemed more and more likely—what would he really do in power? His answers to that question were suspect. Once he said he would return to the Sierra Maestra to help the poor people there. Another time, when asked if he wanted to be president, he gave a nondenial denial, saying he was too young to be president under Cuba's Constitution of 1940.

While gathering background in Washington, Karl Meyer connected with Castro's Movement. "By chance, the 26th of July representative, Ernesto Betancourt, became a friend of mine."[4] If Meyer could get assigned to go to Cuba, Betancourt could make the necessary connections to Castro. "I was writing about Batista and wanted to go to Cuba," Meyer recalled, "but was afraid if I asked the paper, they'd just say no."[5]

He solved that problem by not asking. He put to use a proven practice—so often successful that journalists considered it an unwritten principle. When reporters faced obstacles—such as stubborn editors or newspaper protocol—they found it easier to go get the story and afterward ask if it was all right. Editors, of course, almost never turned down a good story. At that point, protocol and seniority were irrelevant.

Taking the practice to heart, Meyer bypassed his boss, Bob Esterbrook, and the news editors entirely. He applied to take a vacation in late August and told Esterbrook that he was "just going on a holiday." As planned, Betancourt arranged connections with the 26th of July Movement in Cuba. Meyer was "warned by knowledgeable persons that I could be arrested if my identity were known by the government." Like the media sleuths who preceded him, he played "make-believe—I was a 'college teacher' on vacation."[6]

By late August, the news from Cuba indicated the rebels were on the move. The shortwave radio broadcast Charles Shaw heard on August 20 was, in fact, a "tremendous victory," made possible, Jules Dubois learned, because of the captured army war codes.[7] In New York, *Time* magazine's Sam Halper was fed up-to-date information from Jay Mallin in Havana, who bypassed Cuban censorship to report one rebel success after another. Mallin also provided *Time* with a map that showed the increased swath of countryside Castro now claimed as "free Cuba." The expansion of rebel control was facilitated by a change in the army's strategy. Instead of encircling the Sierra Maestra to contain the rebels, the army pulled back to safe positions holding key cities.

These developments caused *Time*'s editors to alter their outlook: "Five months ago many Cubans thought that Rebel Chief Fidel Castro was through. His much touted 'total war' against President Fulgencio Batista was a total failure; the general strike in Havana that started literally with a bang ended with a whimper as local leaders went into hiding, shrilly blaming one another for the fiasco. That was early April. Last week, reports sifting through heavy censorship indicated that Castro has made a notable comeback. Despite the rebels' continued grandstanding and disorganization, the swelling tide of popular discontent has carried them back to a position of strength."[8]

The rebels now were better armed and organized. One key factor was the unity pact, approved in July in Caracas, which recognized Castro's militant movement for what it was—the leading hope for overturning Batista. Dubois considered that consolidation of anti-Batista combatants, including former president Prío Socarrás, as the "turning point of the civil war." The Caracas Pact established a united Civilian Revolutionary Front (CFR), directed mainly by Castro loyalists, with at least three emphases—delivering weapons to the rebels, lobbying the U.S. Congress and the White House, and ending U.S. military support (weapons and training) for President-General Batista's army.[9]

S lipping into Cuba in late August, Meyer sent Esterbrook a telegram from Santiago. "I felt that if something happened to me," Meyer said, "it would be terrible." His telegram said vaguely that he had "the possibility of a deal" and had "to go up some mountains." He waited only twenty-four hours for a response. When none came, he went ahead.[10]

In the Sierra Maestra ten days later, Meyer had completed his mission. He had more than enough new information for a story. Incredibly, he spent three of those days with a very cooperative Fidel Castro. On September 2, when he was ready to head back to Santiago and Havana, a downpour made the forest impassable. Hurricane Ella, a category-3 storm that had been gaining strength in the Caribbean, now slammed onto Cuba's southeastern coast around Santiago. Winds peaked at 115 m.p.h., disrupting telephone and telegraph service. Torrential rainfall flooded the province disastrously, chasing hundreds from their homes and drowning herds of cattle. Five people were reported killed. In the Sierra Maestra, rainfall made streams impassable. After spending its fury against the mountains where Meyer was taking cover, Ella in a single day weakened to a tropical storm.

Arriving back in Santiago, Meyer was greeted by a messenger who handed him Esterbrook's dated reply to his telegram. "A boy came running—'tenemos un telegram.'" It read: "Business prospects sound excellent." Esterbrook's reply suggested Meyer could take as long as he needed, so he spent "an extra week in Havana talking to people." In all, he was in Cuba for three weeks—long enough, he thought, to assess Cuba's political factions and their relative power.[11] "At that time, the anti-Batista movement was a broad coalition—liberals, professionals were one part, and Che Guevara and the militant nucleus another part. The part I mainly talked to was the liberal spectrum. . . . I did not see the militant side. . . . I think that skewed my perspective. . . . We all assumed that the centrist group in the revolution would prevail, which wasn't the case."[12]

Returning to work in Washington, Meyer got journalism's equivalent of a hero's welcome—an "atta boy" moment for the resourceful young man. The Post editors seemed unworried that the scoop was delivered to them by an editorial writer doing the work of a reporter. The scoop was the thing. Similarly, at the New York Times in February 1957, the concern about Herbert Matthews's reporting on Castro did not seem to arise until after the Times gave its front page to his scoop.

Young Meyer had done well, bringing home enough material for more than one story. The Post encouraged him as he turned his notes and recollections into a six-part series. Moreover, the newspaper published an advertisement promoting both the writer and his series starting on Sunday, September 14. The promotional ad featured their reporter's "rebel rendezvous":

This Sunday read: A *Washington Post* reporter's personal account of his 3-day visit with Cuban Rebel Fidel Castro.... In a cunningly camouflaged mountain hut, high up in Cuba's Sierra Maestra, sits Fidel Castro at the center of his rebel realm. It takes three days of hazardous climbing to get there, by horse and by foot. *Washington Post* reporter Karl Meyer, disguised as a vacationing school teacher, was able to reach Castro's mountain hide-out in safety. There, he met with the fiery rebel chief for three days ... watching, asking questions, listening. The six-part report on Meyer's rebel rendezvous will start Sunday in the Outlook Section.

The promotional ad included two photographs. One showed Meyer astride a white horse, reins in hand, and smiling at the lens. The other was a photo of Fidel Castro standing and holding a large walkie-talkie to his ear with a long Cuban cigar in his mouth, apparently a favorite nine-inch Gran Corona.[13] Mid-September was a heady time for Meyer, first with the ads and photos and then with his first story, his scoop, splashed across the front page of a Sunday Outlook section. Meyer, with the cooperation of Castro, had made his mark at the *Post*.

The first installment ritually documented the hero's journey. The difference this time was that Castro now was much more important than he had been when Herbert Matthews first met him. Meyer described the climb as hard for a "city boy." As if coaching others who might want to come, Meyer cautioned, "You need a jeep, a car and several horses—but mostly you need a strong pair of legs—to visit Fidel Castro in his mountain fortress in Cuba's Sierra Maestra. It took me three days of climbing to get there." The climb was "too steep and treacherous—rains coat the rocks with slime—and the last lap is a shin-breaking clamber through nettled trees up an endless slope." Finally, he reached the "cunningly camouflaged hut"—the "aerie" or eagle's nest mentioned in the story's headline—a symbol for seclusion, safety, secrecy, and power where "Fidel Castro sat at the center of his rebel realm." Admitted to the "hut," Meyer first sat among the troops in a room that "smelled of kerosene and rice stew (the staple dish in the mountains). It was filled with crouching rebels—including several rebel girls—who joked amiably with the gold-toothed cook as he stirred the stew. All, including the cook, carried six-shooters in their belts."[14]

At last, a bodyguard stepped "from a shoebox-sized back room and said, 'Meet the *comandante*.'" Castro assumed a characteristic pose, "sprawled across a bed" with a cigar "clamped between his teeth." Thus began the first of "four long talks with Castro" over three days. Meyer searched for a comparison, initially likening the *comandante*'s charismatic manner to that of a shrewd politician: "the knack of the amiable squeeze of the shoulder, the apt joke and the direct and attentive gaze. But combined with this is the ability to stoke to white heat the fervent, even fanatic, idealism which propels so many of his supporters."[15]

Castro's answers to political questions seemed straightforward and "surprisingly moderate." Castro said his main aim was to defeat the dictator and replace him with a "freely chosen president in a Cuba without censorship and police brutality." His social views, Meyer reasoned, seemed "vague, but incline to a kind of welfare state liberalism."[16]

Castro predicted imminent victory. He said that "in three months, three-fourths of the island will be in rebel hands." His men had turned back the army's summer offensive, and now he had the momentum. With a "strong element of bravado" Castro declared, "we grow stronger and the government grows weaker every day." Castro said Raúl was enlarging the second front and the rebels now were receiving "an abundant supply of seized and smuggled weapons—from semi-automatic rifles to machineguns and walkie-talkies."[17]

Meyer confirmed the "tremendous victory" that Charles Shaw had reported from shortwave radio. In that victory the rebels captured 422 soldiers, and Castro freed nearly all after a brief indoctrination about the goals of the revolution. Meyer talked with three prisoners still being held—one major and two captains—who were allowed to "stroll freely around rebel headquarters and are allowed to carry pistols." Castro's treatment of prisoners impressed Meyer. Andrew St. George had documented how Batista's troops tortured and killed captives, but Castro's strategy almost from the beginning was to tend to the wounded, indoctrinate them, and release them. "Thus, in one move," Meyer wrote, "Castro both saved on food bills and won a propaganda victory."[18]

Castro now was receiving more arms and money, some of it from taxes on sugarcane growers. The earlier tactic of burning sugarcane to harm the economy "was a mistake," Castro said. Instead, the rebels now taxed the harvest. "We now tell farmers they can pay taxes to Batista and get their crops out—or pay us, only less." Since the unity agreement of the Caracas Pact, more money was coming from exiles and from wealthy Cubans, a claim Meyer confirmed in interviews in Havana. One 26th of July member said he collected $250,000 from friends in one week.[19]

Meyer was told that the rebels had three hospitals and were building a fourth. The one he visited was "impressively clean and spacious" with ten beds and extra hammocks, with "ample stocks of drugs, bandages and plasma." In a camouflaged outpatient clinic where local farmers came to be treated, he talked with three doctors who had abandoned their practice to join Castro in the hills.[20]

Meyer's second installment tried to answer the question, Who *was* Fidel Castro? The article was a biographical overview, somewhat more insightful than what St. George had published in *Cavalier* almost a year earlier. Meyer's article cast Castro as a family man who had given up his profession as lawyer for *la causa*. Fidel had been "married to an attractive wife" but was now divorced. He was the father of a son, Fidelito, and beamed when he showed Meyer a framed photo of his smiling ten-year-old boy and said, "This is my son." Meyer concluded that "Castro could easily have led a life of comfort and calm. Instead, at 32, Castro has spent 11 years in the hazardous twilight of revolutionary movements." Castro had been actively fighting the dictatorship since 1953, even from prison. Why? "I like to fight," Castro said.[21]

What was he fighting *for*? Castro said he admired "three aspects of American life: its melting pot of nationalities, economic abundance and political liberty," and he wanted his revolution to establish the same "constitutional guarantees and economic opportunity." When the dictatorship falls, Castro said, a free election will be held, within months.[22]

What about President-General Batista's charge that Communists dominated the 26th of July Movement? Castro answered the perfunctory Communist question almost exactly as Raúl in July had answered Shaw. "Sitting on a box of grenades and waving his hands for emphasis," Fidel dismissed Batista as a generic dictator unworthy of a response. The Communist accusation was "the eternal charge of all dictators." But Castro did concede that, practically speaking, there could be some radicals in the Movement. "In every movement," he said, "some people are more radical than others." As for *his* Movement, he provided two absolute denials. "We impose no political orthodoxy on our soldiers. But there is no Communist infiltration."[23]

As an editorial writer now serving as a reporter, Meyer had limited freedom to speculate on the validity of Castro's statements. On the one hand, Meyer respected Herbert Matthews's insistence that Castro was not a Communist. But if not a Communist, what was he? "I assumed that Fidel was more along the [Gamal Abdul] Nasser line," Meyer recalled. "He presented himself as a kind of Franklin Roosevelt New Deal liberal . . . and not having enough evidence" otherwise, Meyer said he had "to report him that way."[24]

What would Castro do when the war ended? That was another now-standard query. Castro had a couple of answers. "He said that after the revolution he was going to retire and be a farmer."[25] Furthermore, he described his desire to devote his time to charitable work. "When it is all over I want to stay here in the Sierra Maestra and help the people to get schools, hospitals, roads and electricity. It is criminal the way the government has done nothing for the people of Oriente."[26] The experience, Meyer later acknowledged, "cured me—I think permanently—of taking at face value what people say in revolutionary situations."[27]

In the Sierra Maestra, the act of getting the interview seemed to be the main point. Meyer and most of the American correspondents favored with the hospitality of the rebel camp and the opportunity to interview Fidel Castro for a scoop had achieved their goal. They determined to record—not question—Castro's statements. They then conveyed Castro's messages uncensored to the United States. As such, Castro's word was *the* word; his words shaped the story. The pattern of American reporting of the revolution seemed remarkably similar to what Walter Lippmann and Charles Merz documented in American journalists' coverage of the Russian Revolution. Their study provided conclusive evidence that the reporting of that revolution was "a case of seeing not what was, but what men wished to see."[28]

As with most of the thirteen journalists, Meyer's stories expressed little or no doubt about Castro's statements. Follow-up questions might have probed how Castro thought he would manage the realities of government—at least in the interim before he took up farming. Here was the most militant *comandante*, who had been fighting for years and had by sheer willpower dominated the recalcitrant Miami exiles and other Cuban contenders. Now, how would he turn over real power to other Cubans, most of whom he had defeated or distrusted, among them former president Carlos Prío Socarrás? How would he manage his own sudden transition from military to civilian life? Considering the exiles' distrust of him, how did Castro expect to slip away with any security for his life into a low-profile role as a farmer helping peasants in the Sierra Maestra?

The correspondents took a very different, distrustful approach toward President-General Batista. Among the thirteen, only Dubois interviewed the dictator, and he found him to be a liar. As a usurper of power that he refused to relinquish, he was increasingly regarded as guilty of, at least, massive corruption and unfathomable brutality. Batista's pronouncements were generally discounted as evasions or found to be false, as when he stated that Fidel

Castro was dead. American journalists tended to focus on the dictator's censorship and reign of terror. In that context, Meyer's third installment in the *Post* focused on the regime's brutality in suppressing dissent and revolutionary activities in Havana and, especially, in Santiago and Oriente Province.

By September, after the army's retreat within fortresses and garrisons, Batista tightened the regime's grip on the country's population centers. The suppression was especially bloody in Santiago, a city seldom visited by tourists. There, Meyer found a reign of terror induced by torture and murder. It was enforced by blue-coated police or brown-clad soldiers armed with machine guns and automatic rifles. The enforcers were "untroubled by the niceties of law." Suspicion of revolutionary activities was enough for arbitrary conviction and execution. "Nearly every night there is shooting in Santiago or on its outskirts. Boys and young men, who because of their rebel sympathies—are automatically regarded as enemies of the state—are found dead in the city streets with an appalling frequency. During my stay of more than a week, Santiago residents estimated that about 30 boys had been murdered."[29]

Meyer detailed the story he heard about one young victim in Santiago. In August, Mario Maceo Quesada, a twenty-three-year-old student, was leaving an 8:30 a.m. mass at San Juan Bosco Church when he was picked up and driven off in a patrol car. "He was driven to a side road and tortured by burning before he was killed. His captors were seen drinking beer at a nearby bar at 10 a.m. At noon his mother identified his body in the city cemetery. The boy's hands were bound. Army officials did not permit his family to reclaim his corpse for burial."

Was this believable? "Your first reaction on hearing stories like these," Meyer acknowledged, "is incredulity." But he believed the stories because his "informants are invariably responsible men—lawyers, doctors, bankers, priests, businessmen, teachers—whose words are sober and temperately stated. Many are eyewitnesses."[30] In Havana, Meyer spotted similar enforcers, although torture was kept from the view of tourists in the hotels, nightclubs, and casinos.

During his days in Santiago and Havana, Meyer met a wide range of citizens who considered Castro's revolution the only alternative to the Batista regime. However, some centrists still hoped they could elect a moderate in the presidential election that was now postponed to November 3. To many, the election was not a solution, but merely a sham to install President-General Batista's political ally, Andrés Rivero Agüero. According to one scenario, Rivero Agüero would then appoint President-General Batista to head the army.

Meyer identified major grievances against Batista, dating from his seizure of power in March 1952. The brutality of the police and army was such that "no class in Cuba is immune from arrest and possible torture." Corruption "has never been worse." The regime had misappropriated taxes and was neglecting roads, schools, electricity, and hospitals to "build more monuments for the government" and pay for the war. And on September 6, 1958, Batista suspended the rights of free speech and assembly for the thirteenth time since April 1956. Newspapers in Cuba were a national joke, Meyer heard, "because they contain no news." International publications continued to be heavily censored. *Life* magazine in early September had followed up Sam Halper's focus on Fidel Castro with an extensive picture story on Raúl featuring Andrew St. George's photographs. Meyer found a copy of *Life* that should have "contained an article on the rebels," but "20 pages had been shorn from the issue."[31]

Meyer was told that "active supporters of the revolution" included "some of the most unlikely revolutionaries"—members of the Rotary Club, the Lion's Club, medical and legal associations, women's organizations, and church groups. In Havana, he discovered that "opposition to the oppressive regime of Batista cuts through all strata of Cuban society." He reported that "it was my impression that the most articulate and thoughtful rebel sympathizers were members of Cuba's small but growing middle class."[32]

Opposition to Batista, however, did not translate into unqualified acceptance of Fidel Castro. Meyer's interviews revealed strong opinions for and against Castro, although hardly anyone accused him of being a Communist. "About Fidel Castro, the leader of the shooting opposition in the distant Sierra Maestra, you find a variety of opinions in the middle class world of Cuba. The attitude varies from idolatry to criticism and distrust." Meyer found intense devotion mostly in the city nearest the Sierra Maestra. "In Santiago," he wrote, "Castro can practically do no wrong. Businessmen who are now dipping into their capital because of losses due to the disturbed economy in Oriente seem indifferent to their personal plight. One merchant I met postponed the purchase of a car to buy rebel bonds (which was tantamount to a gift)."

Men in the business community in Santiago scoffed at reports that Castro was a Communist. Businessmen pointed to their own support of the 26th of July Movement as evidence that Castro was not a front for bolshevism. "My business is worth $2 million a year," one merchant told Meyer. "Tell me how I could back anyone who would take my money away."

But in Havana, Meyer reported, businessmen and other middle-class supporters were much less trusting of Castro. Some reminded him that Castro bungled the general strike in April. Others were wary of Castro's plans "if his movement is toppling the government. None feels he is a Communist, but all worry about his possible immaturity."[33] Despite distrust of Castro, many supported the 26th of July Movement as the only realistic opposition to a regime they detested. "They are busy raising money and smuggling weapons through to Castro's mountain fastness," Meyer wrote, "and are keeping their fingers crossed as to the future."[34]

Meyer's fifth installment was edited to insert news from Radio Rebelde that a large rebel force had opened a new front outside the Sierra Maestra. "This week, the rebel radio reported that six columns—or about 1,000—men had moved into Las Villas province in central Cuba to open a major new front."[35] It was a move that Homer Bigart in February had considered necessary but improbable because Castro had so few men. Evidently his force had grown in size, ambition, and reach.

In that fifth installment Meyer elaborated on President-General Batista's hope "to extricate himself from his present difficulties" by having Andrés Rivero Agüero elected in the promised presidential election. Now, six weeks before the November 3 election, with civil liberties suspended and with "police and soldiers everywhere," Cuba's "stocky strong-man" wanted the election campaign to have "the appearance of a spirited free-for-all in the democratic manner." Meyer noted two possible but unlikely challengers to Rivero Agüero from the "house-broken" opposition. One was the "timeworn" seventy-five-year-old former president (1944–48) Ramón Gran San Martín. The second was the leader of a new Free People's Party, a lawyer, and former diplomat and elected representative, Carlos Marquéz-Sterling.[36]

No candidate represented the revolutionary opposition, and Castro was on record opposing the election as fraud. Meyer noted correctly that "the complex struggle for power among the factions in Cuba's revolutionary opposition may have far more importance in deciding the island's future than the strange election Batista is trying to hold."[37] Despite suspicions that the election was rigged, U.S. ambassador Earl Smith and the U.S. State Department supported it as a legitimate, best course for Cuba. Such persistent U.S. support, Meyer found, disillusioned at least one Havana student: "I like Americans. I like your way of life. But I don't like your government. It is helping Batista."[38]

As tensions increased in Cuba, the U.S. State Department aimed to be perceived as neutral, as Meyer noted in the final installment. "Please, please," one U.S. official said, "don't forget we are trying to be neutral in this fight. Up in the hills, the rebels think we support Batista, but here in Havana the Government complains that we favor the rebels. We are caught in a very difficult situation."[39] Meyer ended the series by quoting an American in Havana who envisioned a possible outcome for U.S.-Cuban relations. "Unless something is done, the Cubans may want to kick out the United States after they have kicked out Batista."[40]

The Cuban election was held as scheduled on November 3, despite protests that Batista's suppression of civil rights prevented centrist opponents from posing a real challenge. As expected, Batista's henchman Rivero Agüero was elected, but Batista intended to rule until his term ended in February. While the U.S. government accepted the results, Herbert Matthews denigrated the election as "farcical" and noted that "neither Fidel Castro nor the by then overwhelming civic resistance movement in the cities paid any attention." In fact, four days after that election, Fidel and Raúl began a joint southeastern offensive aimed to capture Santiago.

In the north, Che Guevara and Camilo Cienfuegos had trekked through the central provinces. By November they reached the Escambray Mountains along the north coast, and established the Movement's third front. There they took leadership of other, less publicized fighters whom Matthews called "the small and sometimes mutually contending forces of the other little guerrilla groups who had been operating in those mountains." They included students who had survived the 1957 attack on the Presidential Palace.[41]

Among the guerrilla fighters in the Escambray Mountains, one experienced American soldier was becoming prominent in the rebels' ranks. Since joining the Escambray rebels in December 1957, William Alexander Morgan had distinguished himself as a military trainer and leader. A former U.S. Army paratrooper, Morgan had such an urge to fight for the revolution that he abruptly abandoned his quiet life in Toledo, Ohio, as well as his wife and two small children. While some questioned his leaving his family—or wondered if he forfeited his U.S. citizenship—others were impressed by his bold gallantry. In any case, William Morgan gave Toledo a local connection with the turmoil in Cuba. His story resonated with editors at the *Toledo Blade*, proud of the newspaper's history of international reporting.

Morgan's Escambray Mountain fighters now joined with Castro's Sierra Maestra guerrillas, under the command of Guevara and Cienfuegos, and targeted central Cuban cities, especially the prize, Santa Clara. With Morgan's role escalating, editors at the *Blade* in late December decided to send reporter Robert Branson to interview Toledo's celebrity soldier.[42]

At the end of November, a female correspondent for *Reader's Digest* arrived in Havana, disguised as a tourist. At thirty-nine, Dickey Chapelle was a renowned freelance photojournalist and writer with extensive experience in covering wars and revolutions. For months, she had been urging her editors to send her to Cuba, arguing that it was time for the conservative *Reader's Digest* to have its own Cuban story since some twenty journalists had already been sent there. By then Henry Luce's *Life* and *Time* had for months devoted money and print to tracking the rebels. "For two years," she wrote, "Fidel Castro had been a magnet for venturesome American newsmen, an off-beat folk hero in the tales of foreign correspondents" who "brought back reports that Castro's forces were taking on planes and armored cars with hunting rifles and shotguns."[43] Of them all, Herbert Matthews most influenced her. Since meeting him, she had wanted this assignment. At last the *Reader's Digest* editors relented, deciding that in one story she could bring their readers up to date by doing what they did best: digesting the entire sweep of the Cuban decade, from Batista's coup in 1952 to Castro's rebellion. She would write the revolution's definitive digest.

Chapelle was confident that she could engage with the rebels in Cuba as she had done with rebels elsewhere, most recently in the Algerian civil war. She already knew people in the 26th of July Movement. "Dickey's excitement," wrote her biographer, "was shared by her New York contacts with the rebel army, two Cubans working at Bab's coffee shop on Forty-Seventh Street and Third Avenue."[44] As she had done in Algeria, she aligned with the rebels' cause, *la causa*. Now, thankfully, the *Reader's Digest* was sending her to "find out what was happening to them."[45]

Her editors had every reason to think she would succeed at what she did so well: covering wars and revolutions from within combat zones. She had got her start in the Pacific toward the end of World War II. As a war photographer for *National Geographic*, she was at the battles of Iwo Jima and Okinawa. *Reader's Digest* editors regarded her as "one of the bravest women around, one of the best reporters and photographers in the business" whose "determination to be where things are happening has carried her into some of the most violent action in a violent world, and her sympathy for people in trouble has led her time and again to disregard personal safety." In 1957, *Reader's Digest* had published Chapelle's first-person account of her imprisonment in Hungary during the October 1956 revolution. On that assignment for *Life* magazine, she had "left the security of the free world" and was caught and jailed. Held for fifty-three days, she attained celebrity status as an American captive behind the "Iron Curtain" in Budapest's notorious Fö Street Prison.[46]

In the summer of 1957, Chapelle had succeeded in covering the revolutionary war in Algeria, under contract with the small Spadea Syndicate press association. To reach the rebels she had circumvented the French military.[47] In an act of daring and stealth, the rebel network in the United States arranged for Chapelle to be "kidnapped" in Madrid, then smuggled into the Algerian mountains, disguised, completely covered, as a Muslim woman.[48] One of the hundreds of photographs she brought back documented her manner of befriending the rebels and listening to their stories. Taken in July 1957, the photograph shows her inside a cave, the rebel command post in the Ksour Mountains. She is seated on the straw-covered earth, drinking Arab coffee and speaking with five rebels of the "Scorpion Battalion."[49] That was the life of action she craved, even though it eventually ended her fifteen-year marriage to her first photography teacher, Tony Chapelle.[50]

After the Algerian war, Dickey Chapelle thought of herself as "an interpreter of violence," having covered "three revolutions in three years" in Europe, the Middle East, and North Africa. In 1958 she recalled poignantly that one editor asked, "You don't mind, do you, if we call you our special correspondent to the bayonet borders of the world?" "I did," she wrote, "but not half as much as I minded the larger truths—that the revolutions had failed. Hungary had fallen to the tanks. Brother still fought against brother in Algeria. Rioting continued in Lebanon. But men continued to hope and fight for a better world."[51] As she had decided with the revolutions in Hungary and Algeria, her special contribution in Cuba would come through giving voice to the rebels.

Cuba, as she saw it, had "two civil wars." Equally important as the "shooting war" was the one she was enlisting for—the war "fought in the press—a battle for global sympathy in which Batista's total censorship was the critical factor." Batista's "oppression was never more effective than against correspondents. He destroyed the profession of reporter in Cuba" with edicts (and bribes) that manipulated and censored the island's press. News of the rebels hardly ever "leaked through Batista's press gag." By U.S. press standards, "the

Fidelista efforts to reply . . . were inept, to say the least."[52] More often than not, news about Fidel Castro came secondhand through U.S. news media.

Chapelle's urgency to fly to Havana clashed at once with the cautions expressed by the 26th of July representatives in Miami who were arranging her connections. The head of the Castro underground, the reasonably paranoid Carlos Busch, warned her not to tell anyone that she was in Miami. "Batista's spies are everywhere," he told her. "A phone call to one of them and the SIM will be waiting for you at the airport in Havana." While she waited, his staff arranged for her to interview Cuban refugees in Miami. Hearing the refugees' "words and voices, many still shrill with fear," she could "piece together a picture of the reign of terror." Before she left Miami, she was forming dominant images of the "looting of Cuba on a lavish scale," police stations with torture chambers, and Cuban Air Force planes dropping "gasoline jelly bombs" on innocent communities.[53]

During the five-day layover, Carlos Busch surprised her by insisting she surrender her boots, the prized marine Kabar trench knife given her in World War II—and most astonishingly, her beloved cameras, the Leicas that were appendages of her personality. Busch "told me bluntly that I'd get through—if I let him ship my cameras and field gear into the Sierra Maestra area clandestinely." By the end of November, security had been tightened. With that photographic gear she couldn't pass as a tourist and so it "would expose the courier who must accompany me to arrest and torture." Even so, she resisted. "I must go with my cameras," she said. She could manage without the boots and the Kabar knife given her by a marine wounded on Iwo Jima—although she carried it as a lucky charm. But what good was a photographer without cameras? Busch did not budge, so she relented, recalling a lesson from her hard-won experiences in Hungary and Algeria, that the "most important rule for negotiating with a jittery underground is *don't argue.*"[54]

Deceptively attired as a tourist, she boarded the plane to Havana. Her Movement escort on the flight was a "plump dark girl" of about twenty-five whose composure Chapelle admired, "for the risks she was taking were real ones. As the plane banked to land, she crossed herself and her lips moved. I discovered I was praying along with her." To Cuban airport authorities, Chapelle appeared as a short, harmless, middle-aged American woman who seemed to be who she said she was: "an employee of a New York firm of portrait photographers on a two-week vacation."[55]

In Havana, contacts alerted her that the military had increased its surveillance in Santiago, where she was headed. "Now word came that the city was virtually besieged by Castro's forces," she noted. "I would need a really good story to tell before I'd be passed through the city proper and out into the province." When her Cubana Airlines flight landed in Santiago, she disembarked wearing spike heels, dangling earrings, and a pale blue fluffy shirtwaist and a new story. She said she had come to see her sweetheart, a U.S. Marine at the Guantánamo Naval Base, showing the suspicious airport security officer "a picture I'd made of a baby-faced Marine with a scarred chin."[56]

In Santiago on December 2, she had the good luck to meet Andrew St. George, who gave her information about Castro and some timely advice. He had been with the rebels since October 23—for more than five weeks. Now he was headed home with his exclusive story for the *New York Times*. In an interview with St. George on November 21, Castro requested "a confidential United States diplomatic representative visit him at his headquarters in the Sierra Maestra . . . to discuss a number of important political issues." Castro "also wants to make certain that the activities of his younger brother, Raúl, do not bring about United States intervention on behalf of the Government of Fulgencio Batista."[57]

St. George told Chapelle no other journalists were in the rebel camp, so she would "probably be the only correspondent with Castro during the month." St. George was now certain that Castro would prevail, and his background information about the summer's battles helped Chapelle explain to *Digest* readers how Castro had managed to repel the Cuban Army. "The civil-resistance arm of the movement," she wrote, "had provided him with mines, and his raiding had given him machine guns. With these, he set up a double ring of ambushes and dug in to wait for the soldiers' advance. In 45 days only a thousand Batista soldiers ever reached the inner ring of mines around Pico Turquino, and none crossed it. Hundreds were captured, disarmed, lectured and released. Batista ordered his troops back into their fortresses along the highways.[58]

St. George also advised Chapelle that the rebels had additional troops and weapons—and now controlled much more territory. This last fact alone had stunned the editors at *Time* magazine when their Havana freelancer Jay Mallin sent a map colored to show how much of the eastern end of the island Castro rightly claimed as "free" Cuba.[59]

Chapelle learned that "Fidel was now ready with a simple, harsh plan." The rebels were now fighting on multiple fronts. Castro held the Sierra Maestra with his brother Raúl, and Major Camilio Cienfuegos had led other troops into the central corridor of eastern Cuba, where they were disrupting trains, trucks, and communications between there and Havana. They had just about cut Cuba in half. A third independent front near the northeastern coast was still active. There, the American soldier-of-fortune Captain William Morgan was leading a separate offensive, contributing to the general advance by distracting the army. Since the end of the summer offensive, Batista's ground forces had weakened, then thinned in numbers. St. George told Chapelle that Castro's strategy of releasing captured soldiers unharmed seemed to be undermining the army's will to fight.[60] In desperation, Batista had ordered his air force into action, and she could expect more bombing and strafing. On the other hand, St. George said he was taking a break as Castro's campaign seemed to be stalled at the gates of Santiago. "I glumly agreed I probably was in the wrong place at the wrong time."[61]

In Chapelle's meeting with St. George, he was astonished that she had no cameras. "Andrew at once told me to beg, borrow, steal—or even buy—new cameras at once since my own certainly would never be given back to me." Chapelle's Movement courier drove her to a photo shop where she bought a 35mm camera. Then she borrowed another one, a Leica, from "one wealthy Castro sympathizer and a lens from another." She recalled securing "a half dozen rolls of dusty film from every drugstore we passed."[62]

Given the rebels' proximity to Santiago, they would no longer be as distant as when Karl Meyer trudged up the mountain in September. Provided with another girl courier, Chapelle walked across a golf course and got into a jeep driven by a bearded rifleman with a 26th of July arm patch. "After a few hours of grinding across cane fields and fording streams, I was deep into Oriente Province," at Raúl's farmhouse headquarters.[63]

Before she reached Fidel's camp, Chapelle witnessed four battles in one week along the Central Highway. During the first battle, she was injured in a jeep accident. It happened when the army fired a mortar barrage from the village of Maffo, and her jeep driver sped in haste from the shelling, lost control, and crashed, dumping her onto the road. "I was lying on my stomach with my arms under me," she recalled. Her right leg was so numb she could only crawl at first; then she realized she was only hobbled by a twisted ankle.

She had been spared the real agony she soon witnessed in a makeshift hospital in a tobacco shed. There she saw a female surgeon trying to help those hit by the mortar shells. In the shed she met a former Cuban newspaper editor, now a rebel known as Capitano Orlando. He said armed conflict was his response to Batista's censorship; bribes and threats had practically destroyed his newspaper. While the press had been silenced, Cuba's radio stations served double duty, as the voice of the government and the servant that jammed U.S. broadcasts and blacked out their newscasts.[64]

"Look, Americana," Capitano Orlando told her, drawing Chapelle's attention to a man with mortar shrapnel in his abdomen. "This man's story you must tell even if you do not tell other stories. For he is not even a Cuban, only one who hates tyranny. He is a Dominican. He fights with us against Batista now so we will fight with him against Trujillo later. If—if—he is ever able to fight again."

"I nodded. I knew why the editor-*capitano* felt this story was important. About one out of every ten rebel fighters I'd seen came from some other Latin American land." Chapelle had been told that Castro had excused non-Cuban volunteers from pledging an oath of loyalty to him "lest they jeopardize their chances to go back home again." Capitano Orlando told her he was headed to see Castro and invited her to join him. Considering her handicap, he "handed me his carbine to use for a crutch."[65]

Chapelle finally reached Fidel Castro's command post a few miles south of the Central Highway inside a cave. She entered the "deep double-ended rock cave in a hillside" that overlooked a muddy side road that the rebels sought to control. The cave was "littered with radio equipment, food crates, cots, boxes of cigars and belts of ammunition." Fidel was gone, directing the siege of Maffo and his ambush of army troops sent to Maffo. Later, she found him riding in a British weapons carrier, changing his command posts almost daily "on the porch or patio of a farmer's house, close enough to the front so we could see the bombing and strafing from the air, and recognize most of the sounds of combat on the ground."[66]

Her timing was fortunate. Shortly afterward, she witnessed the "touching" reunion of the two brothers. "Raúl was returning in triumph to his older brother to report that but for a few city strongholds, all Oriente Province from the main road to the north coast of Cuba had been wrested by his forces from Batista's men. In military language the Castro front at last was consolidated across the Central Highway." The headquarters scene was dominated by the jubilation of victory, casting doubt over rumors Chapelle had heard that the brothers had serious disputes. "Fidel, tremendous in wet and muddy fatigues, laughed deeply as he swung back and forth in a hammock. Raúl spoke shrilly and incessantly about his victories."[67] Chapelle worried about Raúl's fixation with communism, according to her biographer. "Though she personally liked the impish Raúl, his communist ideology disturbed her. She hoped he would come to his senses—he was only twenty-six—once the revolution succeeded. Being naturally optimistic, she hoped, but she also worried."[68]

Chapelle noted the camp's two female leaders. The constant companion to Fidel was Celia Sánchez, who had left a comfortable life in Santiago. It was her father who had established the memorial to José Martí at Pico Turquino, the site where Fidel chose to be filmed by Robert Taber. Now she devoted herself to Fidel. Chapelle observed how Celia Sánchez "hovered there now, thin and febrile in her green twill uniform with five gold religious medals swinging on chains around her neck."

The woman devoted to Raúl was Vilma Espin, code named "Deborah," who had translated during Charles Shaw's interview with Raúl. She had served as assistant to Frank País in Santiago, among other things using her house for storing dynamite. When País was killed in the summer of 1957, police found her code name "Monica" in his notebook. "A couple of days later," she told an interviewer, "I left home, almost by intuition, and the next day they came to look for me and searched the house." She preferred the Sierra Maestra because of "the certainty that you'd die fighting instead of being hunted down. To be hunted down was a terrible thought." Her romance with Raúl and later marriage would be recorded as "one of the love stories of the revolution."[69] As Chapelle observed, Espin smiled "as she toyed with a new Belgian submachine gun presented to her as token of Raúl's triumphs."[70]

Observing Fidel Castro, Chapelle recorded minute details about his mannerisms and moods. Having tracked this hero figure who had so long eluded Batista, she noted his constant activity. He was *numero uno*, the center of attention, conducting meetings, receiving messages, issuing orders, and interrupting everything to transmit over the radio. "He would grasp the walkie-talkie as if it were an enemy's throat and, in a voice to rouse the countryside, begin, *'Urgente, urgente!'* He never spoke in any kind of code and much of Cuba could follow the battles by simply tuning in on the Castro tactical transmissions."[71]

She still depended on the cameras she had bought in Santiago. She asked Castro for her favorite cameras and the Kabar knife that the Movement people in Miami said would be shipped to her. He dismissed her request. "The revolution owes you two cameras," he told her. She found out later that two other reporters' cameras had disappeared. Anyway, for *Reader's Digest*, her notebook supplemented the photography. As for Castro, it was "nearly impossible to photograph him. . . . The emotional tension around him rarely lessened; he conveyed high pressure in every movement and was never still. His normal state of ease was a purposeful forty-inch stride forward, then back. . . . His speaking voice was surprisingly soft and his incessant speech distinct. His manner of giving praise was a bear hug, his encouragement a heavy hand on the shoulder, his criticism an earthquake loss of temper. He reacted with gargantuan anger to every report of dead and wounded." At other "rare times" she thought Castro "revealed a fine incisive mind utterly ill-matching the psychopathic temperament which subdued it. He liked to boast of his encyclopedic knowledge of *Batistiano* soldiers. He said his secret weapon lay in his enemies' minds; they did not want to risk themselves for what they presumably were sworn to defend—the regime of Batista."[72]

Weakening the enemy's morale had been a prominent factor, nearly as important as the use of arms. Chapelle reasoned that Castro lowered the risk factor every time he indoctrinated and released prisoners. She wrote that his catch-and-release strategy—which had also impressed Karl Meyer—"became Castro's secret—and winning—weapon." Government troops, receiving lectures instead of torture, made the "discovery" that "they did not want what they were presumably fighting for—the Batista regime. And they did very much want to live." This, she concluded, was the "final blow to any *Batistiano*'s will to fight." One day close to La Maya, near Santiago, Chapelle witnessed the procedure for 242 captives. "The prisoners were gathered within a hollow square of rebel machine gunners and harangued in the twilight" by Raúl: "We hope that you will stay with us and fight against the master who has so ill-used you. If you decide to refuse this invitation—and I'm not going to repeat it—you will be delivered to the custody of the Cuban Red Cross tomorrow. Once you are under Batista's orders again we hope that you will not take up arms against us." Raúl explained the system. "We took you this time. We can take you again. And when we do, we will not frighten or torture or kill you, any more than we are frightening you in this moment. If you are captured a second or even a third time we will again return you exactly as we are doing now." The next day she watched as all the army troops were sent toward Santiago in buses and trucks marked on their sides with crosses.[73]

The scattered reports of so few rebel deaths persuaded Dickey Chapelle that Castro's losses were not as great as Batista's army claimed. When nine of his men were killed in one battle at Jiguani, Castro assigned Chapelle to photograph their bodies. Castro "insisted I go out to make close-ups of each body," she said, "so their martyrdom will not be forgotten by the world."[74]

After days of observing Castro in camp, Chapelle noted an "overwhelming fault in his character." It was none other than "his inability to tolerate the absence of an enemy: he had to stand—or better, rant and shout—against some challenge every waking moment." This led his "best tactical officers" to shout at him as well, as when she saw an officer "charging up to the commander, standing rock steady and shouting up at the great bearded face, 'Dr. Fidel, I tell you, you have been a fool not to support me! You should have known I needed more shells!'" She too adjusted to the rough edges of camp life and began to shout demands. "Like everyone else in the headquarters, I soon found my own manners conforming. If I'd heard a rumor of a jeep heading for the front but could not find it, I'd rail at any bearded officer that I was tired having Cubans lie to me; where the devil was my jeep?" As a result, in the final weeks of the war, she gained mobility to see more of the fighting.[75]

In her four weeks in the mountains, including ten days in Castro's command post, Chapelle was present during the last successful battles. She came to understand how the rebels scored sudden successes. In addition to Castro's personal charisma and his strategy of releasing Batista's soldiers as defanged enemies, she witnessed the rebels' military intensity in battle. They had overcome the problem of being outgunned. "By all the military theory since Hannibal, Batista's men still held the advantage. The rebels were facing tanks and strafing planes with only rifles and light machine guns," she told *Digest* readers. "But they made up their adversaries' minds with a continuous hail of lead. Regardless of hazard, they kept firing until there was nothing more to shoot at. To this I was repeatedly an eye witness. In fact, in 23 days with the Castro forces in the field, I saw five almost identical actions, each ending in the rebel capture of a town and army garrison. The government soldiers simply retreated behind their ultimate defenses and vainly waited for help from outside while the rebels fired around the clock from a ring of close-in positions until the garrison surrendered." With the surrender of the town, "Castro's men jammed their houses and frequently commandeered them."[76]

Reacting to the occupation of towns, the Batista regime resorted to air power, sending pilots on bombing raids in American B-26s. Suddenly, among the uniformed rebels, Chapelle found herself in the midst of a reign of terror— "bombing, strafing and sometimes mortar fire down on the villages. Once I was in a house photographing some rebels when a low-flying B-26 strafed it, splintering the porch roof. Most terrifying was the use of napalm." These were the "gasoline jelly bombs" she had been told in Miami were being dropped on innocent communities. She had seen Americans use them in World War II on the Pacific islands—against the Japanese. In her self-styled role as an "interpreter of violence," she documented the bombing as a crime against humanity. "Batista's planes did, in fact, drop napalm on civilian villages," she wrote. "I photographed two communities ignited in this way, picking up pieces of the distinctive aluminum containers in which the stuff is air-dropped."[77] She also regarded the bombing of civilians as an illegal use of the B-26s, which had been supplied by the U.S. government for defense of the hemisphere from outside enemies. But the pilots were hitting civilians; Batista was bombing his own people.[78]

With each foray, she became more enamored of the rebels, and they of her. During fighting for the town of La Maya, Chapelle posed, smiling, in a closely bunched group of seven rebel men and women. She purposely kept her hair down rather than in a bun at the back. "While with the bearded ones," she explained, "I kept my hair down since long hair was not a symbol of depri-vation of femininity nor of femininity itself, since the men's hair was long."

Two days before Christmas, Chapelle was at the command post when word arrived that the guerrillas in the Escambray northern front led by Che Guevara and Camilio Cienfuegos now controlled a contested sixty-five-mile-stretch of the Central Highway. Guevara had scored a major success, as CBS's Taber noted, when his men blocked a train carrying troops and several gaso-line tank trucks. "Armor-piercing machine-gun bullets and bazooka rockets began to burst against the train; it was derailed by a dynamite blast, and Gue-vara's guerrillas, approaching closer, began to hurl Molotov cocktails against its sides and under it, turning the seventeen cars into so many ovens. The troops... waved white flags from their firing slits... were disarmed, and put under guard."[79]

It was now safe enough for Chapelle to leave Castro's camp and send her story to New York. At sundown, she joined two scouts in a jeep "to make cer-tain the road lay clear of *Batistianos*." Twelve miles from Santiago, she was taken to a safe house, where she cleaned up and changed clothes. "I walked out a typically groomed tourist with a spotless blouse, brushed hair high un-der a bow, vividly made up, wearing shoes with a mirror shine." From there, escorted by a teenage boy, she began walking—still with the limp—toward Santiago. Batista's bombers were still flying, and she had a scary roadside escape from shells dropped from a B-26. She arrived in a suburb of Santiago and was soon at the American consulate.[80]

Soon after, Chapelle was in Havana and witnessed the revolution's tri-umph. In the early morning of New Year's Day, President-General Batista resigned at the Columbia Army Base, transferring the powers of the presidency to the military. In a last, written command, he ordered "all members of the armed forces and the police agents to obey and co-operate with the new government and with the chiefs of the armed bodies, of which Major General Eulogio Cantillo y Porras has taken charge." Then, with his family, close friends, and suitcases stuffed with cash, Batista fled Cuba on a DC-4 headed to the Dominican Republic.

Jules Dubois learned that Castro was having breakfast on New Year's Day when he was told the news of Batista's flight. "Castro fingered his beard and then exploded, 'This is a cowardly betrayal! A betrayal! They are trying to prevent the triumph of the Revolution!' He rose from the table, went to the door and called out for his men to hear. 'We have to attack Santiago without delay. If they are so ingenuous as to think that they will paralyze the Revolution with a coup d'état, we will show them they are wrong!'"[81] While Castro's troops occupied Santiago without resistance, he ordered Guevara and Cienfuegos to march on Havana and take over Camp Columbia until his arrival.[82]

In Havana, Chapelle witnessed Castro's men entering the city. The "first bearded and uniformed men, and the girls who had fought with them, marched into the capital." She noted that they checked into the Habana Hilton, "which back in the mountains they had proposed to demolish stone by stone" as one of the "symbols of the Batista regime." Dubois credited the bearded rebels—"well-trained Castro *Barbudos*"—with restoring "a notable improvement in public manners, because of their courteous, respectful and sober treatment of civilians and tourists."

Herbert Matthews and his wife Nancie were in Havana, too, having timed their vacation perfectly. On New Year's Eve they were at dinner in the Habana Riviera Hotel with *New York Times* correspondent Ruby Hart Phillips and Ted Scott of the *Havana Post*. In the hours that followed, Matthews "experienced the wild joy" in the capital and "could not repress a sense of personal triumph.... It had been my triumph, along with others." Yet, amid the jubilation, he confessed to an ominous foreboding as he witnessed the delirious victors' attitudes toward the vanquished—the "barely restrained ferocity against *Batistianos*." Then Matthews left Havana to greet Fidel Castro.[83]

A mid the chaos in Havana, a reporter with the *Toledo Blade*, Robert Branson, arrived from Ohio to interview a former Toledo soldier fighting with the rebels. During one year in the Escambray Mountains, William Morgan rose to prominence as a trainer and leader. Castro had just promoted him to major, making Morgan the most prominent former U.S. soldier among about thirty Americans who came to Cuba to fight the Batista regime.[84] Another American veteran, Neill Macaulay, just out of the U.S. Army in August 1958, had been inspired by reading in the U.S. edition of *La Prensa* a story about Donald Soldini, an American who "valiantly joined the forces of Raúl Castro to fight for the liberty of Cuba." Macaulay enlisted by going to the 26th of July Movement's New York office at 2390 First Avenue. Macaulay and his bride had just eloped, so now they planned for her to return to live with her parents and attend the University of Michigan, while he flew to Cuba. There, he was sent west of Havana to Pinar del Río Province to fight in the highlands of the Sierra de los Órganos and Sierra del Rosario.[85]

In Havana, Branson's *Toledo Blade* was interested mainly in Toledo's connection with the successful revolution. Branson tracked down Major William Morgan and found him near exhaustion. He said he had slept only six hours in the last two weeks of fighting. Morgan's force had besieged the southern city of Cienfuegos for weeks, and on New Year's Day marched in and took command of it.[86] He told Branson that he joined the rebels partly to avenge the murder of a friend. In 1957, he said, Cuban police killed an army buddy who was delivering arms to the rebels. In the Escambray Mountains, Morgan eventually commanded as many as five thousand men. "These people," Morgan stated, "have been fighting for things we take for granted in the United States. They wanted their freedom."[87]

Branson asked the Communist question. "I'm an American," Morgan declared. "We have no Communists here in Cuba. We don't want any and we're not going to have any." He said he wanted to return to Toledo but, like the other exiles, was unsure of his citizenship, which had been revoked, at least temporarily. "I'm kind of on the spot. I've been fighting here more than a year and I don't know what my status is with the [United States] Government.... My men fought in 15 or 16 battles—more than any other rebel force—and had heavier losses than the others.... The only thing I can do is sit tight until I see where I stand."[88]

Jules Dubois on the night of January 3 got the first interview with Fidel Castro, "thanks to W. D. Maxwell, editor of the *Chicago Tribune*, who authorized and chartered the plane." His Piper Apache landed at Holguin and was immediately "greeted by hundreds of *barbudos*, who surrounded our plane, smiling and waving." He found Castro in a technological school, in the principal's office, conferring with his commanders. "I bombarded him with questions," Dubois recalled, "some of them very pointed as to whether he harbored any resentment against the United States."

"Look here," Castro told Dubois, "if I have had to be very cautious about my statements in the past, from now on I am going to have to be even more careful."[89]

Dubois, with his persistent concern for press freedom, secured from Castro a written statement that the revolution wanted "to facilitate all the organs of the written press."[90]

Herbert Matthews was also searching for Castro. "I had flown to Camagüey in central Cuba with my wife to meet Fidel as he made his slow journey in a popular delirium westward to Havana. . . . In Camagüey and along the highway we were able to sense the overwhelming surge of popular emotion that was going to leave Fidel Castro no choice but to become his country's Jefe Maximo. No other man, no part, no movement could hold any leading place in Cuban hearts and minds in those early days and weeks. Power—absolute power—was forced upon Castro."

A few days later, Dickey Chapelle was in Havana when Castro arrived, and the citizens had "a day of delirium." Chapelle noted that Castro opened to the public the gates of Batista's stronghold, the huge Camp Columbia Army Base. "There, on the parade ground, with the crowd of 30,000 illuminated by searchlights, he held his final victory celebration. The revolution was over. The movement of the 26th of July had accomplished its mission. 'Free Cuba' was now all Cuba."[91]

EPILOGUE

In Revolutionary Situations

In April 1959, when Castro summoned his thirteen favorite American journalists to the reunion in the Cuban Embassy on 16th Street NW, he was no longer the "rebel chieftain" leading a ragtag band of guerrillas. Nor had he followed the course he had depicted to them—that of seeking a reclusive life in the mountains, farming and helping poor *guajiros*. Perhaps not surprisingly, he had, as some suspected would happen, accepted a central role in the new government, behind his choice as president. As premier of Cuba, he ranked second to the president whom he himself had chosen. In reality, El Comandante was the face of the Revolution, El Maximo, Numero Uno.

For the nine journalists who actually came to the ceremony in the Cuban Embassy, it was the first time they had been together, although they knew each other by reputation and publications, and a few had been in the same places in Cuba at the same time. Andrew St. George had spent the most time with the rebels. He was still hopeful about the revolution and continued to document the new Cuba in words and pictures for *Life* magazine. His hundreds of photographs would become a valuable historical archive, housed at Yale University. Eventually, when he became disillusioned with the revolution, it "was heartbreaking for him. He loved the Cubans," said his wife, Jean. So he started covering the anti-Castro rebels in Miami and elsewhere. Dickey Chapelle said St. George told her simply that he sold his eighteen-karat gold medal, and Jean clarified that her husband donated it to the anti-Castro rebels.

Chapelle was among those whom St. George had helped in their treks to find Fidel Castro. At the media ceremony Chapelle was no longer limping from the jeep accident; her expansive article encompassing the revolution's beginning, middle, and end had just been published in the April issue of *Reader's Digest*.

Five of the thirteen were making sense of their experiences by writing books. The indefatigable Jules Dubois, also recovered from a jeep accident, possessed a wider range of information than any of the others. He had reported on the entire spectrum of the revolution's hot spots—from the attack on the palace of President-General Batista, to the rebels' mountain camps, to the exiles and the spies in Miami. As a champion of the press, Dubois had been hopeful that Castro would restore the freedoms that Batista had suppressed. Since January he had rushed to complete his 389-page book in twenty days, and it had just been published in April by Bobbs-Merrill. In his final editing, Dubois's own caution caused him to make the title reflect his doubt about El Maximo. Now it was titled *Fidel Castro: Rebel, Liberator or Dictator?*

Herbert Matthews on April 5 had reviewed Dubois's book for the *Times*, praising it as "a full, solid, well-documented work that will stand up" and noting that "Dubois is a sincere admirer" of Castro. Matthews was impressed with "how the detail piles up excitingly and copiously"—especially "some of the "dismal facts"—notably the "blindsidedness" of the U.S. ambassador and the State Department in not recognizing in mid-1958 that Castro would win. By April, Matthews found himself defending the revolution against critics, and he would continue to defend it in his own book *The Cuban Story*, published in 1961. In its final chapter on "Journalism," Matthews scolded the press, saying he had "never seen such a big story so misunderstood, so misinterpreted and so badly handled." He would later publish *Castro: A Political Biography* (Allen Lane, 1969) and a broader work, *A World in Revolution* (Scribners, 1971), always maintaining that U.S. foreign policy, notably the economic embargo and the cut in sugar imports, had forced Fidel Castro to turn from nationalism to communism in order to seek massive aid from the Soviet Union. Matthews's personal papers are now housed in the Rare Books and Manuscripts Library of Columbia University's Butler Library, where, behind glass, I was able to see his gold medal engraved to Matthews "with gratitude" and signed by Castro.

At the medal ceremony, Ray Brennan of the *Chicago Sun-Times* seemed recovered from the exhaustion that in December had forced him home to Chicago to be hospitalized. In his strenuous effort to live with the rebels and compete with his *Chicago Tribune* rival, Dubois, Brennan had lost twenty-eight pounds from the deprivations of rebel life, and he had missed Castro's triumphant finish. Now, again following Dubois's lead, Brennan was completing *his* book on the revolution, titled *Castro, Cuba and Justice*, expected to be published that fall by Doubleday.

Robert Taber's experience in creating the "Jungle Fighters" documentary for CBS had been such a highlight of his career that he was drawn back to Cuba. For a time, he too defended the revolution, taking an active role as head of a "Fair Play for Cuba" committee. In his book *M-26: Biography of a Revolution*, published in 1961 by Lyle Stuart, Taber argued against "reactionary voices" in American business and the press that raised the specter of "a dictatorship taking shape in Cuba." Taber's second book, in 1965, *War of the Flea: The Classic Study of Guerrilla Warfare*, expanded on his Cuban experience to explain the success of the twentieth-century phenomenon of guerrilla warfare.

Karl Meyer's first book (*The New America*, 1961) mentioned Castro as one of many "flamboyant foreign leaders" attending the 1960 United Nations General Assembly. Castro was "especially dangerous" because "while North Americans can't 'understand' Castro's anger, many Latin Americans can.... [We] stand a good chance of losing what remains of our influence in Latin America."

Two of the thirteen honorees, Robert Branson and Morton Silverstein, played such brief roles in the revolution that they likely were surprised to be receiving gold medals. Silverstein by April 1959 was working with Mike Wallace in a new CBS interview show. As a freelancer, Silverstein had played an important role in the summer of 1958 during the peak of the Cuban Army's big failed offensive against the rebels. As the only reporter with the rebels at the time, Silverstein relayed Castro's victory to Homer Bigart and the *New York Times*. Branson was the one recipient who had not interviewed either Fidel or Raúl. The *Toledo Blade* had rushed him to Havana to interview the American volunteer soldier from Toledo, Major William Alexander Morgan. In highlighting Major Morgan's military leadership in the Escambray Mountains, Branson showed how American citizens supported what they understood was a battle of the Cuban people for freedom, against dictatorship. In addition to the men who enlisted at the Movement offices in New York, Washington, and Miami, other Americans supported in spirit and with money. A student in Tennessee had written his junior high school essay in support of Castro, and a young community leader in a south Georgia district had "raised money to buy a jeep for Castro's Cuba."

Homer Bigart's absence from the gold medal ceremony was understandable. Bigart had regarded Fidel Castro and Cuba as a distraction from his main work. Since early in 1958 he was busy reporting from newsworthy hotspots elsewhere, notably in the Middle East. Assigned to Cuba by news desk editors as a high-caliber substitute for Herbert Matthews, Bigart had none of Matthews's enthusiasm for the revolution. From the start, he considered Castro's rebel force puny and his revolution hopeless, especially after the general strike failed in April 1958.

Also absent at the embassy was Charles Shaw. He thought so highly of his Cuban reportage and his interview with Raúl Castro that in 1959 he hoped to win broadcasting's coveted Peabody Award. The third absentee was Robert Taber's CBS cameraman, Wendell Hoffman, who had gone on to other assignments. Taber could accept Hoffman's gold medal.

Karl Meyer, whose desk at the *Washington Post* was near enough to the Cuban Embassy, also missed the gold medal presentations. After Castro's victory, Meyer continued to write as an expert on events in Cuba, but far more cautiously than when he wrote his six-part series in September of 1958. On January 2, 1959, Meyer wrote a front-page analysis, noting that Castro's "views are only vaguely known." While Castro's "flamboyant tactics have made him the idol of Cuba's youth, they have aroused widespread mistrust elsewhere."[1] In an analysis three weeks later, on January 25, Meyer wrote that deteriorating U.S.-Cuban relations were caused, according to some diplomats, by cultural misunderstanding:

> The shots fired by Fidel Castro's firing squads have been heard half-way around the world.... In the United States, the aftermath of the revolution has aroused stern words in Congress, condemnation on editorial pages, and even talk about taking some action to show that six million Cubans must be wrong.
>
> The comment in Latin America is far more restrained, and in private some hemisphere representatives here are saying that there may be something to be said for the way the Cubans are wiping out supporters of ousted President Fulgencio Batista.
>
> And in Cuba there is hurt bafflement at criticism here of what the islanders regard as strictly their own business.
>
> The result is that diplomatic sources are citing the reactions to Cuba as a classic example of how differences in national temperament strongly color judgments as to what constitutes political morality.[2]

Since his horseback adventure in the Cuban mountains, Meyer had established his role as an analyst, wisely distancing himself from any appearance of support for Fidel Castro. One month after Castro's victory, on February 5, 1959, Meyer wrote a four-page analysis titled "Who Won What in Cuba?" published in the *Reporter*. Meyer still thought Cuba's future would be guided by its middle class, which had strongly supported Castro "in revolt against . . . graft, favoritism, police brutality, profligate waste of public funds, neglect of education, and the rule by military and landed oligarchs."[3]

In 1959, Meyer wrote reviews of the books published that year by Dubois and Brennan. He praised Dubois and panned Brennan. Dubois's book, published a few weeks before Castro's gold medal ceremony, revealed much unpublicized information basic to understanding Castro's 26th of July Movement. Meyer concluded that Dubois's book was "a reproach to American journalism that so many fundamental data must come to wide attention so late. For example, the theme of vengeance that runs through Castro's rhetoric is noticeable from the outset in the documents that Mr. Dubois quotes extensively." Although Dubois in the spring of 1959 saw "Castro essentially as a democratic leader, impetuous but shrewd," Meyer cautiously declined to agree: "It is perhaps not possible as yet to make a fair judgment on the direction of Castro's revolt."[4] By contrast, Brennan's book, Meyer wrote, "stressed the lurid and the sensational" as well as being "unreliable and tinctured with retrospective romance."[5]

By 1962, after the disastrous U.S.-supported invasion at the Bay of Pigs, Karl Meyer said of Castro, "from the beginning it seems evident that . . . the kind of revolution he evidently had in mind required an enemy image, uniting Cubans under a patriotic banner of resistance to a predatory foreign foe." Meyer's venture in the Cuban revolution had taught him to be less trusting: "It cured me, I think permanently, of taking at face value what people say in revolutionary situations."[6]

In that statement Meyer identified the primary problem in reporting the Cuban revolution. Those who interviewed Fidel Castro—even the skeptical Homer Bigart—usually took what Castro said at face value and passed his message on to their audiences. Several of the thirteen medalists enhanced Castro's image and legitimacy, notably Herbert Matthews, who as an opinion writer bypassed the U.S. press ideal of objectivity; Matthews's views, as he himself said, "set the stage."

On leaving the United States, the others also left behind the ideal of objectivity, or they had a different interpretation of it. Robert Taber and his cameraman Wendell Hoffman seemed to think that objectivity meant giving Castro an opportunity to speak—directly, unfiltered, and unchallenged—to the CBS television audience. As an adventure writer, Andrew St. George was never bound by American journalism's cherished codes; his writing and photography portrayed the rebels in the best light and the Batista dictatorship in the worst; in the end, St. George's disillusionment was profound.

Matthews, Taber, and St. George early on established a pattern for unbalanced coverage that the others tended to follow. Only Jules Dubois troubled himself to interview those opposed to Castro—Batista and the anti-Batista Cuban rebels in Miami.

Early in 1959, Dubois expressed his disillusionment. Like the others, he had been betrayed by his own hope that Castro would restore freedoms in Cuba, including press freedom. Hoping for the best, Dubois exemplified a fundamental problem in covering revolutions. That problem had been identified generations earlier in U.S. press coverage of the Russian Revolution, when reports by newsmen "were dominated by the hopes of the men . . . seeing not *what was*, but what men *wished to see*."

★ APPENDIX ★
"Castro Hails Newsmen"

From the *New York Times*, April 19, 1959, page 4:

CASTRO HAILS NEWSMEN

Gives Medals to Americans
Who Interviewed Him

WASHINGTON, April 19 (UP)—Premier Fidel Castro of Cuba awarded medals tonight to United States newsmen who interviewed him when he was leading the revolution.

They were: Herbert L. Matthews of The New York Times, Sam Halper of the magazine Time, Robert Taber of the Columbia Broadcasting System, Mrs. Georgette (Dickey) Chapelle of the Readers Digest, Ray Brennan of The Chicago Sun Times, Andrew St. George, a free-lance photographer, Morton Silverstein of the Radio Press, Jules Du Bois of The Chicago Tribune and Robert Branson of Michigan.

Others honored but not present were Homer Bigart of The New York Times, Wendell Hoffman of C.B.S., Charles Shaw of WCAU, Philadelphia, and Karl Meyer of the Washington Post and Times-Herald.

★ NOTES ★

1. Walter Lippmann and Charles Merz, "A Test of the News," *New Republic,* August 4, 1920, 3; Leonard Ray Teel, *The Public Press, 1900–1945: The History of American Journalism* (Westport, CT: Praeger, 2006), 91–92.

2. Gabriel García Márquez, Nobel Lecture, December 8, 1982.

3. Robert Taber, *War of the Flea: The Classic Study of Guerrilla Warfare* (1965; Washington, DC: Brassey's, 2002).

4. Maxwell E. McCombs and Donald L. Shaw, "The Agenda-setting Function of Mass Media," *Public Opinion Quarterly* 36, no. 2 (1972): 176–87.

5. Robert M. Entman, "Framing U.S. Coverage of International News: Contrasts in Narratives of the KAL and Iran Air Incidents," *Journal of Communication* 41, no. 4 (Autumn 1991): 6–27, and "Framing: Toward Clarification of a Fractured Paradigm," *Journal of Communication* 43, no. 4 (1993): 51–58.

6. Ernesto Laclau, "Why Do Empty Signifiers Matter in Politics?" in Laclau, *Emancipation(s)* (London: Verso, 1996), 36–46.

CHAPTER 1. THE THIRTEEN

1. "Castro Hails Newsmen; Gives Medals to Americans Who Interviewed Him," *New York Times,* April 19, 1959, 4. The three-paragraph United Press International story was the only mention that Castro awarded medals to the thirteen. The story was slightly inaccurate in that only eleven of the thirteen interviewed Fidel; a Philadelphia broadcaster interviewed his brother Raúl, and a Toledo reporter interviewed a hometown volunteer commander, William Morgan.

2. United Press (Francis McCarthy), "Cuba Wipes Invaders; Leader Is Among 40 Dead," *New York Times,* December 3, 1956, 1; Herbert L. Matthews, "Cuban Rebel Is Visited in Hideout; Castro Is Still Alive and Still Fighting in Mountains," *New York Times,* February 24, 1957, 1.

3. Lillian Guerra, *Visions of Power in Cuba: Revolution, Redemption, and Resistance, 1959–1971* (Chapel Hill: University of North Carolina Press, 2012), 101. Since his victory Castro had made the presentation of medals and pins—many with his picture—a common event. Guerra noted that Andrew St. George was collecting the "handmade and commercially made lapel pins" that were a "constant presence at virtually every political event involving Fidel Castro over the course of 1959–1960." In addition to supporting peace and agrarian reform, special pins were awarded for "'*sacudiendo la mata*' [shaking the tree]," recognizing workers who, Guerra said, "forced out active and tacit former supporters of Batista from their unions and workplaces. The pin decorated with a small tree read '*Sacude*' [Shake it]."

4. Jean Szentgyorgyi, wife of Andrew St. George, confirmed that the medals were of eighteen-karat gold; interview, February 12, 2014. The engraved medal presented to Herbert Matthews

is on exhibit behind glass at the Columbia University Library as part of the Herbert Matthews Collection.

5. Arnold S. DeBeer, "Global News: The Fleeting, Elusive but Essential Feature of Global Journalism," in Arnold S. DeBeer and John C. Merrill, *Global Journalism: Topical Issues and Media Systems,* 5th ed. (Boston: Pearson Education, 2009), 176.

6. Bill Holstein, past president of the Overseas Press Club, interview; during his career as an award-winning foreign correspondent for United Press International, he won the OPC award for coverage of China's economic "opening" to modernization and became UPI's Beijing bureau chief.

7. J. Herbert Altschull, *Agents of Power: The Media and Public Policy* (White Plains, NY: Longman, 1995), 68, 173.

8. This was the assessment of a twenty-first-century media critic. Eric Alterman, "They've Got the Fever . . ." *The Nation,* March 11/18, 2013, 10; see also Eric Louw, "Reporting Foreign Places," in DeBeer and Merrill, *Global Journalism,* 154.

9. "Cuba: Hit-Run Revolt," *Time,* December 10, 1956; "Cuban Mop-Up Ordered: Batista Tells Forces to End Revolt at Minimum Cost," *New York Times,* December 11, 1956, 22.

10. *New York Times,* "Cuban Mop-Up Ordered," 22; *Time,* "Cuba: Hit-Run Revolt."

11. Carlos Franqui, *Diary of the Cuban Revolution* (New York: Viking Press, 1976), 132.

12. Franqui, *Diary,* 132; Anthony DePalma, *The Man Who Invented Fidel: Castro, Cuba, and Herbert L. Matthews of the New York Times* (New York: Public Affairs, 2006), 102. The Batista regime's autocratic control of the press through censorship—as well as with bribes and government advertising—aimed to sustain "the government's hold on power" by controlling political life "but left other aspects of daily life untouched." Carlos Ripoll, "The Press in Cuba, 1952–1960: Autocratic and Totalitarian Censorship," in *The Selling of Fidel Castro,* ed. William E. Ratliff (New Brunswick, NJ: Transaction Books, 1987), 83, 94.

13. Che Guevara, in Franqui, *Diary,* 134.

14. "Cuba: Running-Sore Revolt," *Time,* February 25, 1957. *Time*'s correspondent living in Havana was Jay Mallin, who also freelanced stories for the *Miami News.*

15. Herbert L. Matthews, *The Cuban Story* (New York: Braziller, 1961), 45.

16. Matthews, "Cuban Rebel Is Visited," 1.

17. Matthews, *Cuban Story,* 20.

18. Ibid., 34.

19. Herbert L. Matthews, "Rebel Strength Gaining in Cuba, but Batista Has the Upper Hand," *New York Times,* February 25, 1957, 1, 11.

20. Matthews, *Cuban Story,* 15.

21. Jean Szentgyorgyi, interview, May 25, 2012.

22. In 1957, Cuban police arrested, detained, and sometimes beat several foreign journalists. The U.S. media coverage had sparked interest in Europe. *Le Monde* in Paris and other newspapers sent correspondents. In April and May 1958 *Le Monde*'s special correspondent, Claude Julien, spent three weeks in Cuba, then bypassed Cuban censorship by dispatching his stories from Haiti. His series of six stories appeared May 13–18, 1957, and have been reprinted. Marcel Niedergang, *1959: Castro Prend Le Pouvoir, Les Événements du Monde* (Paris: Éditions du Seuil, 1959), 27–29.

23. Matthews, *Cuban Story,* 16.

24. Jules Dubois, *Fidel Castro: Rebel, Liberator or Dictator?* (Indianapolis: Bobbs-Merrill, 1959).

25. Mario Llerena, *The Unsuspected Revolution: The Birth and Rise of Castroism* (Ithaca, NY: Cornell University Press, 1978), 41.

26. Francis Adams Truslow, *Report on Cuba: Findings and Recommendations of an Economic and Technical Mission* (Baltimore: Johns Hopkins University Press, 1951), 10–15.

1. Matthews, "Cuban Rebel Is Visited," 1, 34; "Cuba Plot Bomb Foiled: Police Say Terrorists Picked Cabarets as Targets," *New York Times*, January 6, 1957, 9; "Cuban Inquiry Sought: Supreme Court Is Petitioned to Investigate Violence," *New York Times*, January 9, 1957, 6. The government was also suspected of retaliatory killings of at least thirty youths found mysteriously shot to death.

2. United Press (Francis McCarthy), "Cuba Wipes Invaders," 1. Later, President Fulgencio Batista explained that he had doubts that Castro was dead but accepted McCarthy's story because the army chiefs believed it. The American ambassador to Cuba, Arthur Gardner, had also been assured that Castro had been killed and buried on December 9. Matthews, *Cuban Story*, 49.

3. Matthews, *Cuban Story*, 21, editorial, *New York Times*, December 4, 1956, and editorial, "Censorship in Cuba," *New York Times*, January 18, 1957.

4. "Cuba Sets Censorship: Curb on News Follows Lifting of Basic Guarantees," *New York Times*, January 16, 1957, 16; "Censors Use Scissors: Cuba Applies Old Means of Handling U.S. Publications," *New York Times*, January 17, 1957; "Batista Gets Appeal; Cuban Publishers Urge Him to Lift Censorship," *New York Times*, February 1, 1957; "Protest Sent to Cuba: Press Group Complains to Batista on Censorship," *New York Times*, February 20, 1957.

5. Peter Khiss, "Cuba Guerrillas Said to Fight On; Castro-Led Rebels Reported Raiding in East—Batista Official Here in Denial," *New York Times*, February 8, 1957, 10.

6. Matthews, "Censorship in Cuba."

7. His report was translated and published in Cuba: Herbert L. Matthews, "Cuba Vista por los Extranjeros: Una Republica Sin Ciudadanos" [Cuba Seen by Foreigners: A Republic without Citizens], *Bohemia*, June 1, 1952.

8. Sugarcane dominated agricultural production, accounting for 31 percent of national income in 1949. Of all agricultural land in 1945, 56 percent was devoted to sugar cultivation, far greater than percentages for corn (9.1), coffee (4.5), bananas and plantains (4.1), tobacco (3.4), rice (2.9), and pineapples (0.7). "Principal Crops Grown in Cuba, 1945," Ministerio de Agricultura, *Memoria del Censo Agricola Nacional*, 1946, Havana 1951, in Michael Patrick McGuigan, "Fulgencio Batista's Economic Policies, 1952–1958" (PhD dissertation, University of Miami, 2012), 6.

9. The flight to Havana from Key West was Pan American World Airways' first scheduled service after its founding in 1927.

10. R. Hart Phillips, "Cuba Liquidates Worst Problems: Sale Here of Surplus Sugar Restores Prosperity—New Industries Big Factor," *New York Times*, January 4, 1957, 74; Diana Rice, "News Notes from the Field of Travel," *New York Times*, January 27, 1957, and "From the Field of Travel," *New York Times*, October 16, 1955, X23; Unpublished notes, Port of Miami File, Historical Association of Southern Florida (HASF), in Arthur Chapman, "Watch the Port of Miami," *Tequesta: The Journal of the Historical Association of Southern Florida* 1, no. 53: 18; Observations during a visit by the author in August 1957.

11. T. J. English, *Havana Nocturne: How the Mob Owned Cuba and Then Lost It to the Revolution* (New York: William Morrow, 2008), 289–90.

12. Kenneth S. Lynn, *Hemingway* (New York: Simon & Schuster, 1987), 575–76.

13. Miguel A. Santin, "Hotel Construction in Puerto Rico at Peak in History of Caribbean," *New York Times*, July 29, 1956, R1; English, *Havana Nocturne*, 150, 203, 210, 211–12; "2 Hurt in Havana Bomb Blast," *New York Times*, January 2, 1957, 4; "'Bebo' Valdés, Giant of Cuban Music, Is Dead," NPR Music, March 22, 2012.

14. Matthews, "Cuban Rebel Is Visited," 34.

15. Truslow, *Report on Cuba*, 10–13.

16. Tad Szulc, *Fidel: A Critical Portrait* (New York: William Morrow, 1986), 255, 264, 267, 273, 279.

17. Ibid., 274, 276. Castro's survival was also attributed to intervention by Archbishop Pérez Serantes and a local priest who put Fidel and Raúl under his protection.

18. Ibid., 280–81. Szulc quoted what Castro ten years later told the French historian Robert Merle.

19. Fidel Castro, *History Will Absolve Me* (Secaucus, NJ: Lyle Stuart, 1984), 31–32.

20. The first edition of *La Historia Me Absolverá* was clandestinely printed and circulated in June 1954. It was dedicated "In memory of the seventy young men who became martyrs of Moncada on July 26, 1953." It was also dedicated to "Haydee Santamaria and Melba Hernandez, two young women who gave an unforgettable example to all women." And it was preceded by "a prayer for peace in all the world and with hope that someday soon no one will need to die in order that his people may be free." For the 1984 publication CBS News anchor Robert Taber recalled his first encounter with Castro in the mountains in the spring of 1957.

21. Szulc, *Fidel*, 213, 320, 324.

22. DePalma, *The Man Who Invented Fidel*, 24.

23. Hugh Thomas, *Cuba: The Pursuit of Freedom* (New York: Harper & Row, 1971), 783–84.

24. Matthews, *Cuban Story*, 21.

25. Ibid.

26. Ibid., 22.

27. Matthews, *Cuban Story*, 22, 45, and "Cuban Rebel Is Visited," 1.

28. Herbert L. Matthews, *The Education of a Correspondent* (New York: Harcourt, Brace and Co., 1946), 4; John Hohenberg, *Foreign Correspondence: The Great Reporters and Their Times*, 2nd ed. (Syracuse, NY: Syracuse University Press, 1995), 169; DePalma, *The Man Who Invented Fidel*, 47.

29. Hohenberg, *Foreign Correspondence*, 169; for a discussion of the war's correspondents and their sympathies, see Michael B. Salwen, *Evelyn Waugh in Ethiopia: The Story behind Scoop* (Lewiston, NY: Edward Mellon Press, 2001), i–vi, 60–68, 277; Evelyn Waugh, *Scoop* (Boston: Little, Brown, 1937).

30. Salwen, *Evelyn Waugh*, 7, 60, 63; Herbert L. Matthews, *A World in Revolution: A Newspaperman's Memoir* (New York: Charles Scribner's & Sons, 1971), 114.

31. Matthews, *World in Revolution*, 21–26.

32. Ibid., 52–53.

33. Matthews, *Education of a Correspondent*, 8.

34. Ibid., 8; Matthews, *Cuban Story*, 22, 45, and "Cuban Rebel Is Visited," 1.

35. Matthews, *Cuban Story*, 16.

36. DePalma, *The Man Who Invented Fidel*, 34–35.

37. Matthews, *Cuban Story*, 16.

38. Ibid.

39. Herbert Matthews, "Four Continents—IV: Latin America," *New York Times*, August 31, 1967, 32.

40. Matthews, *Cuban Story*, 24.

41. Ibid., 24–27; Thomas, *Cuba*, 917.

42. Matthews, "Cuban Rebel Is Visited," 34, and *Cuban Story*, 23–25.

43. Matthews," Cuban Rebel Is Visited," 34.

44. Ibid.

45. Ibid.

46. Ibid., 1.

47. Ibid.

48. Matthews's handwritten notes, Herbert L. Matthews Papers, Rare Book and Manuscript Library, Columbia University; Matthews, "Cuban Rebel," 34.

49. Matthews, *Cuban Story,* 36; photograph in the Herbert L. Matthews Papers, Rare Book and Manuscript Library, Columbia University.

50. Matthews, "Cuban Rebel Is Visited," 34.

51. Ibid.

52. Ibid.

53. Franqui, *Revolucion,* in *Diary,* 136; for more about imagined nations, see Benedict Anderson, *Imagined Communities: Reflections on the Origin and Spread of Nationalism,* rev. ed. (London: Verso, 2006), 141, 144.

54. Matthews, "Cuban Rebel Is Visited," 34.

55. Ibid.

56. Ibid.

57. Szulc, *Fidel,* 168.

58. Matthews, "Cuban Rebel Is Visited," 34.

59. Ibid.

60. Matthews, *Cuban Story,* 43–44, and "Cuban Rebel Is Visited," 34.

61. Herbert L. Matthews, "Old Order in Cuba Is Threatened by Forces of an Internal Revolt," *New York Times,* February 26, 1957, 13.

62. Matthews, "Cuban Rebel Is Visited," 34.

63. Ibid., 1, 34.

64. Matthews, *Education of a Correspondent,* 3.

65. Matthews, "Cuban Rebel Is Visited," 34.

66. Matthews, *Cuban Story,* 41. Matthews later conceded that he "overestimated the size of Fidel's forces.... I had seen about twenty-five rebels and knew there were others nearby—perhaps forty in all. This was correct, but I was wrong to think the group I saw was part of a large force." In April 1959, Castro, on his first visit to New York as Cuba's prime minister, said he had fooled Matthews into believing he had forty or more armed troops by marching the same men repeatedly through the campsite. Actually he had only eighteen men. DePalma, *The Man Who Invented Fidel,* 159.

67. Matthews, "Cuban Rebel Is Visited," 1, and *Cuban Story,* 49.

68. Henry R. Cassirer, interview by Mike Conway, July 21–22, 2003, Annecy-Le-Vieux, videotape recording, Center for American History, University of Texas at Austin (HC-OH), in Mike Conway, *The Origins of Television News in America: The Visualizers of CBS in the 1940s* (New York: Peter Lang, 2009), 251, 255, 286. See also Henry R. Cassirer, *Seeds in the Winds of Change: Through Education and Communication* (Dereham, UK: Peter Francis, 1989), 180–81. In November 1948, Edmond Chester fired Cassirer, giving him no reason.

69. Drew Pearson, *Diaries, 1949–1959,* ed. Tyler Abell (New York: Holt, Rinehart & Winston, 1974), 303.

70. Matthews, *Cuban Story,* 46–47.

71. By 1960, according to the journalism historian John Hohenberg, anonymous sourcing had "become firmly lodged in American journalism." Matt J. Duffy, "Anonymous Sources: A Historical Review of the Norms Surrounding Their Use," *American Journalism* 31, no. 2 (Spring 2014): 244–46; in a later period, the use of unnamed sources during the Vietnam War by *Times* reporter Harrison Salisbury was a likely reason he was passed over for a Pulitzer Prize. Indeed, neither did Matthews's Cuban reports win a Pulitzer. The *Times's* insistence on attribution in war situations was emphasized by foreign news editors. See the controversy over Salisbury's unattributed information about the effects of U.S. bombing of North Vietnam. Seymour Topping, *On the Front Lines of*

the Cold War: An American Correspondent's Journal from the Chinese Civil War to the Cuban Missile Crisis and Vietnam (Baton Rouge: Louisiana State University Press, 2010), 313–18.

72. Matthews, "Rebel Strength Gaining," 11.

73. Ibid., 1.

74. Ibid., 1, 11.

75. Charles W. Kegley, Jr., and Eugene R. Wittkopf, American Foreign Policy: Pattern and Process (New York: St. Martin's Press, 1979), 50–51. The authors cite Neal D. Houghton: "American support for dictatorships through the world is indisputable. Spain. Portugal. The Dominican Republic. Brazil. Greece. Cuba. South Korea. Taiwan. Vietnam. In these and many other cases, the United States has armed and otherwise supported the most ruthless tyrannies in the modern world. Yet the dictatorships share a common characteristic: they were anticommunist."—Neal D. Houghton, ed., Struggle against History: U.S. Foreign Policy in an Age of Revolution (New York: Washington Square Press, 1968).

76. Matthews, "Rebel Strength Gaining," 1.

77. Ibid.

78. Ibid., 11.

79. Ibid., 1–11.

80. "Cuba: Batista at Work," Newsweek, March 24, 1952.

81. Matthews, "Rebel Strength Gaining," 1, 11; English, Havana Nocturne, 19–20, 289–90; Ray Brennan, Castro, Cuba and Justice (Garden City, NY: Doubleday, 1959), 272.

82. Stephen Kinzer, The Brothers: John Foster Dulles, Allen Dulles, and Their Secret World War (New York: St. Martin's Griffin, 2013), 147–60, 164–73; Szulc, Fidel, 315; Thomas, Cuba, 855.

83. Szulc, Fidel, 315; Thomas, Cuba, 855.

84. Szulc, Fidel, 312–13; Douglas Martin, "Melba Hernández, 92, a Confidante of Castro from First Volley, Is Dead," New York Times, March 16, 2014, 24.

85. Fidel Castro, History Will Absolve Me, 52–54, 111.

86. Matthews, "Rebel Strength Gaining," 11, and "Cuba Vista por los Extranjeros."

87. Matthews, "Old Order in Cuba."

88. Ibid.

89. Ibid.

90. Ibid.

91. Ibid.

92. Matthews, Education of a Correspondent, 69, 172; Propaganda by "soldiers of paper and ink" played a key role in the Spanish Civil War. Antony Beevor, The Battle for Spain (London: Weidenfeld & Nicholson, 2006). "In order to sustain false claims made as fighting commenced, battles were often continued long after they were lost," noted book reviewer Piers Brendon, "The Beevorised version: Antony Beevor's The Battle for Spain, a revamped discussion of the Spanish civil war, succeeds brilliantly," The Guardian, June 23, 2006.

93. Matthews, Education of a Correspondent, 69.

94. Ibid., 11.

95. John P. Ferre, "Codes of Ethics: Efforts to Promote Image of Professionalism," in History of the Mass Media in the United States, ed. Margaret A. Blanchard (Chicago: Fitzroy Dearborn, 1998); "No Banker Sways Him, Says Harding," New York Times, April 29, 1923, 1, cited in Steve Ponder, "That Delightful Relationship: Presidents and the White House Correspondents in the 1920s," American Journalism, 14, no 2 (Spring 1997): 172; Teel, The Public Press, 1900–1945, 116–17; Frank Luther Mott, American Journalism, rev. ed. (New York: Macmillan, 1950), 725–27.

96. Mott, American Journalism, 726–27; Teel, The Public Press, 1900–1945, 116–17.

97. Lippmann and Merz, "Test of the News," 3; Teel, *The Public Press, 1900–1945,* 91–92.

98. John Maxwell Hamilton, *Journalism's Roving Eye: A History of American Foreign Reporting* (Baton Rouge: Louisiana State University Press, 2009), 352, 379.

99. Matthews, *World in Revolution,* 29–30.

100. Ibid., 26–27.

101. Matthews, "Old Order in Cuba," 13.

102. Matthews, *World in Revolution,* 5.

CHAPTER 3. THE STAGE IS SET

1. Matthews, *Cuban Story,* 300.

2. A. J. Liebling, *Chicago: The Second City* (New York: Knopf, 1952). "Particularly disappoint-ing to Liebling, one of the period's few serious critics of journalism," wrote J. Weintraub in 1993, "were the city's newspapers, once renowned for their nurturing of literary talent and investigative reporting. Both the *Daily News* and the *Herald-American,* he discovered, had been neutralized by absentee publishers, and of course he could not be expected to stomach the 'foam-flecked-lips' editorials and 'dreamworld' of Colonel McCormick's *Tribune.* The *Sun-Times* launched impressive (albeit futile) crusades against municipal corruption, but the space it devoted to other news was 'below the intellectual subsistence level.' . . . After several months' immersion in Chicago's news-papers, Liebling felt like 'a diver returning to the light' upon reading his first *New York Times*"; J. Weintraub, "Why They Call It the Second City: A. J. Liebling and the Chicago He Knew and Hated," *The Reader,* July 29, 1993, accessed April 21, 2013 at http://www.chicagoreader.com/chicago /why-they-call-it-the-second-city/Content?oid=882456#.UXRIvUQuM1s.gmail.

3. The *Tribune* had a daily circulation of 935,943 to the *Times*'s 557,224. (On Sundays the *Tribune* circulation was 1,303,615, and the *Times*'s up to 1,189,293.) Circulation figures for 1957 are from the *International Yearbook.*

4. "Latin America," in *IPI Survey No.1: Improvement of Information* (Zurich: International Press Institute, 1952), 163; Mary A. Gardner, *The Inter-American Press Association: Its Fight for Free-dom of the Press, 1926–1960* (Austin: University of Texas Press, 1967), 102, 103, 138n, 172, 174. Gardner cites multiple newspaper stories and IAPA records.

5. The reference to the "new deal" was changed perhaps in deference to the *Tribune*'s recently deceased publisher, Colonel Robert McCormick, who during the Great Depression in the 1930s despised President Franklin Roosevelt's "New Deal" that raised taxes on publishers.

6. Herbert L. Matthews, "Rebel Leader Castro Still Fights in Cuba: Batista May Contain, Not Beat Him," *Chicago Daily Tribune,* February 27, 1957, 10F. The story was credited to Matthews and the N.Y. Times–Chicago Tribune Service. The *Tribune* editors noted: "First article in a series by a reporter who has just returned from Cuba." The second installment focused on how Matthews found Castro. "Two Whistles in Dark: Rebels O.K. Reporter; How Meeting with Cuba Chief Was Set Up," *Chicago Daily Tribune,* February 28, 1957, 14F. The third installment was headlined "Cuban Rebel Only 30; His Men Younger; Stronger than Ever, He Boasts in Interview," *Chicago Daily Tri-bune,* March 1, 1957. The fourth installment was headlined "Cuba President Needs Luck to Hang On, Reporter Says," *Chicago Daily Tribune,* March 2, 1957, 6F. The final installment was headlined "Cubans' Fight Called Peril to Old Order; Meaning of Struggle by Rebels Told," *Chicago Daily Tri-bune,* March 3, 1957, 4F.

7. An Associated Press news brief from Havana stated that the Cuban cabinet on March 2 sus-pended constitutional guarantees for forty-five days "to protect Cuba's vital sugar industry from

threatened sabotage by 'insurrectionists and Communists.'" "Suspends Rights," *Chicago Daily Tribune,* March 3, 1957, 4F.

8. George Southworth, "Cuba Confident Rebels Crushed: But Fighting Still Reported," *Miami Herald,* February 23, 1957, 1A.

9. George Southworth, "Castro Termed Only 'Thorn' to Batista: Cuban Newsman Says Dictator's Biggest Headache Is People's Irritation at Unstable Regime," *Miami Herald,* February 26, 1957, 2A; John McMullen, telephone interview with the author, February 12, 2004.

10. Southworth, "Castro Termed Only 'Thorn' to Batista."

11. Ibid.

12. John McMullen, telephone interview with author, February 12, 2004. After Castro invaded Cuba, McMullen said, "the fellow that he [Castro] became acquainted with on our staff was [reporter] Jim Buchanan. Before the revolution actually succeeded Castro was in the mountains. We sent Jim down and warned him not to get involved. So he made that trip OK and came back and did a couple of pretty fair stories. After he made contact with Castro in the mountains he had an association with Castro. He didn't write anything that was offensive to Castro that I know of."

13. Llerena, *Unsuspected Revolution,* 93–94.

14. Ibid., 95.

15. Conway, *Origins of Television News in America,* 269.

16. A. M. Sperber, *Murrow: His Life and Time* (Toronto: Bantam Books, 1987), 354–56.

17. Ibid., 519.

18. Llerena, *Unsuspected Revolution,* 95; Humberto Fontova, "Looking the Other Way on Castro," FrontPageMagazine.com, August 26, 2009. When Don Hewitt, the creator of CBS's *60 Minutes,* died in August 2009, Fontova agreed that "Hewitt may have been a historic figure" but among the "less admirable legacies of the CBS veteran concern the services he rendered to Cuba's communist regime through decades of uncritical coverage" starting with sending Taber to interview Castro; DePalma, *The Man Who Invented Fidel,* 117–18.

19. "Tildada de novela fantástica In entravista Mathews-Castro: Dice el doctor S. Verdeja a nombre que Mathews no se ha entrevistado con Castro," *Diario de la Marina* [Havana], February 28, 1957, 1; "Cuba Brands Castro Interview as Phony," *Times of Havana,* February 28, 1957, 1.

20. "But Matthews Sticks to His Story, Shows New Photo," *Times of Havana,* February 28, 1957, 1.

21. Richard G. "Dick" Cushing to HLM, telegram from Havana, February 26, 1957, Herbert L. Matthews (HLM) Papers, Rare Books and Manuscripts Library (RBML), Columbia University (CU), Box 1, Folder 26.

22. Grayson Kirk to HLM, March 1, 1957; Manuel Bustillo to HLM, February 24, 1957; Arthur Steinmetz to HLM, February 24, 1957, all in Box 1, Folder 26, HLM Papers, RBML, CU.

23. Dr. Raoul Alfonso Gonsé, director, *El Mundo,* La Habana, to HLM, February 25, 1957; Rogelio Pina, Society of Friends of the Republic, Havana, to HLM, March 1, 1957; Arno Ido G. Barron, *Movimiento Revolucionario 26 de Julio New York,* 208 W. 88 St. to HLM, undated; Lidia Castro and Emma Castro to HLM, telegram, Feb. 27, 1957, all in Box 1, Folder 26, HLM Papers, RBML, CU.

24. "The Cuban Censorship," *New York Times,* February 26, 1957, editorial page.

25. HLM to Turner Catledge, March 4, 1957, Box 1, Folder 26, HLM Papers, RBML, CU.

26. Jules Dubois, "Batista Vows Censoring of Press Is Over: Tells Association Men of His Decision," *Chicago Daily Tribune,* March 7, 1957, 11; accompanying Dubois in the interview was the IAPA president, the editor of the Havana daily *El Pais,* Guillermo Martinez Marquez; "Jules Dubois, Famed Latin American Reporter, Is Dead," *Chicago Daily Tribune,* August 17, 1966, 1, 2.

27. "Americas' Press Seeks Firm Right; Mexico City Session Assails Control of Newsprint Import," *New York Times* [Associated Press], October 11, 1953.

28. Peter Kihss, "Nicaragua Holds 200 of Opposition in Somozo Attack: Regime Foes Rounded Up—President Flown to Panama for Four-Hour Surgery," *New York Times*, September 24, 1956, 1. After an assassination attempt in September 1957, Dubois and other correspondents intervened and "the Somoza brothers agreed to permit the dispatch of 'facts' without previous scrutiny . . . relying on the responsibility of correspondents."

29. Gardner, *The Inter-American Press Association*, 32.

30. Ibid., 174.

31. "Jules Dubois, Famed Latin American Reporter, Is Dead," *Chicago Daily Tribune*, August 17, 1966, 1; "Costa Rica Eases Curbs: Censorship Ended for Outgoing Dispatches—Writer Freed," *New York Times*, March 19, 1948, 5; "Dominicans Bar Writer: Trujillo Regime Forbids Entry of U.S. Correspondent," *New York Times*, April 4, 1957; Jules Dubois, "Junta Overthrows Colombia Dictator; Expulsion Order against Tribune Writer Lifted," *Chicago Daily Tribune*, May 11, 1957; "The Press: Freedom Fighter," *Time*, April 15, 1957.

32. Dubois, "Batista Vows"; Associated Press, "Cuba Frees Two Reporters on Plea from U.S.," *Chicago Daily Tribune*, March 6, 1957, 7.

33. Dubois, *Fidel Castro*, 151–52, and "Batista Vows."

34. Dubois, *Fidel Castro*, 151–52, and "Batista Calls Rebel Castro Russian Agent: Vows His Insurrection Will Be Crushed," *Chicago Daily Tribune*, March 11, 1957, 20.

35. Jules Dubois, "3 U.S. Youths Join Cuban Rebel Forces," *Chicago Daily Tribune*, March 9, 1957, 3; Robert Taber, *M-26: Biography of a Revolution* (New York: Lyle Stuart, 1961), 102.

36. Taber, *M-26*, 107; "Batista Decries Killing of 'Fools'; Says He Knew for 3 Days an Attack Was Coming—Prío Says President Will Fall," *New York Times, March 13, 1957*, 3; R. Hart Phillips, "Cuba Suppresses Youths' Uprising, Forty Are Killed; Students Storming Batista's Palace Routed as Tanks and Troops Arrive," *New York Times*, March 14, 1957, 1.

37. Jules Dubois, "Revolt in Havana; 50 Slain: Batista Forces Crush Attack on His Palace: President Blames Assault on 'Pro-Reds,'" *Chicago Daily Tribune*, March 14, 1957, 1.

38. Dubois, "Revolt in Havana, 1; Dubois, *Fidel Castro*, 152–53; Dom Bonafede, "Cuba Calm: Death Toll Rises to 45: Order Is Restored in Havana," *Miami Daily News*, March 14, 1957, 1, 2; Bob Hardin, "Trio Here Tells How Cubans Riddled Room: Beach Quieter, They Find," *Miami Daily News*, March 15, 1957, 18B; Milt Sosin, "Tourists Describe Violence [in Havana]: Witnesses Arrive at Miami Airport: All's Quiet Now, Batista in Saddle," *Miami Daily News*, March 14, 1957, 1. More than a week later, a New York City singer, Gina Goddard, showed off her souvenir of the attack on the palace: a music book from her Havana apartment now with a bullet hole. United Press Photo, *Chicago Daily Tribune*, March 24, 1957, 15; Phillips, "Cuba Suppresses Youths' Uprising."

39. Taber, *M-26*, 110.

40. Taber, *M-26*, 110–11.

41. Dubois, "Revolt in Havana," 1; Dubois, *Fidel Castro*, 152–53; Sosin, "Tourists Describe Violence," 1; Jules Dubois, "The Hemisphere: Cuba: 'Not Afraid to Die,'" *Time*, March 25, 1957, 36.

42. Dubois, "Revolt in Havana," 1, *Fidel Castro*, 152–53, and "Cuba under Reign of Terror: Batista Foe Shot Dead: 2 Found Hanged," *Chicago Daily Tribune*, March 15, 1957, 10; Taber, *M-26*, 116; Dubois, "'Not Afraid to Die,'" 36; [Deaths in] Cuba Rise to 45: Score Wounded in Havana Revolt," *Miami Daily News*, March 14, 1957, 1.

43. Dubois, "Revolt in Havana," 1, 2.

44. Dubois, "Cuba under Reign of Terror," 10, 1, and *Fidel Castro*, 153.

45. Dubois, "Cuba under Reign of Terror," 1, *Fidel Castro*, 153, and "Widow Says Batista Slew Husband: Sought Him Out in Hiding Place," *Chicago Daily Tribune*, March 18, 1957, 9; Phillips, "Cuba Suppresses Youths' Uprising, 2."

46. Jules Dubois, "Batista's Foes Vow to Push Freedom Fight," *Chicago Daily Tribune,* March 16, 1957, 4F.

47. Jules Dubois, "Forces of Rebellion in Cuba Are Closing Ranks and Moving Fast," *Chicago Sunday Tribune,* March 24, 1957, 15, and "Empty Jails, Cubans Tell Batista: Ask More Political Freedom," *Chicago Daily Tribune,* March 7, 1957.

48. Dubois, "Forces of Rebellion."

49. Dubois, "Empty Jails," 13.

50. Dubois, *Fidel Castro,* 5.

51. Charles W. Anderson, "Toward a Theory of Latin American Politics," in Peter G. Snow, *Government and Politics in Latin America: A Reader* (New York: Holt, Rinehart & Winston, 1967), 233–34; Dubois, *Fidel Castro,* 383.

52. Jack Lotto, "Batista Used Himself as 'Bait' in Revolt," *Miami Daily News,* March 16, 1957, 1. In passing, Batista revealed that he was canceling Cuba's congressional elections, supposedly because "the opposition will accept nothing less than general elections"; Dom Bonafede, "Revolt Made Batista Tougher, Cubans Say: Dramatic Uprising Had No Chance of Success," *Miami Daily News,* March 17, 1957, 9A.

53. Herbert L. Matthews, "Una Republica Sin Ciudadanos," *Bohemia,* June 1, 1952, translated in Havana from the *New York Times.* Matthews was identified as a member of the "Junta de Dirección del 'Times' de New York."

54. Dubois, "'Not Afraid to Die.'"

55. Dubois, *Fidel Castro,* 153.

56. Dubois, "Empty Jails."

57. Herbert Matthews, "Whither Cuba," *New York Times,* March 25, 1957, 24.

58. Dubois, "Forces of Rebellion."

CHAPTER 4. CUBA'S JUNGLE FIGHTERS

1. Melvyn P. Leffler, *A Preponderance of Power: National Security, the Truman Administration, and the Cold War* (Stanford, CA: Stanford University Press, 1992); Dexter Filkins, "Collateral Damage: Promoting Their Opening to China, Richard Nixon and Henry Kissinger Countenanced Mayhem in South Asia," review of Gary J. Bass, *The Blood Telegram: Nixon, Kissinger, and a Forgotten Genocide* (2013), *New York Times Book Review,* September 29, 2013, 15; Bass is a professor of politics at Princeton, and Filkins is a staff writer for the *New Yorker,* formerly a correspondent in South Asia for the *New York Times* and the *Los Angeles Times.* Adam Hochschild, "Ian Buruma's Global History of the Pivotal Year 1945, When a New World Emerged from the Ruins of War," review of Ian Buruma, *Year Zero: A History of 1945* (2013), *New York Review of Books,* September 29, 2013, 18. Hochschild's most recent book is *To End All Wars: A Story of Loyalty and Rebellion, 1914–1918.*

2. Matthews, *Cuban Story,* 49. Matthews learned this from Ted Scott of the *Havana Post,* who also said of Batista's public relations counselor, "Ed Chester, of course, is fit to be tied."

3. Taber, *M-26,* 133.

4. Ibid., 133–34.

5. Ibid., 101, 135.

6. Ibid., 132–33.

7. Ibid., 103–6, 113, 118, 133, 137. Taber determined that Prío "had been pouring money into arms for various revolutionary groups in Cuba almost from the beginning of his exile." Eventually the amount reached $5 million or more.

8. Ibid., 135–36.

9. Ibid., 136.

10. Ibid.

11. Ibid., 136–37.

12. Ibid.

13. Llerena, *Unsuspected Revolution,* 104.

14. Ibid., 104–5.

15. Ibid., 105.

16. Shortly after slipping home to New York with his film, Hoffman gave an interview and some of his still photographs to Cuban correspondents Luis Ortega Sierra and Marco A. Martinez for the Havana magazine *Bohemia.* Wendell L. Hoffman, "Yo Condemno El Terrorismo: Rechaza Energicamente Los Atentados Personales," *Bohemia* [Havana] 49, no. 21 (May 26, 1957), 72.

17. Llerena, *Unsuspected Revolution,* 105–8.

18. Marcos and Nicaragua were later identified as Delio Gómez Ochoa and Major Carlos Iglesias, assisted by a coordinator, Marcelo Fernández.

19. Richard Haney, *Celia Sanchez: The Legend of Cuba's Revolutionary Heart* (New York: Algora, 2005), 70; Che Guevara, in Franqui, *Diary,* 174; Thomas, *Cuba,* 936.

20. Hoffman, "Yo Condemno El Terrorismo," 71, 97; Guevara, in Franqui, *Diary,* 174.

21. Hoffman, "Yo Condemno El Terrorismo," 70, 72.

22. Ibid.

23. Ibid., 72, 97.

24. Jon Lee Anderson, *Che Guevara: A Revolutionary Life,* rev. ed. (New York: Grove Press, 2010), 244. The peak, at 6,561 feet, is named for the turquoise hue that covers its steep upper slopes. Today, the climb is described as a "two- to-three-day grind" for which a guide is mandatory, as well as warm clothing. Brendan Sainsbury, *Lonely Planet: Cuba* (Oakland, CA: Lonely Planet Publications, 2009), 395.

25. Emilio Bejel, *José Martí: Images of Memory and Mourning* (New York: Palgrave Macmillan, 2012), 103; Lillian Guerra, *The Myth of José Martí: Conflicting Nationalisms in Early Twentieth-Century Cuba* (Chapel Hill: University of North Carolina Press, 2005), 34.

26. Robert Taber and Wendell Hoffman, "The Jungle Fighters: The Rebels of the Sierra Maestra," CBS, May 20, 1957, excerpted in the documentary *American Experience: Fidel Castro,* a production of WGBH Educational Foundation (PBS), Boston, 2005; distributed by Paramount Home Entertainment., Hollywood, CA.

27. Hoffman, "Yo Condemno El Terrorismo," 98.

28. Transcript of Taber's radio broadcast in Taber, *M-26,* 137–38.

29. Ibid., 138.

30. "In Man's War, U.S. Boys Quit," *Life,* May 27, 1957, 43. Ryan remained a few more months and was promoted to lieutenant. "Castro then sent him back, too, suggesting that he could do more for the rebel cause in the United States in propaganda work." Dubois, *Fidel Castro,* 159. The *Life* display also showed a photograph of "a man facing death"—a "Batista spy" (back to camera) confronted by a rebel rifleman and being interrogated by Camilo Cienfuegos, waving a pistol. The "spy" was later shot. Cienfuegos, described as a romantic cavalryman, was to become commander-in-chief of the army and "the man best loved in Cuba after Castro" until his mysterious death in October 1959. His body was never found, and foul play was suspected. Thomas, *Cuba,* 1247–1248.

31. The reason for this failure—bitterly denounced by students in the urban Directorio Revolutionario—was a mystery, Taber noted. Taber, *M-26,* 137, 139–40.

32. Guevara, in Franqui, *Diary,* 175.

33. Taber, *M-26,* 137–38; Guevara, in Franqui, *Diary,* 175.

34. Don Hewitt's framing of the documentary without rebuttal could have been justified as "documentary vérité"—showing a slice of reality. After the revolution succeeded, one anti-Castro critic argued that Hewitt had "fashioned" a "snow-job" that made him a "Fidel Castro enabler. . . . Fully half of the 'report' consisted of Fidel Castro facing the camera and monologuing into the mic. The liberties, rights and blessings Castro planned for Cuba's people, as transmitted by CBS, made John Stuart Mill appear like Ivan the Terrible. Regarding Castro's heartwarming and eye-misting plans for Cuba—nary a rebuttal was to be heard on this blockbuster CBS 'investigative report.'" Humberto Fontova, "CBS's Don Hewitt—Fidel Castro Enabler," accessed August 24, 2009, www.lewrockwell.com/fontova/fontova77.1.html.

35. "Fidel Castro," American Experience, PBS Home Video, 2005.

36. Taber and Hoffman, "Rebels of the Sierra Maestra"; DePalma, *The Man Who Invented Fidel,* 117.

37. United Press, "Televisó la Columbia en E.U. el documental de la Sierra Maestra; Radiada también una entrevista grabada en le Pico Turquino al lider insurrecto Fidel Castro," *Diario de la Marina* (Havana), May 20, 1957, 1; United Press, "Fidel Castro 'Stars' on Television Program," *Times of Havana,* May 20, 1957, 3.

38. Associated Press, "Documentary exhibited in Miami," May 20, 1957.

39. United Press, "Manifestation in front of the White House," May 20, 1957.

40. Dubois, *Fidel Castro,* 159. Dubois noted that Castro had revolutionary "cells" inside the Guantánamo base, located as it was near the Sierra Maestra. Even before the three teenagers joined Castro, "some arms and ammunition had disappeared from the naval base. Among the stolen weapons were two 81-millimeter mortars. These were taken, apparently, by members of the 26th of July Movement cells on the base and were transported westward for use by the Castro forces, desperately in need of guns of any kind."

CHAPTER 5. MARCHING WITH CASTRO

1. Jean Szentgyorgyi, interview by the author, May 25, 2012.

2. Jean Szentgyorgyi, interview, March 1, 2012; J. L. Anderson, *Che,* 245.

3. Clyde Benton as told to Andrew St. George, "We Counter-Snatched Russia's Most Dangerous Spy," *Real,* November 1955.

4. This and later expeditions by Stanley were jointly sponsored with London's *Daily Telegraph,* but the *Herald* took the initiative and paid most of the expenses. Tim Jeal, *Stanley: The Impossible Life of Africa's Greatest Explorer* (London: Faber & Faber, 2007), 198–200. Bennett's father, James Gordon Bennett Sr., who founded the *Herald* in 1835, was also inventive, often beating his competition by increasing the speed of newsgathering. He was known for using homing pigeons that carried reporters' stories above the chaotic New York streets to the *Herald*'s rooftop. For international scoops, he sent reporters aboard sloops to meet ships from Europe and interview passengers before they docked in New York. James L. Crouthamel, *Bennett's New York Herald and the Rise of the Popular Press* (Syracuse, NY: Syracuse University Press, 1989).

5. *Cavalier,* April 1957.

6. Szentgyorgyi, interview by author, May 25, 2012.

7. Jean Szentgyorgyi, interview by author, October 2, 2014.

8. Ibid.

9. Szentgyorgyi, interview by author, May 25, 2012; Andrew St. George, "How I Found Castro, the Cuban Guerrilla," *Cavalier*, October 1957, 23.

10. St. George, "How I Found Castro," 24.

11. Norman Lewis (1908–2003) was a distinguished British novelist and venerated travel writer who described the world before globalization. As a literary traveler he was unsurpassed, being able, Cyril Connolly observed, to "write about the back of a bus and make it interesting." Lewis, who served in the British Intelligence Corps from 1939 to 1945, wrote a number of suspense novels, among them *Cuban Passage: A Novel* (New York: Pantheon, 1982), set in Batista's Havana. Beyond his two dozen books, he contributed to newspapers and magazines as a roving correspondent, covering, among other things, the Algerian struggle for independence from France. Considered outstanding among his nonfiction was *Naples '44* (Pantheon, 1978), which recounted his wartime experiences in Italy, where he served as a liaison officer with the local population. He later shared much-cited insights into Sicilian organized crime and related themes *in The Honored Society: A Searching Look at the Mafia* (New York: Putnam, 1964). Wolfgang Saxon, "Norman Lewis, 95, Author Known for Exotic Travels," *New York Times*, July 25, 2003, accessed August 14, 2011; and Richard Newbury, "Norman Lewis: The Semi-Invisible Man," *La Stampa*, December 16, 2008.

12. Lewis, *Cuban Passage*, 5–6.

13. Graham Greene, *Our Man in Havana* (London: William Heinemann, 1958; New York: Viking, 1958); Norman Sherry, *The Life of Graham Greene, Vol. 3: 1955–1991* (London: Penguin, 2004; New York: Penguin Group, 2005), 133, 135.

14. St. George, "How I Found Castro," 23, 26–27.

15. Ibid., 27.

16. Over time, Guevara recorded that he became suspicious of St. George. "At first he showed only one of his faces—the less bad one—that of a Yankee journalist. Honestly, he didn't seem to me as dangerous as he proved he was in our second interview, when he openly showed himself to be an agent." Over time, Guevara detested St. George as one of many who "tried to make use of the revolution for their own ends." Ernesto Che Guevara, *Reminiscences of the Cuban Revolutionary War*, authorized edition with corrections by Guevara (New York: Ocean Press, 2006), 72; J. L. Anderson, *Che*, 246–47.

17. St. George, "How I Found Castro," 25, 26; J. L. Anderson, *Che*, 245. When Taber left, St. George also photographed the remaining runaway, Charles "Chuck" Ryan, who proudly displayed his rifle and bandolier as a "full-fledged forest fighter."

18. Guevara, *Reminiscences*, 72; Franqui, *Diary*, 179.

19. St. George, "How I Found Castro," 55.

20. Guevara, *Reminiscences*, 72–73; Timothy O. Wickham-Crowley, *Guerrillas and Revolution in Latin America: A Comparative Study of Insurgents and Regimes since 1956* (Princeton, NJ: Princeton University Press, 1992), 52–53. Wickham-Crowley estimated that by 1958, Castro had 300 to 450 peasants as guerrilla fighters, accounting for 50 to 70 percent of his rebel force.

21. St. George, "How I Found Castro," 55.

22. Wickham-Crowley, *Guerrillas and Revolution*, 38; see also Ramón L. Bonachea and Marta San Martín, *The Cuban Insurrection, 1952–1959* (New Brunswick, NJ: Transaction, 1974), 39–40, 60.

23. St. George, "How I Found Castro," 55; Dubois, *Fidel Castro*, 204; J. L. Anderson, *Che*, 246.

24. St. George, "How I Found Castro," 55.

25. Ibid.

26. Ada Ferrer, *Insurgent Cuba: Race, Nation, and Revolution, 1868–1898* (Chapel Hill: University of North Carolina Press, 1999), 15–16, 22–36, 94, 105–6, 141–47.

27. St. George, "How I Found Castro," 56.

28. Ibid.

29. Matthews, *Cuban Story,* 144–45; Robert E. Quirk, *Fidel Castro: The Full Story of His Rise to Power, His Regime, His Allies, and His Adversaries* (New York: W. W. Norton, 1993), 55–56.

30. For a discussion of the ethics of "overly moralizing" by "representing distant suffering" in detail, see Tim Markham, *The Politics of War Reporting: Authority, Authenticity and Morality* (Manchester, UK: Manchester University Press, 2011), 103.

31. St. George, "How I Found Castro," 56.

32. Ibid.

33. Franqui, *Diary,* 71–77. The woman was Melba Hernandez. The other woman in the attack was Haydée Santamaría.

34. Dubois, *Fidel Castro,* 84–86, 208–9.

35. St. George, "How I Found Castro," 56; Matthews, *Cuban Story,* 146.

36. Dubois, *Fidel Castro,* 98–99.

37. St. George, "How I Found Castro," 56.

38. Ibid.

39. St. George misspelled the name *Gramma* instead of *Granma.* It was supposedly named for the grandmother of its first American owner.

40. St. George, "How I Found Castro," 56. Actually the Granma was smaller than Castro's measurements, forty-three feet long and built to accommodate twelve to twenty passengers.

41. Ibid.

42. Ibid., 57.

43. Ibid., 58.

44. Guevara, *Reminiscences,* 73; Franqui, *Diary,* 179. St. George's wife, Jean, afterward insisted that her husband was only a journalist and had never worked for the FBI or the CIA, as some suspected. In agreement with her, Jay Mallin, the Havana correspondent for *Time* magazine and the *Miami News,* said St. George was "absolutely not an agent.... He was not working for an American agency. The CIA wouldn't talk to him.... That doesn't mean he wasn't working for someone else. But he did a remarkable job, going up there and photographing Castro and his men.... He went up repeatedly.... On one occasion he had to hide in a water barrel in the bushes because there was a Batista patrol." Jay Mallin, interview by phone, September 11, 2008.

45. St. George, "How I Found Castro," 58.

46. Ibid.

47. Ibid.

48. Ibid.

49. Ibid.

50. Ibid.

51. Ibid., 58–59.

52. Jean Szentgyorgyi, interview, March 1, 2012.

53. St. George, "How I Found Castro," 58.

CHAPTER 6. THE TWO HAVANAS

1. "The Press: Freedom Fighter," *Time,* April 15, 1957; an editor's note in the *Tribune* later reminded readers that "last April 3, the Dominican Republic, on orders of Generalissimo Rafael Leonidas Trujillo to his brother, Hector, president, issued a decree barring Dubois from obtain-

ing a visa. The move followed charges of free press suppression in the Dominican republic by the Inter-American Press Association's freedom of the press committee of which Dubois was chairman." Jules Dubois, "Colombia Expels Tribune Reporter," *Chicago Tribune,* May 10, 1957, 1.

2. Dubois, "Colombia Expels Tribune Reporter," 1, 12, and "3 Ex-Ministers Ask Military to Oust Dictator," *Chicago Tribune,* May 10, 1957, 1. Dubois lowered the riot death count from fifty to thirty-three. Jules Dubois, "Junta Overthrows Colombia Dictator; Expulsion Order against Tribune Writer Lifted," *Chicago Tribune,* May 11, 1957, 1, and "The Press: Freedom Fighter." For a discussion of modern writers on the subject of Latin American dictatorships, especially the work of Gabriel García Márquez, see Peter Gay, *Modernism: The Lure of Heresy* (New York: W. W. Norton, 2008), 496–97.

3. "Cuba: Sugar and Strife," *Newsweek,* May 6, 1957, 63.

4. Ibid.

5. "Bombings, Sabotage Hit Cuba; Hundreds Jailed," *Chicago Tribune,* May 24, 1957, 10; Jules Dubois, "Cuban Army Clashes with Rebel Forces; Report Casualties in Oriente," *Chicago Tribune,* May 29, 1957, 11.

6. Dubois, *Fidel Castro,* 163.

7. Leonard Ray Teel, *Ralph Emerson McGill: Voice of the Southern Conscience* (Knoxville: University of Tennessee Press, 2001), 35–42.

8. *Chicago Tribune,* "Bombings, Sabotage Hit Cuba."

9. Dubois, "Cuban Army Clashes with Rebel Forces."

10. Jules Dubois, "Prío Men Map a Plan to End Strife in Cuba," *Chicago Tribune,* May 27, 1957, 26.

11. Batista maintained a wide spy ring; when Castro was in Mexico "the number of Batista's spies in Mexico City increased." Dubois, *Fidel Castro,* 97.

12. Samuel Farber, *The Origins of the Cuban Revolution Reconsidered* (Chapel Hill: University of North Carolina Press, 2006), 117.

13. "They say that I was a terrible president of Cuba," Prío Socarrás later confided to Arthur Schlesinger Jr. "That may be true. But I was the best president Cuba ever had." Joan Didion, *Miami* (New York: Simon & Schuster, 1987; rpt. London: Granta Books, 2005), 12. Didion's book portrayed *el exilio* life in the Cuban exile community over a span of several generations.

14. Thomas, *Cuba,* 757–58.

15. "Un Presidente Cordial: El Supo Distingue . . . Asegure La Paz Con Prío Socarrás." Accessed December 11, 2013, at http://www.latinamericanstudies.org/prio/prio-1948.jpg; Thomas, *Cuba,* 759.

16. Thomas, *Cuba,* 77.

17. Didion, *Miami,* 11. Didion noted that "a photograph of the occasion shows Señora de Prío, quite beautiful, boarding the plane in what appears to be a raw silk suit, and a hat with black fishnet veiling. She wears gloves, and earrings. Her makeup is fresh. The husband and father, recently the president, wears dark glasses, and carries the younger child, Maria Elena, in his arms."

18. Jon Lee Anderson, "Letter from Havana: Private Eyes: A Crime Novelist Navigates Cuba's Shifting Reality," *New Yorker,* October 21, 2013, 71.

19. Didion, *Miami,* 13–14.

20. "The events at the palace had nearly destroyed us," wrote Enrique Rodriguez Loeches. "Almost without arms, without houses, without money, without automobiles, we survived solely on courage and dignity." On April 16, Batista's police tracked down remnants of the student revolutionaries and shot them as they fled from an apartment at 19 Humboldt Street. Franqui, *Diary,* 170–73.

21. Dubois, *Fidel Castro,* 159–60.

22. Ibid., 160.

23. Ibid., 161.

24. "Landing Fizzles in Cuba; 27 Rebels Land but 2 Caught," *Miami Herald*, May 25, 1957, 1; Dubois, "Batista to Rap Exile Prío in Gripe to U.S.; Hints He's Rebel Chief and Liable to Ouster," *Chicago Daily Tribune*, June 3, 1957, 4; Dubois, *Fidel Castro*, 179.

25. Dubois, *Fidel Castro*, 161, 179, 138. Castro, scolded by Bayo, replied: "I want everyone in Cuba to know I am coming. I want them to have faith in the 26th of July Movement. It is a peculiarity all my own although I know that militarily it might be harmful. It is psychological warfare."

26. Ibid.

27. Ibid., 208–10.

28. Ibid., 178–79.

29. Ibid., 161, 179, 209. Mata Hari (1876–1917) was the stage name of the Dutch exotic dancer Gertrude Margarete Zelle, who was executed by the French, allegedly for spying, on October 15, 1917. During the First World War, she was accused of conducting espionage for Germany that led to the deaths of thousands of French soldiers.

30. Fidel Castro, in Franqui, *Diary*, May 28, 1957, 180.

31. Dubois, "Cuban Army Clashes with Rebel Forces," 11.

32. Fidel Castro, in Franqui, *Diary*, May 28, 1957, 180–81; Taber, *M-26*, 140–41.

33. Fidel Castro, in Franqui, *Diary*, May 28, 1957; Guevara, *Reminiscences*, 95. The prisoner release policy was intended to affect army morale, stressing that the revolution was against the dictator, not against the soldiers.

34. Fidel Castro, in Franqui, *Diary*, May 28, 1957, 181.

35. Taber, *M-26*, 141.

36. Jules Dubois, "Demand End of Terrorism in Santiago," *Chicago Tribune*, June 1, 1957, 2.

37. "Batista Will Try Fire Bombs," *Miami Herald*, June 3, 1957, 1.

38. Jules Dubois, "Batista Must Quit to Pacify Cuba, Says Prío," *Chicago Tribune*, June 6, 1957, 14.

39. William Kennedy, "'United Rally' Here Draws 1,100: Cuba Rebels Form Anti-Batista Front," *Miami Herald*, June 24, 1957, 1–2.

40. Justo Carillo to Alejandro [Fidel Castro], July 25, 1957, in Franqui, *Diary*, 210.

41. Jules Dubois, "5 Cuban Rebels Make Thru Batista's Line," *Chicago Tribune*, August 30, 1957, 3F.

42. Jules Dubois, "Cuban Rebels Weigh Setting Up Government," *Chicago Tribune*, July 22, 1957, 2.

CHAPTER 7. THIS IS ABSOLUTELY FALSE

1. Jean Szentgyorgyi, interview, May 26, 2012. She was always amazed at his writing in English, down to his spelling. "The interesting thing is, I think, that in nearly 50 years of typing up his work, I never encountered a misspelled word."

2. St. George, "How I Found Castro," 23.

3. Ibid.

4. *Life*'s circulation grew from 3.2 million (1941) to 5.2 million (late 1940s) to 8.5 million (1972); *Look*'s circulation was 7.7 million (1971). Therese L Lueck, "The Age of Mass Magazines," in *The Media in America: A History*, 9th ed., ed. Wm. David Sloan (Northport, AL: Vision Press, 2014), 417, 419.

5. "In Man's War, U.S. Boys Quit," *Life*, May 27, 1957, 43.

6. Andrew St. George, "Inside Cuba's Revolution," *Look*, February 4, 1958, 24–30.

7. After leaving *Life* as its executive editor, Wilson Hicks became director of student publications at the University of Miami (1955–70), where he advised the next generation of journalists, among them Mel Frishman, Joseph B. Treaster, and Leonard Ray Teel.

8. "Speaking of Pictures," *Life*, July 19, 1937, 12. A 1932 Gallup Poll "Survey of Reader Interest" confirmed the most widely read sections of the paper were the ones with special rotogravures.

9. Mott, *American Journalism*, 683; "Look Out," *Time*, January 11, 1937; Margaret Bourke-White, *Portrait of Myself* (New York: Simon & Schuster, 1963).

10. Beginning in February 1937, three months after Luce's *Life*, Gardner Cowles's *Look* by the mid-1950s had advertising revenue of $23 million (up from $6 million in 1946), and guaranteed circulation was at an all-time high: 3,700,000. "The Press: Shakeup at *Look*," *Time*, January 11, 1954.

11. William Attwood, "Memo from Havana: A Reporter Raises Some Questions," *Look*, March 3, 1959. Attwood, who became *Look*'s editor, got an interview with Castro in 1959.

12. *Coronet*'s circulation was 3.1 million in 1961: Lueck, "The Age of Mass Magazines," 419; *Coronet* was described as "so richly illustrated that it became a collector's item." David A. Smart, publisher of *Esquire* and *Coronet*, "believed the magazine was something the public ought to like, and if it did not make money it could be supported by *Esquire*'s profits." Jack A. Nelson, "The Genius of Passion: Esquire, Coronet, and Ken Magazines," paper presented at annual conference of the Association for Education in Journalism and Mass Communication (AEJMC), Portland, OR, July 1988.

13. Andrew St. George, "A Visit with a Revolutionary," *Coronet*, February 1958, 74.

14. Frank Luther Mott, *American Journalism: A History, 1690–1960*, 3rd ed. (New York: Macmillan, 1962), 839.

15. Turner Catledge, *My Life and the Times* (New York: Harper & Row, 1971), 266, 257; DePalma, *The Man Who Invented Fidel*, 127–28.

16. Lippmann and Merz, "Test of the News." In a review of the reprint of Lippmann's book *Liberty and the News*, Michael Schudson noted that "when these pictures come from distant places, brought to us by a press without much self-discipline or sophistication or intellectual weight, our actions—our votes, our choices—are at the mercy of a flawed picture of the world that various media provide." Michael Schudson, "Lippmann and the News," *Nation*, December 13, 2007.

17. Joseph Pulitzer, "The College of Journalism," *North American Review* 178 (May 1904): 641–80; a condensed revision appeared in *Review of Reviews*, June 1904, 735–37. One highly visible critic of Pulitzer's vision, H. L. Mencken, in 1924 scoffed at journalism "trade schools" that were "seldom manned by men of any genuine professional standing, or of any firm notion of what journalism is about." H. L. Mencken, "Editorial," *American Mercury* (October 1924): 155–58. See also Teel, *The Public Press, 1900–1945*, 9–13, 118.

18. Walter Lippmann, *Liberty and the News* (New York: Harcourt, Brace & Howe, 1920).

19. "Canons of Journalism, Adopted by the American Society of Newspaper Editors, April 1923," *World's Work*, November 1924, 45; Willis J. Abbott, "The A.S.N.E. and Its Ethical Code," *New Republic*, May 22, 1929, 15–16.

20. The absence of an international code of ethics was confirmed by William J. Holstein, a past president of the Overseas Press Club, interview with the author, July 9, 2009; J. Herbert Altshull, *Agents of Power: The Media and Public Policy* (White Plains, NY: Longman, 1995), 68.

21. Holstein, interview, July 9, 2009. One standard practice in advance of sending a journalist to a war zone was a briefing by a senior correspondent with experience in that country; such briefing mostly dealt with practical, not ethical matters. Thus, when the *New York Times* assigned

David Halberstam to Vietnam to head its bureau, the outgoing head, Homer Bigart, briefed him in a three-page letter about how to work and live in Saigon. Halberstam's subsequent ethical quandaries about U.S. policies there were based on his own professional ethics rather than on a code of ethics for U.S. overseas correspondents. Homer Bigart to David Halberstam, August 6, 1962, David Halberstam Collection, Gottlieb Archives, Boston University, Boston.

22. DePalma, *The Man Who Invented Fidel,* 58–59. On a battlefield story in which Matthews documented intervention by Mussolini's Italian troops in Spain against the Loyalist government forces, his editors, suspecting Matthews to be sympathetic with the Loyalist cause, changed "Italian" to "Insurgent."

23. Herbert L. Matthews, "From the Sierra Maestra to Havana, the Ideals Never Changed," review of Jules Dubois, *Fidel Castro: Rebel, Liberator or Dictator?* (1959), in *New York Times,* April 5, 1959, BR3.

24. Franqui, *Diary,* 236.

25. His Excellency, President of the Republic General Fulgencio Batista y Zaldívar, Letter to the President and Members, Cuban Publishers Association, October 9, 1957, IAPA Annal, 1957, 163–67.

26. St. George, "A Visit with a Revolutionary," 74, 78.

27. Ibid.

28. Ibid., 74, 78–79.

29. St. George, "A Visit with a Revolutionary," 74–76.

30. Ibid.

31. Ibid., 76. For insight about common sense as an errant social motivator, see Duncan J. Watts, *Everything Is Obvious Once You Know the Answer: Why Common Sense Fails Us* (New York: Crown Business, 2011).

32. St. George, "A Visit with a Revolutionary," 76.

33. Szulc, *Fidel,* 184–209.

34. St. George, "A Visit with a Revolutionary," 76.

35. Szulc, *Fidel,* 205.

36. St. George, "A Visit with a Revolutionary," 76–77.

37. Ibid., 78.

38. Ibid., 78–79.

39. Fidel Castro, "Why We Fight," *Coronet,* February 1958, 80–81. The same title had been used for a World War II film series commissioned by the U.S. government to show why Americans were fighting.

40. Ibid.

41. Ibid., 80.

42. Ibid., 80–84.

43. Ibid., 84–85.

44. Fulgencio Batista to the President and Members of the Cuban Publishers Association, October 9, 1957, reprinted in the *Annals of the Inter-American Press Association,* 1958, 164–65; Castro, "Why We Fight," 86.

45. "Exclusive: Inside Cuba's Revolution: In a Savage Civil War, Fidel Castro and 1,000 Rebels Fight Cuba's 'Rifle Rule,'" *Look,* vol. 22, February 4, 1958, 30.

46. Ibid., 27; translation of the song required poetic license because in Spanish *cama* means "bed," not "pillow," which is *almohada.*

47. Ibid., 26–27.

48. Ibid., 28.

49. Ibid. 28–29.

50. Ibid., 24–26.

51. Ibid., 30.

52. Ibid.

CHAPTER 8. IT IS NECESSARY TO HAVE FAITH

1. "Homer Bigart's Perilous Trip to See Markos," *New York Herald Tribune,* July 25, 1948; "Homer Bigart in Rebel Greece Finds Route to Markos Arduous," *Herald Tribune,* July 26, 1948; "Homer Bigart at Greek Front Finally Reaches Gen. Markos," *Herald Tribune,* July 27, 1948; "Markos Still Open to Peace Bid," *Herald Tribune,* July 28, 1948. All four stories were reprinted in *Forward Positions: The War Correspondence of Homer Bigart,* compiled and edited by Betsy Wade (Fayetteville: University of Arkansas Press, 1992), 111–23.

2. Homer Bigart, "Rebel Chief Offers Batista Plan to End Cuban Revolt; Castro, in Interview, Demands Army's Departure from Oriente Province, Then Election Supervised by O.A.S., " *New York Times,* February 26, 1958, 1, and "Castro Declares He Will Win Soon," *New York Times,* February 27, 1958, 10.

3. Bigart, "Rebel Chief Offers Batista Plan," 3; Dubois, *Fidel Castro,* 168–72.

4. Bigart, "Rebel Chief Offers Batista Plan," 3.

5. Ibid.

6. Ibid.

7. Ibid.

8. Homer Bigart, "Castro Declares He Will Win Soon," 10.

9. Bigart, "Rebel Chief Offers Batista Plan," 3.

10. Bigart, "Castro Declares He Will Win Soon," 10.

11. Taber, *M-26,* 218–19.

12. Sir Edward Creasy, *The Fifteen Decisive Battles of the World from Marathon to Waterloo.* First published in 1851, the book "became one of the great Victorian best-sellers, rivaling Charles Darwin's *Origin of the Species* in the frequency with which it was published—38 times in 43 years between 1851 and 1894." John Keegan, *The Face of Battle* (New York: Viking, 1976), 56.

13. DePalma, *The Man Who Invented Fidel,* 130–31.

14. Taber, *War of the Flea,* 29–31.

15. Ibid., 30.

16. Bigart, "Castro Declares He Will Win Soon," 10.

17. Ibid.

18. Brennan, *Castro, Cuba and Justice,* 201; Dubois, *Fidel Castro,* 212.

19. Dubois, *Fidel Castro,* 212–13.

20. Brennan, *Castro, Cuba and Justice,* 192–93. Lucero a few weeks earlier had killed Colonel Fermin "The Vermin" Cowley, who was responsible for the deaths of several rebels. In February, another of the Movement's attacks was against government finances when they set fire to the clearinghouse of Havana, burning half a million dollars in checks.

21. Brennan, *Castro, Cuba and Justice,* 192–93; Dubois, *Fidel Castro,* 213.

22. Brennan, *Castro, Cuba and Justice,* 192–93.

23. Meyer Lansky's first contact with Batista was in 1933, according to one historian. That year, "Lansky came to [Lucky] Luciano with an astounding proposition. . . . He wanted to 'buy in' with the Cubans so that the Mob could begin to develop its own gambling infrastructure on the island.

The person Lansky had set his sights on was a young military man on the rise in Cuba named Fulgencio Batista." Soon after, the various mob leaders raised a bribe of $500,000. Lansky and his gofer Joseph "Doc" Stracher took the cash in suitcases and showed it to Batista. "Batista just stared at the money without saying a word," Stracher recalled. "Then he and Meyer shook hands and Batista left.... We gave Batista a guarantee of between $3 and $5 million a year, as long as we had a monopoly at the casinos at the Hotel Nacional and everywhere else on the island where we thought tourists would come. On top of that he was promised a cut of our profits." T. J. English, *Havana Nocturne* (New York: HarperCollins, 2008), 15–16.

24. Ibid., 172.

25. Charles Ashman, *The CIA-Mafia Link* (New York: Manor Books, 1975), 92; Pearson, *Diaries*, 449.

26. Homer Bigart, "Foes of Batista Split on Strike; Prío Bars Aid to Supporters If Not Recognized on Rebels' Central Board," *New York Times*, March 5, 1957, 15.

27. Ibid.

28. DePalma, *The Man Who Invented Fidel*, 132.

29. Ibid., 137.

30. Ibid.; Werner Wiskari, "U.S. Embargo Set on Arms to Cuba; Shipment Halted; Rifles Ordered by Batista Are Held Up—Rochester Concern Is Indicted," *New York Times*, April 3, 1958.

31. Manuel Márquez-Sterling, in collaboration with R. Rembert Aranda, *Cuba, 1952–1959: The True Story of Castro's Rise to Power* (Wintergreen, VA: Kleiopatria Digital Press, 2009), 142–43.

32. Thomas, *Cuba*, 983. For the comment on Castro, Thomas cites Earl E. T. Smith, *The Fourth Floor* (New York, 1962), 81.

33. Thomas, *Cuba*, 615, 619, 678; Brennan, *Castro, Cuba and Justice*, 38–40; Teel, *Ralph Emerson McGill*, 18, 42–45.

34. Inter-American Press Association (Sociedad InterAmericana de Prensa, Inc.), Minutes of the Annual Meeting, Washington, DC, October 1957, 147. Dubois continued to work in cooperation with the Cuban head of IAPA, the editor Guillermo Martínez Márquez.

35. Norman Lewis, "Our Far-Flung Correspondents: Cuban Interlude," *New Yorker*, May 3, 1958, 80.

36. Dubois, *Fidel Castro*, 241–42.

37. Jules Dubois, "Batista Tries 8 Officers for Plotting against Him," *Chicago Tribune*, April 8, 1958, 11.

38. Homer Bigart, "U.S. Correspondents Held," *New York Times*, April 8, 1958, 3; Brennan, *Castro, Cuba and Justice*, 210–21; Dubois, *Fidel Castro*, 255.

39. Brennan, *Castro, Cuba and Justice*, 210–11.

40. Ibid.

41. Ibid.

42. Ibid.

43. Ibid.

44. Dubois, *Fidel Castro*, 273.

45. Jay Mallin, interview with author, August 14, 2011.

46. Dubois, *Fidel Castro*, 222–23, 234.

47. Dubois wrote that the 1957 strike was "a spontaneous expression of repudiation of daily brutality, tortures, killings, and a protest against corrupt government and equally corrupt labor leaders who had become millionaires within a few years, notably Eusebio Mujal, secretary general of the CTC." Ibid., 173.

48. Ibid., 245–46.

49. Ibid.

50. Ibid.

51. Ibid., 246–47; Castro on March 28 proposed that the strike should include all opposition groups, including the Communists, but his Havana organizing committee decided that there was not enough time to involve all opposition groups. "This was the first occasion that Castro showed himself willing to collaborate with the Communists," Hugh Thomas wrote. Thomas, *Cuba,* 988 and fn3.

52. Pearson, *Diaries,* 449.

53. Ibid.

54. The characterization of Chicago journalists was from political insider David Axelrod in Michael S. Schmidt, "Obama's 'Hemingway' Draws on Various Inspirations," *New York Times,* January 20, 2015, A14; "The Press: Nose for News," *Time,* November 30, 1959; "Crime: Death on the Steps," *Time,* December 28, 1959.

55. English, *Havana Nocturne,* 50, 316.

56. Brennan, *Castro, Cuba and Justice,* 12–13, 16, 134; English, *Havana Nocturne,* 50, 58–59, 104, 269, 289–92.

57. Jules Dubois, "Strike Call Touches Off Gun Battles; 7 to 30 Reported Slain in Capital," *Chicago Tribune,* April 10, 1958, 1; Dubois, *Fidel Castro,* 251–53.

58. Dubois, *Fidel Castro,* 252–53.

59. Brennan, *Castro, Cuba and Justice,* 216–17.

60. Dubois, *Fidel Castro,* 252.

61. Brennan, *Castro, Cuba and Justice,* 220–21.

62. Sam Halper, "The Hemisphere: This Man Castro," *Time,* April 14, 1958.

63. Jay Mallin, interview with author, August 14, 2011.

64. Therese L. Lueck, "The Age of Mass Magazines, 1900–Present," in *The Media in America: A History,* ed. Wm. David Sloan, 8th ed. (Northport, AL: Vision Press, 2011), 407.

65. Hamilton, *Journalism's Roving Eye,* 353.

66. Sam Halper, "The Hemisphere: This Man Castro," 35–36, and "Castro on Eve of His Big Bid," *Life,* April 14, 1958, 26–27.

67. Halper, "The Hemisphere: This Man Castro," 35–36.

68. Ibid., 35.

69. Ibid., 35–36. It is likely that the unnamed "captain" was Che Guevara.

70. Ibid., 36.

71. Ibid.; Halper, "Castro on Eve," 27.

72. Halper, "The Hemisphere: This Man Castro," 36, and "Castro on Eve," 26–27.

CHAPTER 9. HOW CAN WE PROVE WE ARE NOT SOMETHING?

1. DePalma, *The Man Who Invented Fidel,* 136; Brennan, *Castro, Cuba and Justice,* 225.

2. Dubois, *Fidel Castro,* 266–67. The CRM suffered numerous casualties. Dubois noted that in mid-June the bodies of two young sisters in the CRM, Maria and Cristina Giral, were found, badly bruised with blackened eyes, indicating they had been tortured before both were shot in the breast and abdomen. They had been seized because police suspected their brother in the CRM's failed attempt to assassinate Batista's former minister of interior, Santiago Rey. Dubois noted that the murders of the sisters "added to the determination of many Cuban men and women to fight Batista to the bitter end."

3. Ibid., 256–57.

4. Ibid., 257.

5. Brennan, *Castro, Cuba and Justice,* 226–28.

6. Ibid., 245.

7. Ibid., 225–26.

8. Ibid., 228.

9. Ibid.

10. Taber, *M-26,* 263.

11. Brennan, *Castro, Cuba and Justice,* 229.

12. Ibid., 228–29.

13. Ibid.

14. Ibid., 229.

15. Ibid., 230.

16. Ibid., 228.

17. Homer Bigart, "Cuban Army Push Reported Halted; Castro Rebels Beat Troops in Battle, New Yorker, Back from Visit, Says," *New York Times,* July 10, 1958, 8; Emanuel Perlmutter, "Castro Expected to Act," *New York Times,* July 3, 1958, 4.

18. Bigart, "Cuban Army Push."

19. Ibid.

20. Ibid.

21. Ibid.

22. Perlmutter, "Castro Expected to Act," 4.

23. Dubois, *Fidel Castro,* 270.

24. Ibid., 270–72.

25. Ibid., 273.

26. Ibid., 172.

27. Ibid., 274.

28. Ibid., 274–77.

29. Ibid., 277–78.

30. Shaw's biographical background and photograph, submitted in 1958 with his Peabody Award application, George Foster Peabody Radio and Television Awards, Collection No. 58014 NWR, Hargrett Rare Book and Manuscript Library, University of Georgia Libraries, Athens.

31. Charles Shaw, "As I See It," WCAU radio broadcast, July 3, 1958, transcript, 1, 5, George Foster Peabody Radio and Television Awards, Collection No. 58014 NWR, Hargrett Rare Book and Manuscript Library.

32. Ibid.

33. Shaw, "As I See It," WCAU radio broadcast, July 24, 1958, transcript, 1, George Foster Peabody Radio and Television Awards, Collection No. 58014 NWR, Hargrett Rare Book and Manuscript Library.

34. Ibid., 1–4.

35. Shaw, "As I See It," broadcast, WCAU radio, July 25, 1958, transcript, 2, George Foster Peabody Radio and Television Awards Collection No. 58014 NWR, Hargrett Rare Book and Manuscript Library.

36. Ibid., 2–3.

37. Ibid.

38. Ibid., 3.

39. Ibid., 1–2.

40. Shaw, "As I See It," broadcast, WCAU radio, July 28, 1958, transcript, 1–3, George Foster Peabody Radio and Television Awards Collection No. 58014 NWR, Hargrett Rare Book and Manuscript Library.

41. Ibid., 4.

42. Shaw, "As I See It," broadcast, WCAU radio, July 29, 1958, transcript, 1–2, George Foster Peabody Radio and Television Awards Collection No. 58014 NWR, Hargrett Rare Book and Manuscript Library.

43. Ibid., 4.

44. Shaw, "As I See It," broadcast, WCAU radio, July 30, 1958, transcript, 1–3, George Foster Peabody Radio and Television Awards Collection No. 58014 NWR, Hargrett Rare Book and Manuscript Library.

45. Ibid., 4.

46. Shaw, "As I See It," broadcast, WCAU radio, July 31, 1958, transcript, 1, George Foster Peabody Radio and Television Awards Collection No. 58014 NWR, Hargrett Rare Book and Manuscript Library.

47. Ibid., 1–6.

48. Shaw, "As I See It," broadcast, WCAU radio, September 25, 1958, transcript, 1, George Foster Peabody Radio and Television Awards Collection No. 58014 NWR, Hargrett Rare Book and Manuscript Library.

49. Shaw, "As I See It," broadcast, WCAU radio, August 20, 1958, transcript, 1, George Foster Peabody Radio and Television Awards Collection No. 58014 NWR, Hargrett Rare Book and Manuscript Library.

50. Ibid., 4.

51. Ibid., 5.

52. Shaw, "As I See It," broadcast, WCAU radio, August 20, 1958, transcript, 3.

53. Dubois, *Fidel Castro*, 280–83.

54. Shaw, "As I See It," broadcast, WCAU radio, August 20, 1958, transcript, 3–4.

55. Peabody Awards archives: http://www.peabodyawards.com/search-site/1959/null/null. Charles Shaw did not win a 1959 Peabody Award for radio. That year three radio awards went to CBS network radio for *The World Tonight,* to NBC network radio for *Family Living '59,* and to WCCO radio in Minneapolis for *Local Public Service.* It was obviously now the age of television, which garnered eleven awards, including one for Shaw's former boss, Edward R. Murrow, who shared the award with Fred Friendly for *The Lost Class of '59.* Unlike Shaw, Murrow had made the move to television.

56. Shaw, Addendum to Peabody Archives Application, September, 1958.

CHAPTER 10. LIBERATOR OR DICTATOR?

1. Chris Hedges, "Public Lives: Sounding Out Words of Caution during Wartime," *New York Times,* July 12, 2002.

2. Karl E. Meyer, interview by telephone, April 5, 2009.

3. Ibid.

4. Ibid.

5. Ibid.

6. Ibid.

7. Dubois, *Fidel Castro,* 289–90.

8. "CUBA: Comeback," *Time,* August 25, 1958, 28.

9. Dubois, *Fidel Castro,* 299–302.

10. Meyer, interview, April 5, 2009; Karl E. Meyer, "Report on Rebel Cuba: A Visit to Castro Aerie," *Washington Post and Times Herald,* September 14, 1958, E1; Meyer, interview. The headline word "aerie" likened Castro's mountain hideout to the nest of a bird, such as an eagle, built on a cliff or other high place.

11. Meyer, interview, April 5, 2009.

12. Meyer, "Report on Rebel Cuba: A Visit to Castro Aerie," E1.

13. "Display Ad 63," *Washington Post and Times Herald,* September 12, 1958, D5; for Cuban cigar types and lengths, see "Le Guide des principaux formats Des Havanes." After the Gran Corona, the next longest was the Promiente at 7 5/8 inches.

14. Meyer, "Report on Rebel Cuba: A Visit to Castro Aerie," E1.

15. Ibid.

16. Ibid.

17. Ibid.

18. Ibid., E1–2.

19. Ibid.

20. Ibid.

21. Karl E. Meyer, "Report on Rebel Cuba: Castro Says He Fights for Rights and Opportunities Found in the U.S.," *Washington Post and Times Herald,* September 15, 1958, A1.

22. Ibid., A6.

23. Ibid.

24. Meyer, interview, April 5, 2009.

25. Ibid.

26. Meyer, "Report on Rebel Cuba: Castro Says He Fights for Rights and Opportunities Found in the U.S.," A6.

27. Ibid.; Meyer, interview, April 5, 2009.

28. Lippmann and Merz, "Test of the News," 1–42; Teel, *The Public Press, 1900–1945,* 91–92; Ronald Steel, *Walter Lippmann and the American Century* (New Brunswick, NJ: Transaction, 1999).

29. Karl E. Meyer, "Report on Rebel Cuba: Teen-Age Boys Tortured, Murdered for Sympathy with Castro's Cause," *Washington Post and Times Herald,* September 16, 1958, A22.

30. Ibid.

31. The censored article in *Life* was "Inside *Rebel Cuba* with Raúl Castro (Fidel's brother)," *Life,* September 1, 1958; Karl E. Meyer, "Report on Rebel Cuba: Rotarians, Doctors, Women Back Castro Revolt," *Washington Post,* September 17, 1958, A7.

32. Ibid.

33. Ibid.

34. Ibid.

35. Karl E. Meyer, "Report on Rebel Cuba: Foes Attack Batista-Called Election," *Washington Post,* September 18, 1958, A16.

36. Ibid. Carlos Márquez Sterling, the son of former secretary of state Manuel Márquez Sterling under President Ramón Grau San Martin, had served in government from 1936 to 1948.

37. Ibid.

38. Ibid.

39. Karl E. Meyer, "Report on Rebel Cuba: Neutrality Difficult in Castro's Revolt," *Washington Post,* September 19, 1958, A5.

40. Ibid.

41. Herbert Matthews, *Castro: A Political Biography* (London: Allen Lane, 1969), 113.

42. Robert Branson, "Leader of Castro's Jungle Fighters Wants to Return Home to Toledo; Morgan Uncertain of Status in Eyes of U.S. Government," *Toledo Blade,* January 6, 1959; David Grann, "The Yankee *Comandante*: A Story of Love, Revolution and Betrayal," *New Yorker,* May 28, 2012, 46–71; Jack Lessenberry, review of Aran Shetterly, *The Americano: Fighting for Freedom in Castro's Cuba* (2007) in *Toledo Blade,* October 21, 2007.

43. Dickey Chapelle, *What's a Woman Doing Here? A Reporter's Report on Herself* (New York: William Morrow, 1962), 257.

44. Roberta Ostroff, *Fire in the Wind: The Life of Dickey Chapelle* (New York: Ballantine, 1992), 247.

45. Chapelle, *What's a Woman Doing Here?* 225.

46. Dickey Chapelle, "Nobody Owes Me a Christmas," *Reader's Digest,* December 1957.

47. Chapelle, *What's a Woman Doing Here?* 221.

48. Ibid., 219–20, 238.

49. Ostroff, *Fire in the Wind,* photos starting p. 220.

50. Chapelle, whose birth name was Georgette Meyer, was working for Trans World Airlines when she took the photo class with Tony Chapelle, who was TWA's publicity photographer. After the divorce, she changed her first name to Dickey, after her favorite explorer, Admiral Richard Byrd. "Despite mediocre credentials, Chapelle managed to become a war correspondent for National Geographic, posted with the Marines during World War II." "Dickey Chapelle," Topics in Wisconsin History, Wisconsin Historical Society, www.wisconsinhistory.org/topics/chapelle.

51. Chapelle, *What's a Woman Doing Here?* 255.

52. Dickey Chapelle, "Remember the 26th of July! The Story of Fidel Castro and the Liberation of Cuba," *Reader's Digest,* April 1959, 240–41.

53. Chapelle, *What's a Woman Doing Here?* 255.

54. Ibid., 257.

55. Ibid., 258; Ostroff, *Fire in the Wind,* 249.

56. Chapelle, *What's a Woman Doing Here?* 258–59.

57. Andrew St. George, "Castro Seeking U.S. Talks on Cuban Political Issues," *New York Times,* December 11, 1958, 1.

58. Chapelle, "Remember the 26th of July!" 241.

59. Mallin, interview with author, August 14, 2011.

60. Chapelle, "Remember the 26th of July!" 241–42.

61. Chapelle, *What's a Woman Doing Here?* 261.

62. Ibid., 261.

63. Ibid., 261–62.

64. Ibid., 262–67.

65. Ibid., 266.

66. Chapelle, "Remember the 26th of July!" 247–48.

67. Chapelle, *What's a Woman Doing Here?* 268–70.

68. Ostroff, *Fire in the Wind,* 261.

69. Jane McManus, ed., *From the Palm Tree: Voices of the Cuban Revolution* (Secaucus, NJ: Lyle Stuart, 1983), 32, 49, 69.

70. Chapelle, *What's a Woman Doing Here?* 268–70.

71. Chapelle, "Remember the 26th of July!" 248, and *What's a Woman Doing Here?* 270.

72. Ostroff, *Fire in the Wind,* 262; Chapelle, *What's a Woman Doing Here?* 269–71.

73. Chapelle, "Remember the 26th of July!" 242, and *What's a Woman Doing Here?* 272–73.

74. Chapelle, *What's a Woman Doing Here?* 270–71.

75. Ibid.

76. Chapelle, "Remember the 26th of July!" 245.

77. Ibid.

78. Ostroff, *Fire in the Wind,* 252.

79. Taber, *M-26,* 290.

80. Chapelle, *What's a Woman Doing Here?* 274–77.

81. Dubois, *Fidel Castro,* 345.

82. Ibid., 352; Matthews, *Castro: A Political Biography,* 122.

83. Chapelle, Remember the 26th of July!" 248–50; Dubois, *Fidel Castro,* 353; Matthews, *Cuban Story,* 87–88; Matthews, *Castro: A Political Biography,* 122.

84. Robert Branson, "Leader of Castro's Jungle Fighters," *Toledo Blade,* January 5, 1959, 1; Michael D. Sallah, "Cuba's Yankee Comandante—William Morgan Stunned His Family by Leaving Toledo in 1957 to Join the Revolutionary Forces of Fidel Castro, but Met a Cruel End," *Toledo Blade,* March 3, 2002.

85. Neill Macaulay, *A Rebel in Cuba: An American's Memoir* (Chicago: Quadrangle Books, 1970), 1, 12, 25, 62.

86. Dubois, *Fidel Castro,* 348–49.

87. Branson, "Leader of Castro's Jungle Fighters."

88. Ibid. On March 11, 1961, William Morgan was executed by a Cuban firing squad, charged with plotting to overthrow the Castro regime allegedly because he opposed its ties with the Soviet Union. Forty-six years later, the *Toledo Blade* discovered that Morgan's citizenship was never officially revoked because the paperwork was never processed and signed. Officially, the U.S. State Department in 2007 confirmed that "Mr. Morgan shall be deemed never to have relinquished his U.S. nationality." His second wife, Olga Rodriguez Morgan, whom he married while fighting with Castro's rebels, escaped to Toledo and in 1985 remarried, following the advice Morgan gave her in his final letter from prison. He begged her not to "let your life become lifeless and sad. If you should find someone who you should love and who respects you, marry him; because knowing that you are happy, I will be also." Robin Erb, "Morgan Gains Citizenship; Toledoan Killed after Cuba Revolt," *Toledo Blade,* April 13, 2007; Grann, "The Yankee Comandante," 71.

89. Dubois, *Fidel Castro,* 353–55.

90. Ibid., 354–55.

91. Chapelle, "Remember the 26th of July!" 251–52.

EPILOGUE

1. Karl E. Meyer, "Castro's Triumph over Batista Leaves Cuba's Future Blurred," *Washington Post,* January 2, 1959, A1.

2. Karl E. Meyer, "Some Views Restrained: Reactions to Executions by Castro Colored by National Temperaments," *Washington Post,* January 25, 1959, A5.

3. Karl E. Meyer, "At Home & Abroad: Who Won What in Cuba?" *Reporter,* February 5, 1959, 20–23. In response to a letter from a reader of his February 5 essay, Karl Meyer in the March 5 issue traced the breakdown of U.S.-Cuban relations to the former ambassador. Meyer stated that "the complaint made about our former ambassador to Cuba, Earl E. T. Smith, is that he jeopardized his country's interest by sticking his nose into politics. . . . The post in Havana during the

civil war called for the skills of a seasoned career diplomat, familiar with Latin America and able to hew to the line of strict neutrality set in Washington. However admirable Mr. Smith's skills as Republican fund raiser, sportsman, and financier, his Cuban tour required different talents. It may be meddlesome for the American press to point this out, but that is one of the drawbacks of democracy." "Cuba," *Reporter,* March 5, 1959, 7.

4. Karl E. Meyer, "Is Castro a Washington or a Nasser?" review of Jules Dubois, *Fidel Castro: Rebel, Liberator or Dictator?* (1959), *Washington Post,* April 5, 1959, E6.

5. Karl E. Meyer, "Castro Revisited," review of Ray Brennan, *Castro, Cuba and Justice* (1959), *Washington Post,* October 11, 1959, E6.

6. Karl Meyer, interview with the author, April 9, 2009.

★ BIBLIOGRAPHY ★

PRIMARY SOURCES

Newspaper and Magazine Articles

Associated Press. "Americas' Press Seeks Firm Right; Mexico City Session Assails Control of Newsprint Import," *New York Times,* October 11, 1953.

——. "Cuba Frees Two Reporters on Plea from U.S.," *Chicago Daily Tribune,* March 6, 1957, 7.

——. "Documentary Exhibited in Miami," May 20, 1957.

Attwood, William. "Memo from Havana: A Reporter Raises Some Questions," *Look,* March 3, 1959.

"Batista Decries Killing of 'Fools'; Says He Knew for 3 Days an Attack Was Coming—Prío Says President Will Fall," *New York Times,* March 13, 1957, 3.

"Batista Gets Appeal; Cuban Publishers Urge Him to Lift Censorship," *New York Times,* February 1, 1957.

"Batista Will Try Fire Bombs," *Miami Herald,* June 3, 1957, 1.

"'Bebo' Valdés, Giant of Cuban Music, Is Dead," NPR Music, March 22, 2012.

Bigart, Homer. "Castro Declares He Will Win Soon: In Interview, Rebel Leader with Battle Force of 400 Is Certain of Victory," *New York Times,* February 27, 1958, 10.

——. "Cuban Army Push Reported Halted; Castro Rebels Beat Troops in Battle, New Yorker, Back from Visit, Says," *New York Times,* July 10, 1958, 8.

——. "Foes of Batista Split on Strike; Prío Bars Aid to Supporters If Not Recognized on Rebels' Central Board," *New York Times,* March 5, 1957, 15.

——. "Homer Bigart at Greek Front Finally Reaches Gen. Markos," *New York Herald Tribune,* July 27, 1948.

——. "Homer Bigart in Rebel Greece Finds Route to Markos Arduous," *New York Herald Tribune,* July 26, 1948.

——. "Markos Still Open to Peace Bid," July 28, 1948.

——. "Rebel Chief Offers Batista Plan to End Cuban Revolt: Castro, in Interview, Demands Army's Departure from Oriente Province, Then Election Supervised by O.A.S.," *New York Times,* February 26, 1958, 1, 3.

——. "U.S. Correspondents Held," *New York Times,* April 8, 1958, 3.

"Bombings, Sabotage Hit Cuba; Hundreds Jailed," *Chicago Tribune,* May 24, 1957, 10.

Bonafede, Dom. "Cuba Calm: Death Toll Rises to 45: Order Is Restored in Havana," *Miami Daily News,* March 14, 1957, 1, 2.

———. "Revolt Made Batista Tougher, Cubans Say: Dramatic Uprising Had No Chance of Success," *Miami Daily News,* March 17, 1957, 9A.

Branson, Robert. "Leader of Castro's Jungle Fighters," *Toledo Blade,* January 5, 1959, 1.

———. "Leader of Castro's Jungle Fighters Wants to Return Home to Toledo; Morgan Uncertain of Status in Eyes of U.S. Government," *Toledo Blade,* January 6, 1959.

Brendon, Piers. "The Beevorised Version: Antony Beevor's *The Battle for Spain,* a Revamped Discussion of the Spanish Civil War, Succeeds Brilliantly," *Guardian* [England], June 23, 2006.

"But Matthews Sticks to His Story, Shows New Photo," *Times of Havana,* February 28, 1957, 1.

"Canons of Journalism, Adopted by the American Society of Newspaper Editors, April 1923," *World's Work,* November 1924, 45.

Castro, Fidel. "Why We Fight," *Coronet,* February 1958, 80–81.

"Censors Use Scissors: Cuba Applies Old Means of Handling U.S. Publications," *New York Times,* January 17, 1957.

Chapelle, Dickey. "Nobody Owes Me a Christmas," *Reader's Digest,* December 1957, 219–20, 238.

———. "Remember the 26th of July! The Story of Fidel Castro and the Liberation of Cuba," *Reader's Digest,* April 1959, 240–41.

"Costa Rica Eases Curbs: Censorship Ended for Outgoing Dispatches—Writer Freed," *New York Times,* March 19, 1948, 5.

"Crime: Death on the Steps," *Time,* December 28, 1959.

"Cuba: Batista at Work," *Newsweek,* March 24, 1952.

"Cuba Brands Castro Interview as Phony," *Times of Havana,* February 28, 1957, 1.

"Cuba: Comeback," *Time,* August 25, 1958, 28.

"Cuba: Hit-Run Revolt," *Time,* December 10, 1957.

"The Cuban Censorship," *New York Times,* February 26, 1957.

"Cuban Inquiry Sought: Supreme Court Is Petitioned to Investigate Violence," *New York Times,* January 9, 1957, 6.

"Cuban Mop-Up Ordered; Batista Tells Forces to End Revolt at Minimum Cost," *New York Times,* December 11, 1956, 22.

"Cuba Plot Bomb Foiled: Police Say Terrorists Picked Cabarets as Targets," *New York Times,* January 6, 1957, 9.

"Cuba: Running-Sore Revolt," *Time,* February 25, 1957.

"Cuba Sets Censorship: Curb on News Follows Lifting of Basic Guarantees," *New York Times,* January 16, 1957, 16.

"Cuba: Sugar and Strife," *Newsweek,* May 6, 1957, 63.

"[Deaths in] Cuba Rise to 45: Score Wounded in Havana Revolt," *Miami Daily News,* March 14, 1957, 1.

"Dominicans Bar Writer: Trujillo Regime Forbids Entry of U.S. Correspondent," *New York Times*, April 4, 1957.

Dubois, Jules. "Batista Calls Rebel Castro Russian Agent: Vows His Insurrection Will Be Crushed," *Chicago Daily Tribune*, March 11, 1957, 20.

———. "Batista Must Quit to Pacify Cuba, Says Prío," *Chicago Tribune*, June 6, 1957, 14.

———. "Batista's Foes Vow to Push Freedom Fight," *Chicago Daily Tribune*, March 16, 1957, 4F.

———. "Batista Tries 8 Officers for Plotting against Him," *Chicago Tribune*, April 8, 1958, 11.

———. "Batista to Rap Exile Prío in Gripe to U.S.; Hints He's Rebel Chief and Liable to Ouster," *Chicago Daily Tribune*, June 3, 1957, 4.

———. "Colombia Expels Tribune Reporter," *Chicago Tribune*, May 10, 1957, 1.

———. "Cuban Army Clashes with Rebel Forces; Report Casualties in Oriente," *Chicago Tribune*, May 29, 1957, 1.

———. "Cuban Rebels Weigh Setting Up Government," *Chicago Tribune*, July 22, 1957, 2.

———. "Cuba under Reign of Terror: Batista Foe Shot Dead; 2 Found Hanged," *Chicago Daily Tribune*, March 15, 1957, 10.

———. "Demand End of Terrorism in Santiago," *Chicago Tribune*, June 1, 1957, 2.

———. "Empty Jails, Cubans Tell Batista: Ask More Political Freedom," *Chicago Daily Tribune*, March 7, 1957, 13.

———. "5 Cuban Rebels Make Thru Batista's Line," *Chicago Tribune*, August 30, 1957, 3F.

———. "Forces of Rebellion in Cuba Are Closing Ranks and Moving Fast," *Chicago Sunday Tribune*, March 24, 1957, 15.

———. "Junta Overthrows Colombia Dictator; Expulsion Order against Tribune Writer Lifted," *Chicago Tribune*, May 11, 1957, 1.

———. "Prío Men Map a Plan to End Strife in Cuba," *Chicago Tribune*, May 27, 1957, 26.

———. "Revolt in Havana; 50 Slain: Batista Forces Crush Attack on His Palace; President Blames Assault on 'Pro-Reds,'" *Chicago Daily Tribune*, March 14, 1957, 1.

———. "Strike Call Touches Off Gun Battles; 7 to 30 Reported Slain in Capital," *Chicago Tribune*, April 10, 1958, 1.

———. "3 Ex-Ministers Ask Military to Oust Dictator," *Chicago Tribune*, May 10, 1957, 1.

———. "3 U.S. Youths Join Cuban Rebel Forces," *Chicago Daily Tribune*, March 9, 1957, 3.

———. "Widow Says Batista Slew Husband: Sought Him Out in Hiding Place," *Chicago Daily Tribune*, March 18, 1957, 9.

Halper, Sam. "Castro on Eve of His Big Bid," *Life*, April 14, 1958, 26–27.

———. "The Hemisphere: This Man Castro," *Time*, April 14, 1958.

Hardin, Bob. "Trio Here Tells How Cubans Riddled Room: Beach Quieter, They Find," *Miami Daily News*, March 15, 1957, 18B.

"The Hemisphere: Cuba: 'Not Afraid to Die,'" *Time*, March 25, 1957, 36.

Hoffman, Wendell L. "Yo Condemno El Terrorismo: Rechaza Energicamente Los Atentados Personales," *Bohemia* [Havana] 49, no. 21 (May 26, 1957): 72.

"Hurt in Havana Bomb Blast," *New York Times*, January 2, 1957, 4.

"In Man's War, U.S. Boys Quit," *Life,* May 27, 1957, 43.

"Inside Cuba's Revolution: In a Savage Civil War, Fidel Castro and 1,000 Rebels Fight Cuba's 'Rifle Rule,'" *Look* 22 (February 4, 1958): 30.

Kihss, Peter. "Cuba Guerrillas Said to Fight On; Castro-Led Rebels Reported Raiding in East—Batista Official Here in Denial," *New York Times,* February 8, 1957, 10.

——. "Nicaragua Holds 200 of Opposition in Somozo Attack: Regime Foes Rounded Up—President Flown to Panama for Four-Hour Surgery," *New York Times,* September 24, 1956, 1.

"Landing Fizzles in Cuba; 27 Rebels Land but 2 Caught," *Miami Herald,* May 25, 1957, 1.

Lewis, Norman. "Our Far-Flung Correspondents: Cuban Interlude," *New Yorker,* May 3, 1958, 80.

"Look Out," *Time,* January 11, 1937.

Lippmann, Walter, and Charles Merz. "Test of the News," *New Republic,* August 4, 1920, 1–42.

Lotto, Jack. "Batista Used Himself as 'Bait' in Revolt," *Miami Daily News,* March 16, 1957, 1.

Matthews, Herbert L. "Cuban Rebel Is Visited in Hideout; Castro Is Still Alive and Still Fighting in Mountains," *New York Times,* February 24, 1957, 1.

——. "Cuban Rebel Only 30; His Men Younger, Stronger than Ever, He Boasts in Interview," *Chicago Daily Tribune,* March 1, 1957.

——. "Cubans' Fight Called Peril to Old Order; Meaning of Struggle by Rebels Told," *Chicago Daily Tribune,* March 3, 1957, 4F.

——. "Cuba President Needs Luck to Hang On, Reporter Says," *Chicago Daily Tribune,* March 2, 1957, 6F.

——. "Cuba Vista por los Extranjeros: Una Republica Sin Ciudadanos" [Cuba Seen by Foreigners: A Republic without Citizens], *Bohemia,* June 1, 1952.

——. "Editorial," *New York Times,* December 4, 1956.

——. "Four Continents—IV: Latin America," *New York Times,* August 31, 1967, 32.

——. "From the Sierra Maestra to Havana, the Ideals Never Changed," review of Jules Dubois, *Fidel Castro: Rebel, Liberator or Dictator?* (1959).

——. "Old Order in Cuba Is Threatened by Forces of an Internal Revolt," *New York Times,* February 26, 1957, 13.

——. "Rebel Leader Castro Still Fights in Cuba: Batista May Contain, Not Beat Him," *Chicago Daily Tribune,* February 27, 1957, 10F.

——. "Rebel Strength Gaining in Cuba, but Batista Has the Upper Hand," *New York Times,* February 25, 1957, 1, 11.

——. "Two Whistles in Dark: Rebels O.K. Reporter; How Meeting with Cuba Chief Was Set Up," *Chicago Daily Tribune,* February 28, 1957, 14F.

——. "Una Republica Sin Ciudadanos," *Bohemia,* June 1, 1952, translated in Havana from the *New York Times.*

——. "Whither Cuba," *New York Times,* March 25, 1957, 24.

McCarthy, Francis. "Castro Hails Newsmen; Gives Medals to Americans Who Interviewed Him," *New York Times,* April 19, 1959, 4.

Mencken, H. L. "Editorial," *American Mercury* (October 1924), 155–58.

Meyer, Karl E. "Display Ad 63," *Washington Post and Times Herald,* September 12, 1958, D5.

———. "Report on Rebel Cuba: Castro Says He Fights for Rights and Opportunities Found in the U.S.," *Washington Post and Times Herald,* September 15, 1958, A1.

———. "Report on Rebel Cuba: Foes Attack Batista-Called Election," *Washington Post,* September 18, 1958, A16.

———. "Report on Rebel Cuba: Neutrality Difficult in Castro's Revolt," *Washington Post,* September 19, 1958, A5.

———. "Report on Rebel Cuba: Rotarians, Doctors, Women Back Castro Revolt," *Washington Post,* September 17, 1958, A7.

———. "Report on Rebel Cuba: Teen-Age Boys Tortured, Murdered for Sympathy with Castro's Cause," *Washington Post and Times Herald,* September 16, 1958, A22.

———. "Report on Rebel Cuba: A Visit to Castro Aerie," *Washington Post and Times Herald,* September 14, 1958, E1.

"No Banker Sways Him, Says Harding," *New York Times,* April 29, 1923, 1.

Perlmutter, Emanuel. "Castro Expected to Act," *New York Times,* July 3, 1958, 4.

Phillips, Ruby Hart. "Cuba Liquidates Worst Problems: Sale Here of Surplus Sugar Restores Prosperity—New Industries Big Factor," *New York Times,* January 4, 1957, 74.

———. "Cuba Suppresses Youths' Uprising; Forty Are Killed; Students Storming Batista's Palace Routed as Tanks and Troops Arrive," *New York Times,* March 14, 1957, 1.

"The Press: Freedom Fighter," *Time,* April 15, 1957.

"The Press: Nose for News," *Time,* November 30, 1959.

"The Press: Shakeup at *Look,*" *Time,* January 11, 1954.

"Protest Sent to Cuba: Press Group Complains to Batista on Censorship," *New York Times,* February 20, 1957.

Pulitzer, Joseph. "The College of Journalism," *North American Review* 178 (May 1904): 641–80.

———. "The College of Journalism," *Review of Reviews,* June 1904, 735–37.

Rice, Diana. "From the Field of Travel," *New York Times,* October 16, 1955, X23.

———. "News Notes from the Field of Travel," *New York Times,* January 27, 1957.

St. George, Andrew. "Castro Seeking U.S. Talks on Cuban Political Issues," *New York Times,* December 11, 1958, 1.

———. "How I Found Castro, the Cuban Guerrilla," *Cavalier,* October 1957.

———. "Inside Cuba's Revolution," *Look,* February 4, 1958, 24–30.

———. "A Visit with a Revolutionary," *Coronet,* February 1958, 74.

———. "We Counter-Snatched Russia's Most Dangerous Spy," *Real,* November 1955.

Santin, Miguel A. "Hotel Construction in Puerto Rico at Peak in History of Caribbean," *New York Times,* July 29, 1956, R1.

Sosin, Milt. "Tourists Describe Violence [in Havana]: Witnesses Arrive at Miami Airport: All's Quiet Now, Batista in Saddle," *Miami Daily News,* March 14, 1957, 1.

Southworth, George. "Castro Termed Only 'Thorn' to Batista: Cuban Newsman Says Dictator's Biggest Headache Is People's Irritation at Unstable Regime," *Miami Herald,* February 26, 1957, 2A.

———. "Cuba Confident Rebels Crushed: But Fighting Still Reported," *Miami Herald,* February 23, 1957, 1A.

"Tildada de novela fantástica in entravista Mathews-Castro: Dice el doctor S. Verdeja a nombre que Mathews no se ha entrevistado con Castro," *Diario de la Marina* [Havana], February 28, 1957, 1.

United Press. "Cuba Wipes Invaders; Leader Is among 40 Dead," *New York Times,* December 3, 1956, 1.

———. "Fidel Castro 'Stars' on Television Program," *Times of Havana,* May 20, 1957, 3.

———. "Manifestation in Front of the White House," May 20, 1957.

United Press Photo. *Chicago Daily Tribune,* March 24, 1957, 15.

"Un Presidente Cordial: El Supo Distingue . . . Asegure La Paz Con Prío Socarras." Accessed on December 11, 2013, at http://www.latinamericanstudies.org/prio/prio -1948.jpg.

Wiskan, Werner. "U.S. Embargo Set on Arms to Cuba; Shipment Halted; Rifles Ordered by Batista Are Held Up—Rochester Concern Is Indicted," *New York Times,* April 3, 1958.

Television and Radio Broadcasts

Shaw, Charles. "As I See It," WCAU radio broadcast, July 3, 24, 25, 28, 29, 30, 31, August 20, September 25, 1958.

Taber, Robert, and Wendell Hoffman. "The Jungle Fighters: The Rebels of the Sierra Maestra," CBS network, May 20, 1957. Excerpts from the CBS documentary *American Experience: Fidel Castro,* a production of WGBH Educational Foundation (PBS), Boston, 2005; distributed by Paramount Home Entertainment, Hollywood, CA.

Interviews

Holstein, William J. [Overseas Press Club past president]. Interview with the author by telephone, July 9, 2009.

Mallin, Jay. Interview with the author by telephone, September 11, 2008.

———. Interview with the author, August 14, 2011.

McMullen, John. Interview with the author by telephone, February 12, 2004.

Meyer, Karl E. Interview with the author by telephone, April 5, 2009.

Szentgyorgyi, Jean. Interview with the author by telephone, March 1, May 25, 26, 2012, October 2, 2014.

Correspondence and Archives

Batista, Fulgencio. "His Excellency, President of the Republic General Fulgencio Batista y Zaldívar, Letter to the President and Members, Cuban Publishers Association," October 9, 1957, InterAmerican Press Association Annal, 1957, 163–67.

"Chapelle, Dickey." Topics in Wisconsin History, Wisconsin Historical Society, www.wisconsinhistory.org/topics/chapelle.

David Halberstam Collection. Howard Gotlieb Archival Research Center, Boston University, Boston.

Herbert L. Matthews Papers, Box 1, Folder 26, Rare Book and Manuscript Library, Columbia University.

    Barron, Arno Ido G., to Herbert L. Matthews, undated.

    Bustillo, Manuel, to Herbert L. Matthews, February 24, 1957.

    Castro, Lidia, and Emma Castro, to Herbert L. Matthews, February 27, 1957.

    Cushing, Richard G., to Herbert L. Matthews, February 26, 1957.

    Gonsé, Raoul Alfonso, to Herbert L. Matthews, February 25, 1957.

    Kirk, Grayson, to Herbert L. Matthews, March 1, 1957.

    Matthews, Herbert L., to Turner Catledge, March 4, 1957.

    Pina, Rogelio, to Herbert L. Matthews, March 1, 1957.

    Steinmetz, Arthur, to Herbert L. Matthews, February 24, 1957.

Inter-American Press Association (Sociedad InterAmericana de Prensa, Inc.). Minutes of the Annual Meeting, Washington, DC, October 1957, 147.

IPI [International Press Institute]. Survey No.1: Improvement of Information (Zurich: International Press Institute, 1952).

Peabody Radio and Television Awards. Collection No. 58014 NWR, Hargrett Rare Book and Manuscript Library, University of Georgia Libraries, Athens.

Books

Brennan, Ray. *Castro, Cuba and Justice*. Garden City, NY: Doubleday, 1957.

Castro, Fidel. *History Will Absolve Me*. Secaucus, NJ: Lyle Stuart, 1984.

Catledge, Turner. *My Life and the Times*. New York: Harper & Row, 1971.

Chapelle, Dickey. *What's a Woman Doing Here? A Reporter's Report on Herself.* New York: William Morrow, 1962.

Dubois, Jules. *Fidel Castro: Rebel, Liberator or Dictator?* Indianapolis: Bobbs-Merrill, 1959.

English, T. J. *Havana Nocturne: How the Mob Owned Cuba—and then Lost It to the Revolution*. New York: William Morrow/HarperCollins, 2008.

Franqui, Carlos. *Diary of the Cuban Revolution*. New York: Viking, 1976.

Lewis, Norman. *Cuban Passage*. Pantheon, 1982.

Liebling, A. J. *Chicago: The Second City*. New York: Knopf, 1952.

Llerena, Mario. *The Unsuspected Revolution: The Birth and Rise of Castroism*. Ithaca, NY: Cornell University Press, 1978.

Macaulay, Neill. *A Rebel in Cuba: An American's Memoir*. Chicago: Quadrangle Books, 1970.

Matthews, Herbert L. *Castro: A Political Biography*. London: Allen Lane, 1969.

——. *The Cuban Story*. New York: Braziller, 1961.

——. *The Education of a Correspondent*. New York: Harcourt, Brace, 1946.

——. *A World in Revolution: A Newspaperman's Memoir*. New York: Charles Scribner's & Sons, 1971.

McManus, Jane, ed. *From the Palm Tree: Voices of the Cuban Revolution*. Secaucus, NJ: Lyle Stuart, 1983.

Niedergang, Marcel. *1959: Castro Prend Le Pouvoir; Les Événements du Monde*. Paris: Éditions du Seuil, 1959.

Pearson, Drew. *Diaries, 1949–1959*. Ed. Tyler Abell. New York: Holt, Rinehart & Winston, 1974.

Taber, Robert. *M-26: Biography of a Revolution*. New York: Lyle Stuart, 1961.

——. *War of the Flea: The Classic Study of Guerrilla Warfare*. 1965; Washington, DC: Brassey's, 2002.

Truslow, Francis Adams. *Report on Cuba: Findings and Recommendations of an Economic and Technical Mission*. Baltimore: Johns Hopkins University Press, 1951.

Other

Unpublished notes, Port of Miami File, Historical Association of Southern Florida (HASF), in Arthur Chapman, "Watch the Port of Miami," *Tequesta: The Journal of the Historical Association of Southern Florida* 1, no. 53: 18.

SECONDARY SOURCES

Newspaper and Magazine Articles

Alterman, Eric. "They've Got the Fever ..." *Nation*, March 11/18, 2013, 10.

Anderson, Jon Lee. "Letter from Havana: Private Eyes: A Crime Novelist Navigates Cuba's Shifting Reality," *New Yorker*, October 21, 2013, 71.

Duffy, Matt J. "Anonymous Sources: A Historical Review of the Norms Surrounding Their Use," *American Journalism* 31, no. 2 (Spring 2014): 244–46.

Filkins, Dexter. "Collateral Damage: Promoting Their Opening to China, Richard Nixon and Henry Kissinger Countenanced Mayhem in South Asia," review of Gary J. Bass, *The Blood Telegram: Nixon, Kissinger, and a Forgotten Genocide* (2013), *New York Times Book Review*, September 29, 2013, 15.

Fontova, Humberto. "CBS's Don Hewitt—Fidel Castro Enabler," accessed on August 24, 2009, www.lewrockwell.com/fontova/fontova77.1.html.

———. "Looking the Other Way on Castro," *FrontPage*Magazine.com, August 26, 2009.

Grann, David. "The Yankee *Comandante*: A Story of Love, Revolution and Betrayal," *New Yorker*, May 28, 2012, 46–71.

Hedges, Chris. "Public Lives: Sounding Out Words of Caution during Wartime," *New York Times*, July 12, 2002.

Hochschild, Adam. "A Brutal Peace: Ian Buruma's Global History of the Pivotal Year 1945, When a New World Emerged from the Ruins of War," review of Ian Buruma, *Year Zero: A History of 1945* (2013), in *New York Review of Books*, September 29, 2013, 18.

Martin, Douglas. "Melba Hernández, 92, a Confidante of Castro from First Volley, Is Dead," *New York Times*, March 16, 2014, 24.

Newbury, Richard. "Norman Lewis: The Semi-Invisible Man," *La Stampa*, December 16, 2008.

Ponder, Steve. "That Delightful Relationship: Presidents and the White House Correspondents in the 1920s," *American Journalism* 14, no. 2 (Spring 1997): 172.

Saxon, Wolfgang. "Norman Lewis, 95, Author Known for Exotic Travels," *New York Times*, July 25, 2003.

Schudson, Michael. "Lippmann and the News," *The Nation*, December 13, 2007.

Weintraub, J. "Why They Call It the Second City: A. J. Liebling and the Chicago He Knew and Hated," *The Reader*, July 29, 1993.

Books, Essays, Papers, and Dissertations

Altschull, J. Herbert. *Agents of Power: The Media and Public Policy*. White Plains, NY: Longman, 1995.

Anderson, Charles W. "Toward a Theory of Latin American Politics." In *Government and Politics in Latin America: A Reader*, ed. Peter G. Snow. New York: Holt, Rinehart & Winston, 1967, 233–34.

Anderson, Jon Lee. *Che Guevara: A Revolutionary Life*, rev. ed. New York: Grove Press, 2010.

Ashman, Charles. *The CIA-Mafia Link*. New York: Manor Books, 1975.

Bejel, Emilio. *José Martí: Images of Memory and Mourning*. New York: Palgrave Macmillan, 2012.

Bonachea, Ramón L., and Marta San Martín. *The Cuban Insurrection, 1952–1959*. New Brunswick, NJ: Transaction, 1974.

Bourke-White, Margaret. *Portrait of Myself*. New York: Simon & Schuster, 1963.

Cassirer, Henry R. *Seeds in the Winds of Change: Through Education and Communication*. Dereham, UK: Peter Francis Publishers, 1989.

Conway, Mike. *The Origins of Television News in America: The Visualizers of CBS in the 1940s*. New York: Peter Lang, 2012.

Creasy, Sir Edward. *The Fifteen Decisive Battles of the World from Marathon to Waterloo.* London: Richard Bentley & Sons, 1851.

Crouthamel, James L. *Bennett's New York Herald and the Rise of the Popular Press.* Syracuse, NY: Syracuse University Press, 1989.

DeBeer, Arnold S., and John C. Merrill. *Global Journalism: Topical Issues and Media Systems.* 5th ed. Boston: Pearson Education, 2009.

DePalma, Anthony. *The Man Who Invented Fidel: Castro, Cuba and Herbert L. Matthews of the New York Times.* New York: Public Affairs, 2006.

Didion, Joan. *Miami.* New York: Simon & Schuster, 1987; rpt. London: Granta Books, 2005.

Farber, Samuel. *The Origins of the Cuban Revolution Reconsidered.* Chapel Hill: University of North Carolina Press, 2006.

Ferre, John P. "Codes of Ethics: Efforts to Promote Image of Professionalism." In *History of the Mass Media in the United States,* ed. Margaret A. Blanchard. Chicago: Fitzroy Dearborn, 1998.

Ferrer, Ada. *Insurgent Cuba: Race, Nation, and Revolution, 1868–1898.* Chapel Hill: University of North Carolina Press, 1999.

Gardner, Mary A. *The Inter-American Press Association: Its Fight for Freedom of the Press, 1926–1960.* Austin: University of Texas Press, 1967.

Gay, Peter. *Modernism: The Lure of Heresy.* New York: W. W. Norton, 2008.

Greene, Graham. *Our Man in Havana.* London: William Heinemann, 1958; New York: Viking Press, 1958.

Guerra, Lillian. *The Myth of José Martí: Conflicting Nationalisms in Early Twentieth-Century Cuba.* Chapel Hill: University of North Carolina Press, 2005.

———. *Visions of Power in Cuba: Revolution, Redemption, and Resistance, 1959–1971.* Chapel Hill: University of North Carolina Press, 2012.

Guevara, Ernesto Che. *Reminiscences of the Cuban Revolutionary War.* Authorized edition with corrections by Guevara. New York: Ocean Press, 2006.

Hamilton, John Maxwell. *Journalism's Roving Eye: A History of American Foreign Reporting.* Baton Rouge: Louisiana State University Press, 2009.

Haney, Richard. *Celia Sanchez: The Legend of Cuba's Revolutionary Heart.* New York: Algora Publishing, 2005.

Hohenberg, John. *Foreign Correspondence: The Great Reporters and Their Times,* 2nd ed. Syracuse, NY: Syracuse University Press, 1995.

Houghton, Neal D., ed. *Struggle against History: U.S. Foreign Policy in an Age of Revolution.* New York: Washington Square Press, 1968.

Jeal, Tim. *Stanley: The Impossible Life of Africa's Greatest Explorer.* London: Faber & Faber, 2007.

Keegan, John. *The Face of Battle.* New York: Viking, 1976.

Kegley, Charles W., Jr., and Eugene R. Wittkopf. *American Foreign Policy: Pattern and Process.* New York: St. Martin's Press, 1979.

Leffler, Melvyn P. *A Preponderance of Power: National Security, the Truman Administra-tion, and the Cold War.* Stanford, CA: Stanford University Press, 1992.

Lewis, Norman. *Cuban Passage: A Novel.* New York: Pantheon, 1982.

——. *The Honored Society: A Searching Look at the Mafia.* New York: Putnam, 1964.

Lippmann, Walter. *Liberty and the News.* New York: Harcourt, Brace & Howe, 1920.

Lueck, Therese L. "The Age of Mass Magazines." In *The Media in America: A History,* 9th ed. Ed. Wm. David Sloan. Northport, AL: Vision Press, 2014.

Lynn, Kenneth S. *Hemingway.* New York: Simon & Schuster, 1987.

Markham, Tim. *The Politics of War Reporting: Authority, Authenticity and Morality.* Manchester, UK: Manchester University Press, 2011.

Márquez-Sterling, Manuel, and R. Rembert Aranda. *Cuba, 1952–1959: The True Story of Castro's Rise to Power.* Wintergreen, VA: Kleiopatria Digital Press, 2009.

McGuigan, Michael Patrick. "Fulgencio Batista's Economic Policies, 1952–1958." PhD dissertation, University of Miami, 2012.

Mott, Frank Luther. *American Journalism,* rev. ed. New York: Macmillan, 1950.

——. *American Journalism: A History, 1690–1960,* 3d ed. New York: Macmillan, 1962.

Nelson, Jack A. "The Genius of Passion: *Esquire, Coronet* and *Ken* Magazines." Paper presented at annual conference of the Association for Education in Journalism and Mass Communication (AEJMC), Portland, OR, July 1988.

Ostroff, Roberta. *Fire in the Wind: The Life of Dickey Chapelle.* New York: Ballantine, 1992.

Quirk, Robert E. *Fidel Castro: The Full Story of His Rise to Power, His Regime, His Allies, and His Adversaries.* New York: W. W. Norton, 1993.

Ripoll, Carlos. "The Press in Cuba, 1952–1960: Autocratic and Totalitarian Censorship." In *The Selling of Fidel Castro,* ed. William E. Ratliff. New Brunswick, NJ: Transac-tion, 1987.

Sainsbury, Brendan. *Lonely Planet: Cuba.* Oakland, CA: Lonely Planet Publications, 2009.

Salwen, Michael B. *Evelyn Waugh in Ethiopia: The Story behind Scoop.* Lewiston, NY: Edward Mellon Press, 2001.

Sherry, Norman. *The Life of Graham Greene. Vol. 3, 1955–1991.* New York: Penguin Group, 2005.

Smith, Earl E. T. *The Fourth Floor.* Washington, DC: U.S. Cuba Press, 1962.

Sperber, A. M. *Murrow: His Life and Times.* Toronto: Bantam, 1987.

Szulc, Tad. *Fidel: A Critical Portrait.* New York: William Morrow, 1986.

Teel, Leonard Ray. *The Public Press, 1900–1945: The History of American Journalism.* Westport, CT: Praeger, 2006.

——. *Ralph Emerson McGill: Voice of the Southern Conscience.* Knoxville: University of Tennessee Press, 2001.

Thomas, Hugh. *Cuba: The Pursuit of Freedom.* New York: Harper & Row, 1971.

Topping, Seymour. *On the Front Lines of the Cold War: An American Correspondent's*

Journal from the Chinese Civil War to the Cuban Missile Crisis and Vietnam. Baton Rouge: Louisiana State University Press, 2010.

Watts, Duncan J. *Everything Is Obvious Once You Know the Answer: Why Common Sense Fails Us.* New York: Crown Business, 2011.

Waugh, Evelyn. *Scoop.* Boston: Little, Brown, 1937.

Wickham-Crowley, Timothy O. *Guerrillas and Revolution in Latin America: A Comparative Study of Insurgents and Regimes since 1956.* Princeton, NJ: Princeton University Press, 1992.

★ INDEX ★

Brennan, Ray, 3, 4, 119, 141–42, 153; on Batista as thief, 134; biography of, 118, 133; on competition with Dubois, 118, 133; description of, 133; on general strike, 134–35, 141; on Havana Mob, 125–26, 133–34; on Juan Fangio kidnap, 125; in Moncada prison, 129–30; on rebel propaganda, 142; as suffering exhaustion, 185; as witness to mass assault, 142–44. *See also* gold medal U.S. correspondents

bribery: by Batista for Cuban press loyalty, 54; for Batista by mobsters, 134; by Castro in Mexico, 84

British Intelligence, 72, 73

Buehlman, Victor J., 46

Burdett, Winston, 59

Camagüey Province, 136, 183

Camp Columbia, 47, 135, 181, 183

Cannel, Ed, 119; in Moncada prison, 129

Cantillo y Porras, Eulogio, 181

Capa, Robert, 19

Capital Times (Madison, WI), 159

Capri Hotel, 134

Carney, William P., 18, 35

Carnival (July), 153

Carrillo, Justo, 100

Casa Grande Hotel (Santiago): arrest of U.S. reporters at, 129; Shaw rendezvous at, 153

casinos, 119; Capri hotel and casino, 134; new construction of, 126

Castro, Emma, 43

Castro, Fidel, 1, 2; on accuracy of rifle scopes, 23, 78; as advocate of democracy, 24, 118; anti-colonial/anti-imperialist sentiments of, 10, 24–25; applause in Miami for, 100; arms embargo sought by, 24, 118; award of gold medals by, 3–4; Batista assassination attempt criticized by, 53; on Batista's exodus, 181; on benefit from discontent, 161; biography of, 15–16, 30–31, 39, 46, 56, 78–84, 111–12; bullets rationed by, 6; catch-and-release combat strategy of, 23, 164, 178; charge of Communism denied by, 9, 31, 117; cigars supplied to, 112; coastal invasion by, 5, 29; as combat director, 177; Constitution of 1940 supported by, 24, 31, 158; death of reported, 5; described by Batista, 45–46,

137; described by Chester, 27; duplicity of on troop count, 26; on economic warfare, 114, 122; elections and free press promised by, 114; fighting for democratic Cuba, 24; first armed attack by, 6; Free Cuba established by, 24, 76, 116; fundraising by, 164; on general strike, 121–24, 131–32, 134–37; guerrilla tactics by, 98–99, 123–24; *History Will Absolve Me* by, 31; impact on tourism of, 126; on ineligibility for presidency, 113, 158; legitimacy through U.S. press, 137; Mafia reward for, 126, 133; manifesto by, 123, 131; martyrs exalted by, 178; middle- and upper-class support for, 121–22; nationalization plan denied by, 114; opposition to 1958 election by, 169; on Pact of Caracas, 158; peace plan of, 120; on Pino de Agua victory, 124; political program outlined by, 113; on power struggle with exiles, 120, 158; as premier, 1, 184; presidency declined by, 10, 113, 139, 158, 164; press freedom promised by, 113; revolutionary laws proposed by, 31; sabotage strategy of, 24, 120–21; secret weapon of, 178; tyrants denounced by, 117–18; U.S. journalists sought by, 60; victory interviews with, 182–83; weapons captured by, 123; "Why We Fight" statement of, 112–14. *See also* Movimiento 26 de Julio (26th of July Movement)

—described by journalists: as agitator and bum, 151; as distrusted by anti-Batista groups, 56; as forceful young orator, 111; as incessant speaker with gargantuan anger, 178; as leader of Cuba's youth, 28, 32; as messiah and zealot, 134; as off-beat folk hero, 171; as potential dictator worse than Batista, 56; as resembling General Stonewall Jackson, 77; as Robin Hood figure, 104; as shrewd politician, 164; as swashbuckling young lawyer, 6; as too young, fiery, militaristic, anti-Yanqui, 56; as unable to tolerate absence of an enemy, 179; as very cautious, 183; as "well-born, well-to-do daredevil," 29, 5

Castro, Raúl, 6, 10, 15, 22, 175; attacks on second front by, 144; Communist ideology of, 176; Communist questions answered by, 147–48, 155–56; described by journalists, 151; doctrines of Martí cited by, 148; execution squad led by, 116; kidnap of U.S. servicemen by, 146–47, 149, 150; *Life* magazine story on, 168; physical description of, 154; presidential election called fake by, 155; and second Oriente front 142, 164; victories reported by, 176

Catholic Church: general strike alarms bishops, 133; and support of Castro, 151, 156

Catledge, Turner: as newsroom managing editor, 43–45; agrees with Matthews, 105

Cavalier, 3, 8, 89, 102–3; Batista displeased by St. George article, 109

censorship (in Cuba), 4, 9, 11, 13, 16, 21, 22, 27, 29, 39, 40, 42, 43, 48–49; by bribery, threats, and punishment, 128; bypassed by reporters and rebel radio, 26, 132, 151, 157, 161; of *Life* magazine, 168; of *New York Times,* 27; opposition to, 37; by periodic decrees, 1; self-censorship, 152; on television, 49; tightening of, 131; total censorship, 172–73. *See also* Batista, Fulgencio

Chapelle, Dickey, 3, 4; aided by St. George, 174–75; aligned with rebel cause, 171; biography of, 171–72; on Castro as magnet for reporters, 171; on confiscation of cameras, 173, 177; in Cuba for *Reader's Digest,* 173–82; Cuban exile stories heard by, 173; enamored with rebels, 180; at Fidel Castro command post, 176–79; identical battles noted by, 179; influence of Matthews on, 171; as interpreter of violence, 172; in jeep accident, 175; on napalm use, 179; posing as tourist and army sweetheart, 174; on Raúl's Communist ideology, 176; at Raúl's farmhouse, 175; on Raúl's victories, 176; on rebels celebrating victory in Havana, 183; with 26th of July Movement, 171, 173. *See also* gold medal U.S. correspondents

Chester, Edmund, 42; as Batista's publicity agent, 27; biography of, 27; on controlled interviews, 52–53; denial strategy of, 27; on Pearson interview with Batista, 27; on quitting Batista, 126; on restoring limited freedom, 91

Chiang Kai-Shek, 138

Chicago, IL, 37; mobsters in, 119

Chicago Sun-Times, 3, 118, 129; Cuba ignored by, 119; on jailing of Brennan, 129–30

Chicago Tribune, 3, 8, 37–38, 44–45, 118; on fearless reputation of Dubois, 90

Cienfuegos, Camilio: on aborted navy rebellion, 98; march to Havana by, 181; in third front (with Che Guevara), 170, 174. *See also* spies

Civic Resistance Movement (CRM), 141

Civilian Revolutionary Front (CFR), 161

code of ethics. *See* ethical standards

Cold War, 28–29, 30, 55–56; media concern with, 104, 152; *realpolitik* during, 24

Collier's, 19

Collingwood, Charles, 59

Columbia Broadcasting System, 3–4, 27, 42–44, 55; first evening newscast, 41; on Taber in Havana, 47. *See also* Hewitt, Don

Columbia University, 42

communism: anti-Communist stance of Batista, 56; Chinese Communists, 138; crypto Communists, 104; Cuban Communists, 132; editors' questions about, 1, 104; Greek Communist guerrillas, 120; pro-Communists, 28; Soviet Communists, 55

—accusations of, dismissed: by Fidel Castro, 9–10, 117, 132; by Matthews, 28, 31, 130; by Raúl Castro, 148, 155; by St. George, 110; by U.S. embassy, 110–11

Constitution of 1940: Castro's pledge to restore, 10; democracy established by, 15

Coronet, 3, 104; Castro's manifesto in, 112–14

corruption: cited by international bankers, 14–15; traced to Batista, 30

Costa Rica, 44

Cowles, Gardner, 104

Cowles, John, 104

Cowley, Fermin, 96

Creasy, Edward, 123

Cuban Air Force: bombing of Sierra Maestra mountains by, 6, 24; on *guajiros* as victims, 29; on *guajiros'* deaths, 143; napalm use by, 143, 179

Cuban Army, 7; confinement strategy of, encircling rebels, 59; doubled, 112; poor training of, 143; retreat to key cities by, 161

Cuban cigars, 23, 112; Gran Corona, 163

26th of July Movement ("M-26"), 7, 9, 17; and
access to cash, 60; and Chapelle, 171, 173;
and Dubois, 131–32; and Matthews's stories,
40; and Meyer, 160; on New York office's
anti-Batista press releases, 105; pact with Directorio Revolucionario, 53; and Shaw, 151;
and St. George, 69, 73, 109; and Taber, 41, 60

unemployment in Cuba, 14–15
United Press: bureau chief, 47; erroneous
story about Castro's death, 12
unity pact, 161. *See also* Pact of Caracas
University Students Federation (FEU), 47
Urrutia, Manuel Lleo: choice as president
confirmed by unity pact, 158; favored by
Castro, 120; on right of revolution, 77
U.S. citizens as rebel fighters: Macaulay, 182;
Morgan, 170–71, 181–82; Soldini, 182
U.S. Congress, 127; Senate Special Judiciary
Committee to Investigate Crime in Inter-
state Commerce, 134

U.S. Embassy, Havana, 38, 44, 45, 56, 58; and
sons of U.S. servicemen joining rebels, 46;
and U.S. servicemen as rebel hostages, 147;
and violation of arms agreement, 146–47
U.S. Information Agency (Havana), 42
U.S. Naval Base, Guantánamo, 147
U.S. State Department, 45; arms embargo
enforced by, 147; Batista's friends in, 28; and
collateral damage of foreign policy, 56; and
embargo violation, 146–47; and U.S. servicemen as rebel hostages, 147

Verdeja, Santiago, 27

Wallace, Mike, 3
Washington Post and Times-Herald, 3, 159;
Meyer's series publicized by, 162–63
Waugh, Evelyn, 18
WCAU (CBS affiliate, Philadelphia), 149
Wollam, Park, 130